Hope you enjoy my book, and know some of the places.

Best Wishes

from Barry

Wild Britain

BARRY PAYLING

Wild Britain

The author has stated to the publishers that, except in such minor respects not affecting the substantial accuracy of the work, the contents of the book are true.

A CIP catalogue record for this book is available from the British Library.

ISBN: 978-1-909461-10-9 (Hardback)

10 9 8 7 6 5 4 3 2 1

Every effort has been made to obtain the necessary permissions with reference to copyright material, both illustrative and quoted. We apologise for any omissions in this respect and will be pleased to make the appropriate acknowledgements in any future edition.

VG Designed and typeset in *The Sans*, *Glober* and *Sabon* by Nathan Ryder www.v-graphics.co.uk

Printed and bound in China on behalf of Latitude Press Ltd.

Dedicated to my mother and father
who introduced me to
beautiful places.

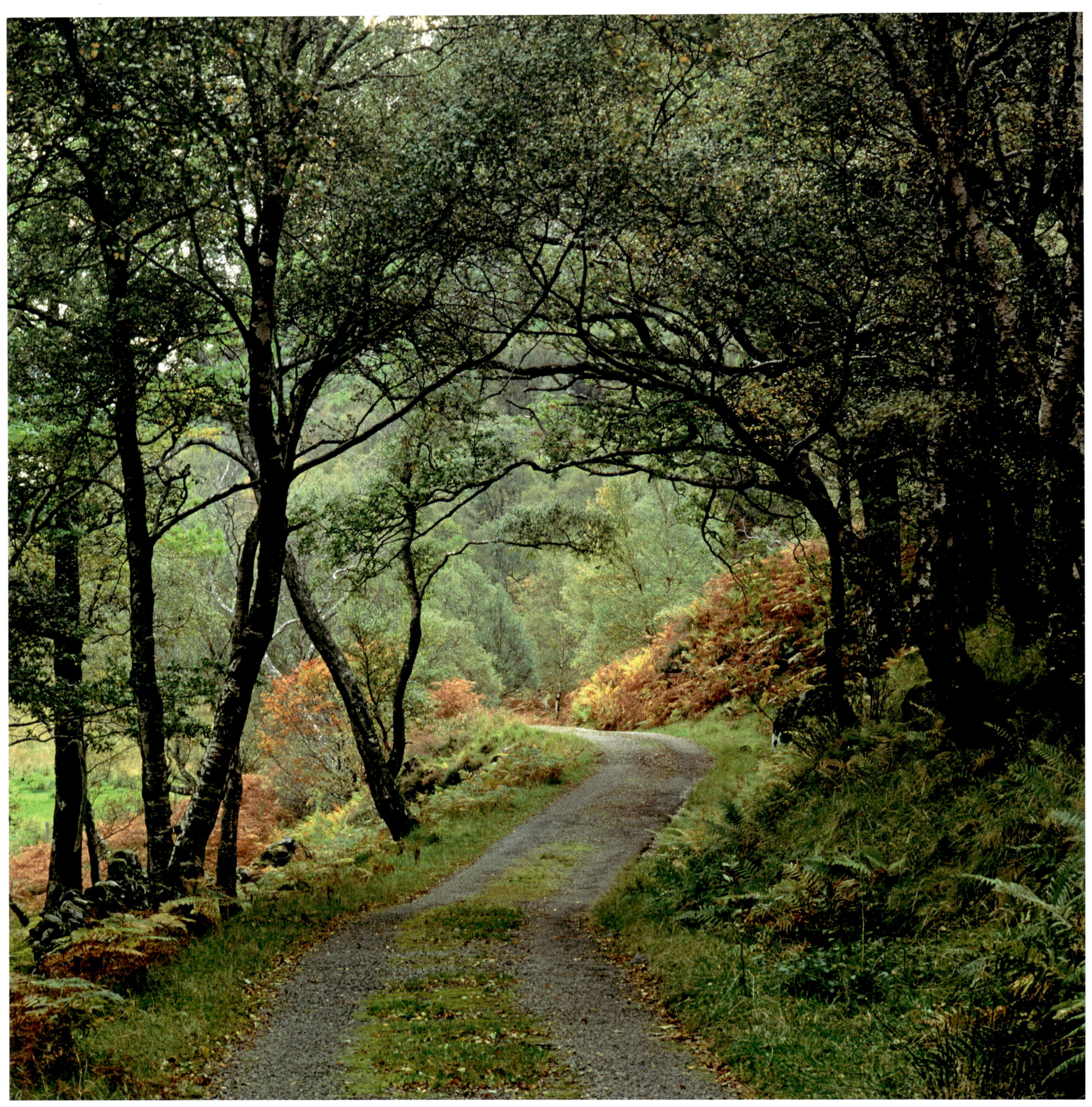

The road to Loch Mere – Wester Ross – Scotland

They paved paradise and put up a parking lot
With a pink hotel a boutique and a swingin' hot spot
Don't it always seem to go
That you don't know what you got 'til it's gone
They paved paradise and put up a parking lot

They took all the trees and put 'em in a tree museum
And they charged the people a dollar and a half just to see 'em
Don't it always seem to go
That you don't know what you've got 'til it's gone
They paved paradise and put up a parking lot

AS SUNG BY JONI MITCHELL

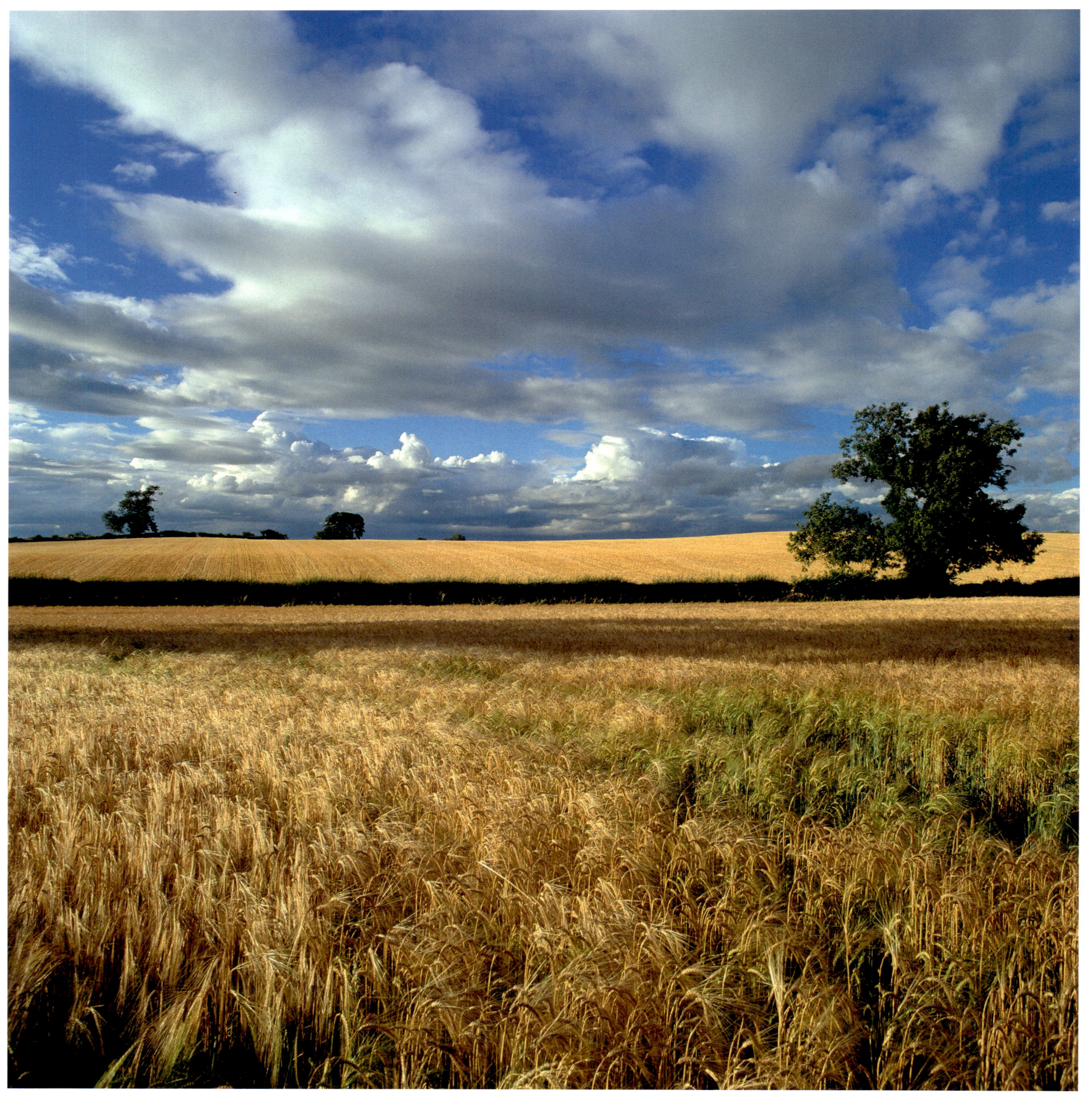

Middleham – North Yorkshire – England

FOREWORD

I owe my love of the great outdoors to my parents. Living in industrial South Yorkshire, parents in the 1950s and 60s, in this area at least, often took their holidays on the east coast in places like Bridlington, Scarborough and Skegness.

Working down mines and in steelworks, fathers were tired, thirsty men. Holidays for many of them were spent lying on the beach during the day, followed by evenings in the pub.

My father, however, was neither a drinker nor a smoker and, probably due to this, we became one of the few families on our street (at the time) to own a car. So, instead of travelling east, we headed north to remote areas of England and Scotland. In those days, in a Ford Popular with three gears, northern Scotland took a journey lasting two days to complete.

I must admit, at ten years old, when my friends returned from their holidays with stories of their fathers' drinking exploits, I did wonder if I had missed something. Looking back now, though, I thank goodness my parents were different, introducing me to some of the magical places I still visit to this day.

My father would venture down every track possible in his quest to find 'where this goes' and I developed his acumen for getting to know places intimately. We stayed in a place and explored it, consequently getting involved with the soul of the location. When returning to our bed and breakfast at night, we might have travelled just four miles in a day, whereas our fellow guests had completed a two-hundred mile round trip.

You'll no doubt see from my photographs that many of them are of things which could be found in your local hedge bottom, as from an early age my photographic eye was trained to be on what was right there in front of me.

I believe that my photographic ability has nothing to do with technical knowledge; it's simply that I am always looking for that special shot. For example, travelling by train to London with a fellow photographer, I constantly scanned the scenery for places or things that would provide interesting subjects in the future. My companion, on the other hand, whiled away the journey playing with his mobile phone.

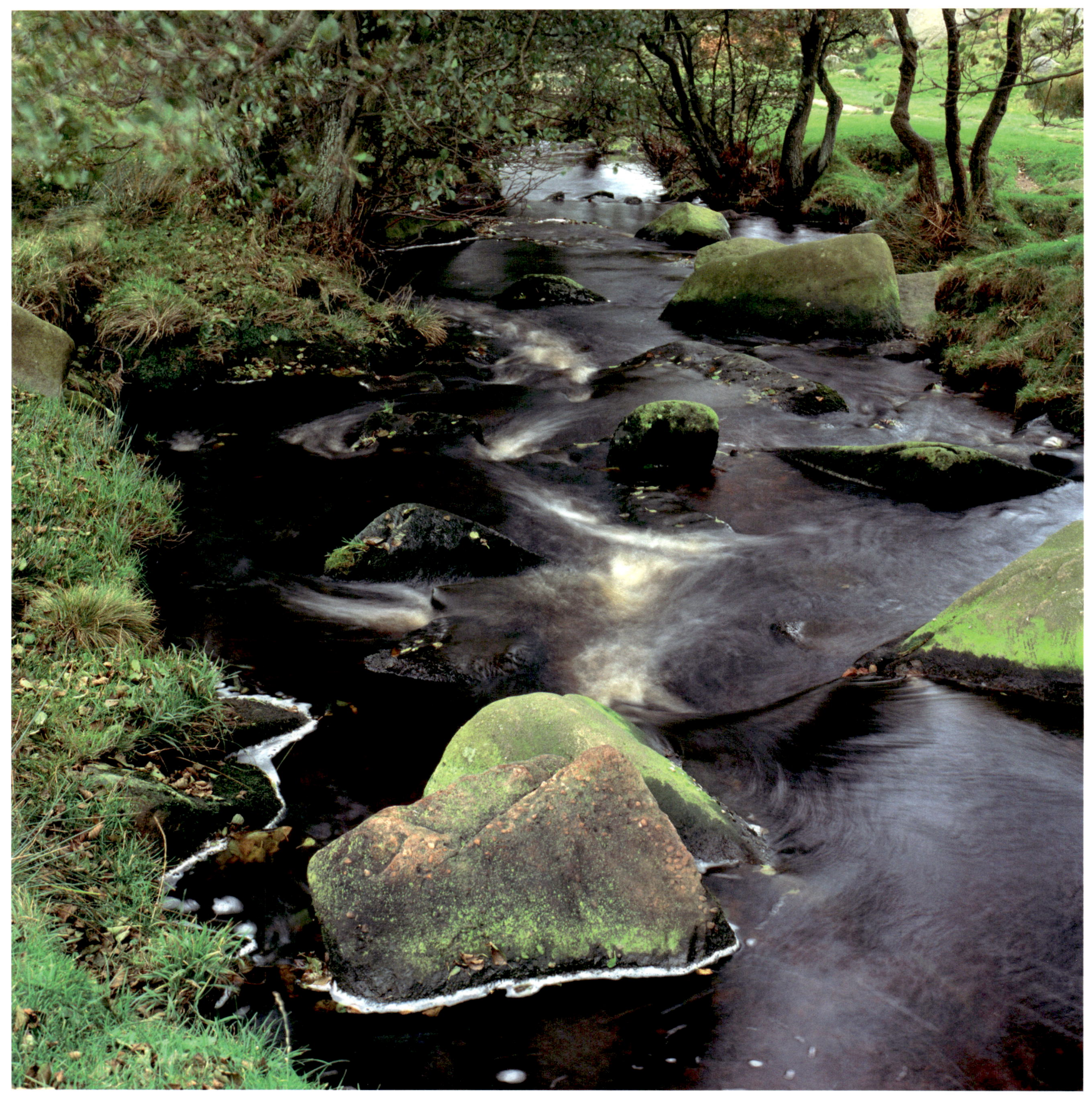

Burbage Brook – Derbyshire – England

EARLY DAYS

Like many other amateur photographers in the second half of the last century, I started out with a Kodak Box Brownie camera. Even as a young teenager of thirteen I knew I was taking decent photographs with good lighting and composition, but realised I could achieve better quality by moving up to a 35mm camera. Once again, like many budding photographers of the time, I bought a 35mm Zenith camera (Russian) and, after a while, moved to another 35mm maker – Minolta (Japanese). In the latter half of the twentieth century, the Japanese dominated the 35mm SLR camera market.

When redundancy came from my administrative post, my hobby as a part-time photographer was due to become a full-time occupation, and serious decisions had to be made regarding my livelihood. Good cameras had to be bought and a medium format (6cm x 6cm) was my choice. Many photographers had one medium format camera with a 35mm camera as a back-up, but I decided that having a back-up exactly the same would be more suitable.

I had a look at all the options and one system stood out amongst all others – Hasselblad. It had a reputation as the best medium format camera in the world and, undoubtedly, its build quality was exceptional. However, I went to buy with an open mind and was ready to be advised by the dealer I had chosen in Leeds.

The guy there had all the medium format cameras you could ever wish to see and, one by one, he took them off the shelf in order to demonstrate their individual qualities – Bronica, Mamiya, Rollei, Pentax and Hasselblad. He praised each one, but on taking hold of the Hasselblad, he kissed it on top, saying 'and this, my friend, is the best camera in the world; a thing of sheer beauty and quality of build that none of these others can hold a light to; a camera with a system to match and lenses, also, that are the best in the world.'

At that point I ordered a Hasselblad 500CM and its motor-driven equivalent, a Hasselblad 500ELM. A short while later, as I became busier and needed an assistant, I purchased a further two for his use. My redundancy money had gone, but it was, undoubtedly, a great business decision. The dearest camera cost me £750 and twenty-two years later I traded it in for £650. Try doing that with a modern digital camera that depreciates in value in an alarming fashion!

I must admit I take more care with my equipment now than when I first started out, mainly because a more relaxed style is developed with time and experience. I did have a few accidents, but the robust nature of the cameras ensured very little damage was caused and my decision to buy Hasselblad has proved prudent. There is also the tremendous back-up given by Hasselblad; for example, over the years, their public face at many events was Derek Gatland who, through his help and expertise, kept many professional photographers working.

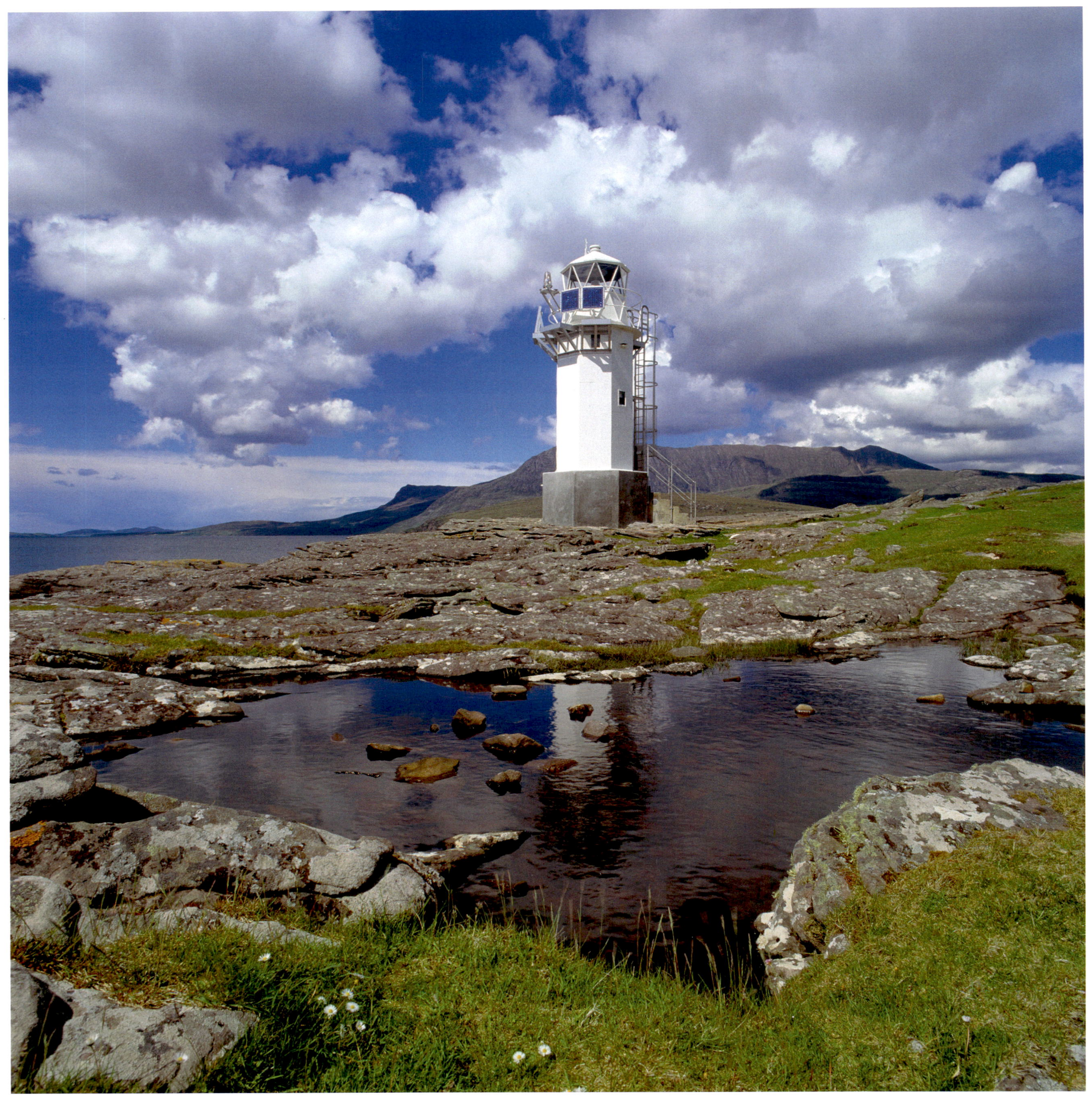

Rhue Lighthouse – Wester Ross – Scotland

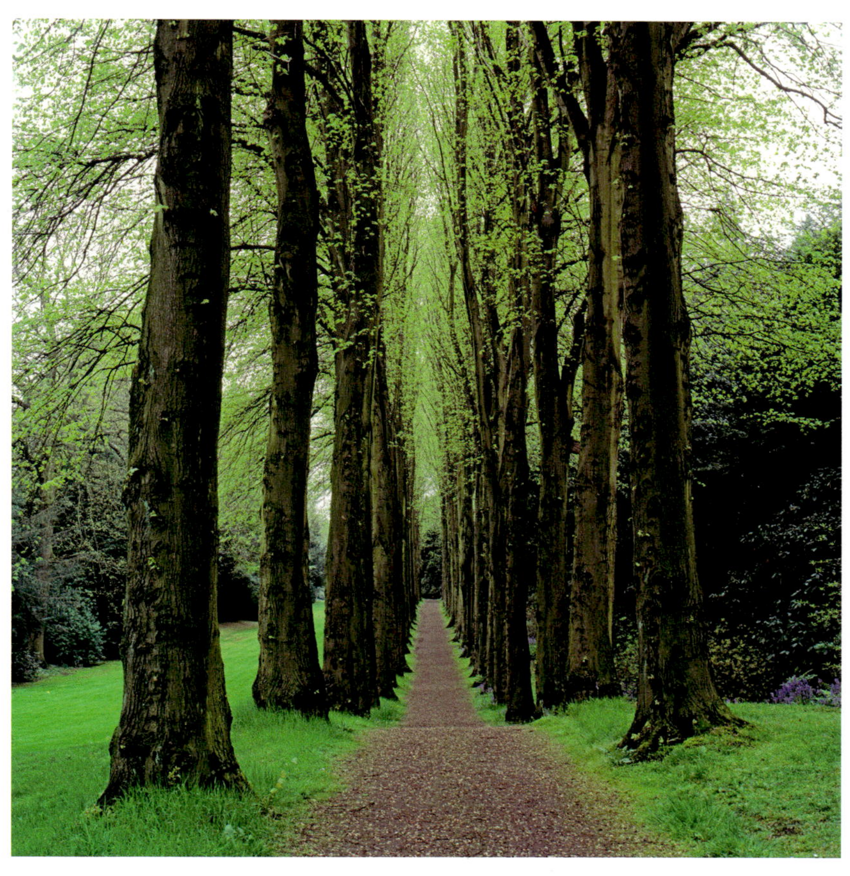

Wentworth Castle – South Yorkshire – England

Wentworth – South Yorkshire – England

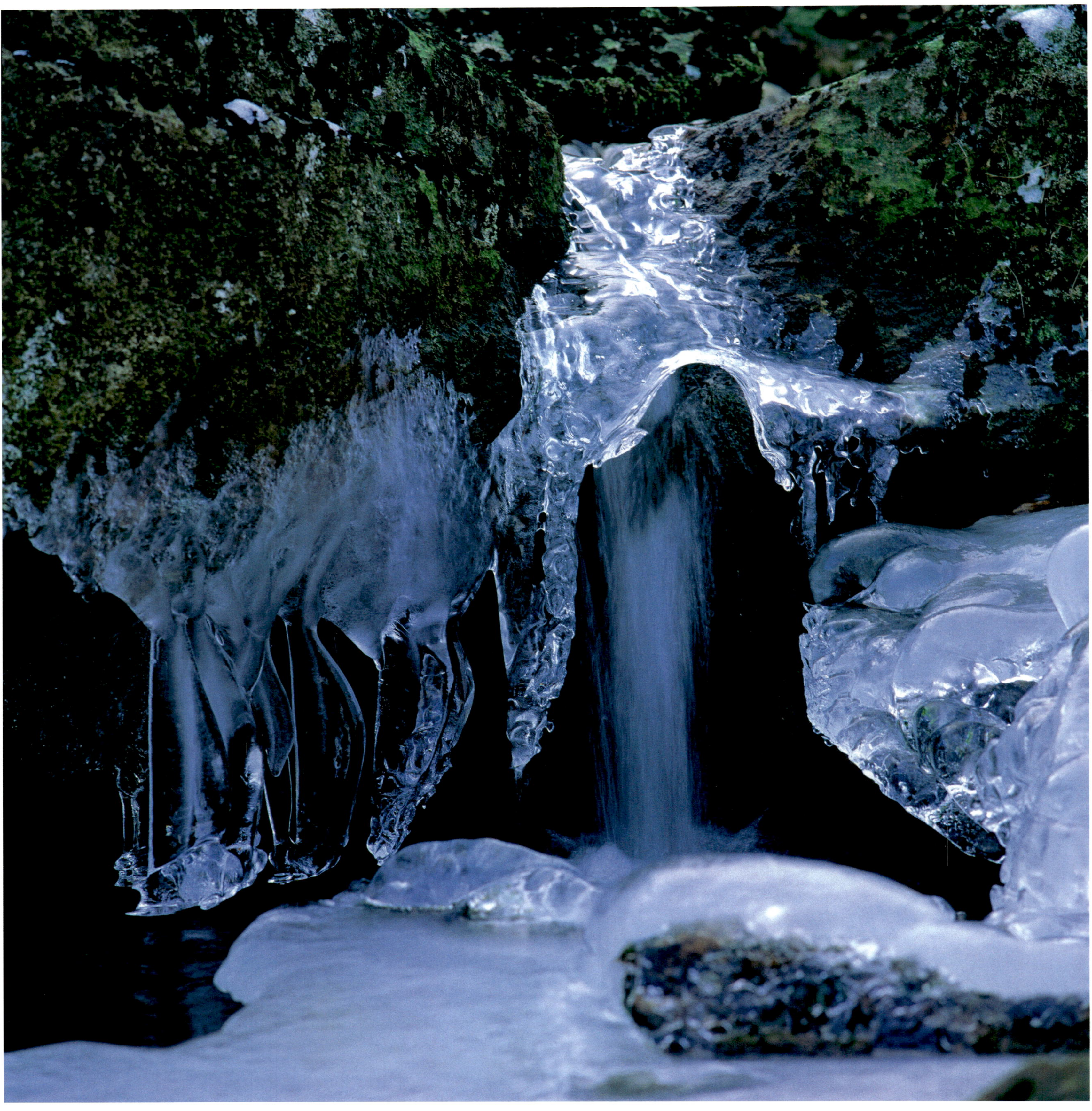

STANDING AND STARING

On a walk with a friend in Derbyshire I shouted and asked for him to wait for me, as I wanted to take a photograph. He's a quick walker and by the time I'd taken the photographs I wanted, I knew he'd be a long way in front.

As I snapped away, he walked back to me and, interested in the shots I was taking, looked through the viewfinder to see what lay therein. With a look of astonishment and, as if feeling a pang of guilt at what he had passed, he said I reminded him of an advert on the television.

After some trying to explain the advert and its content, slowly and surely I knew the one he meant, and I was pleased he appreciated the message, especially in these frenzied times, for he was alluding to the words of William Henry Davies:

'A poor life this if, full of care,
We have no time to stand and stare.'

The shot opposite and the two shots overleaf were all taken within a couple of minutes of one another.

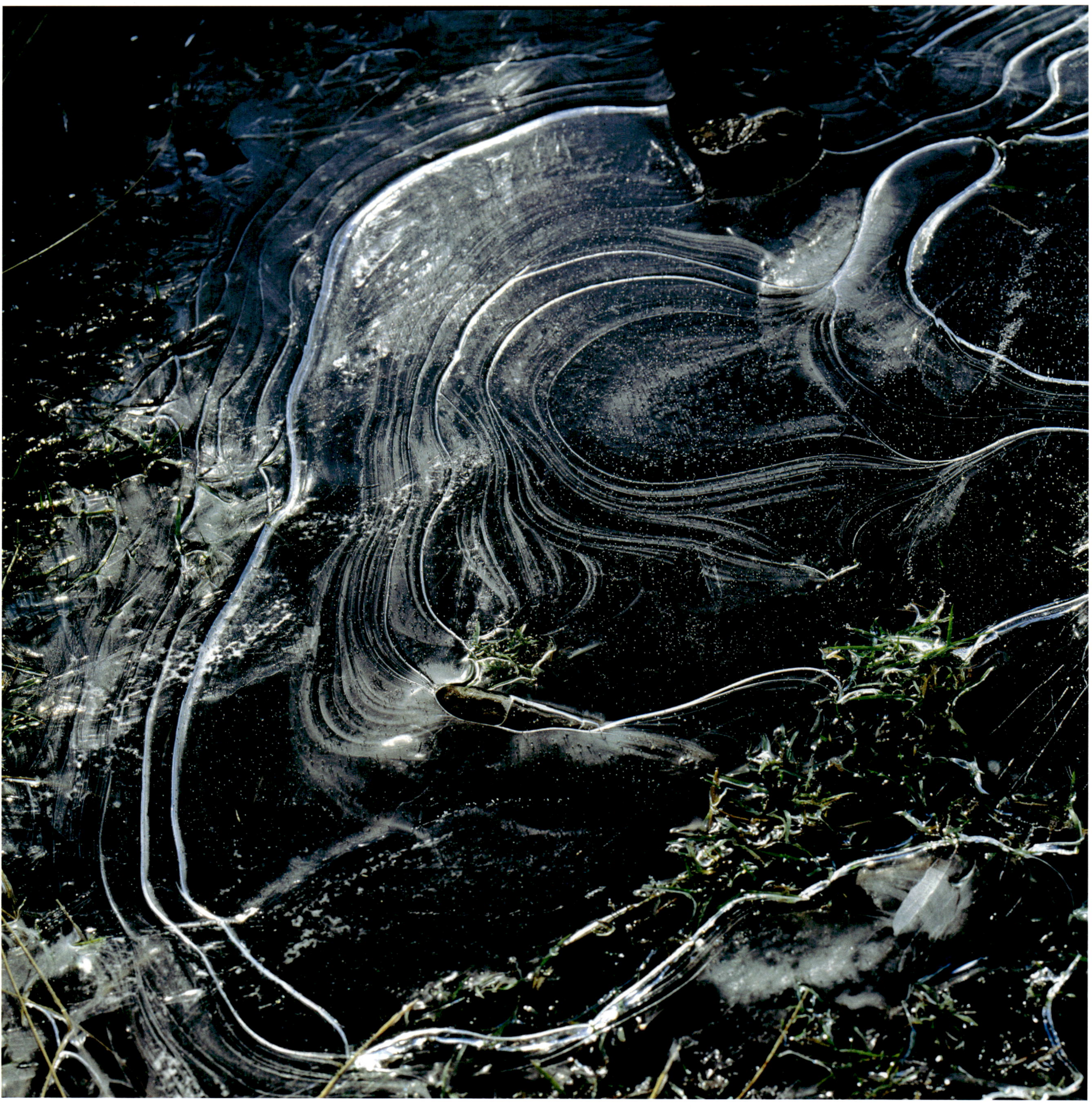

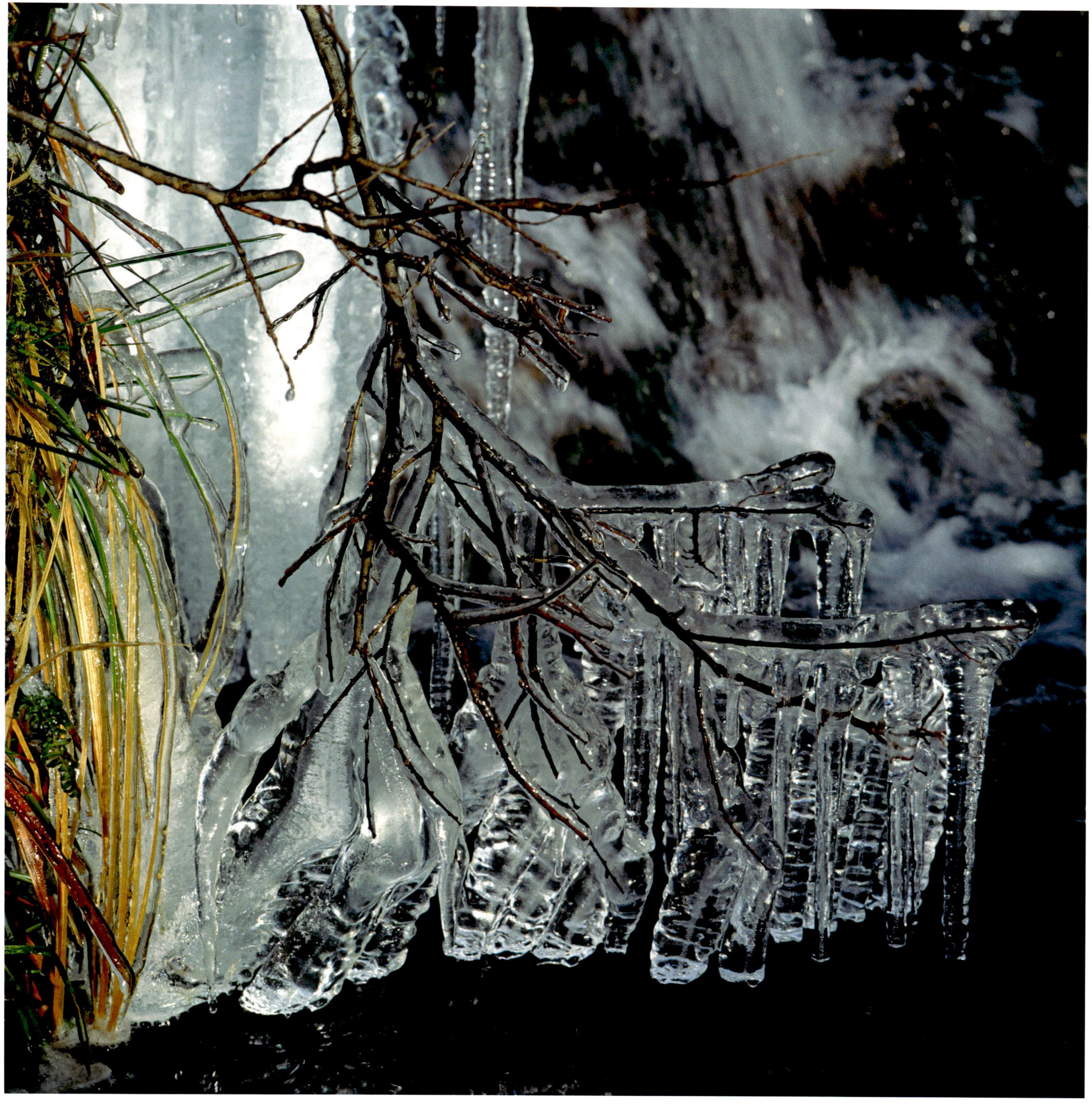

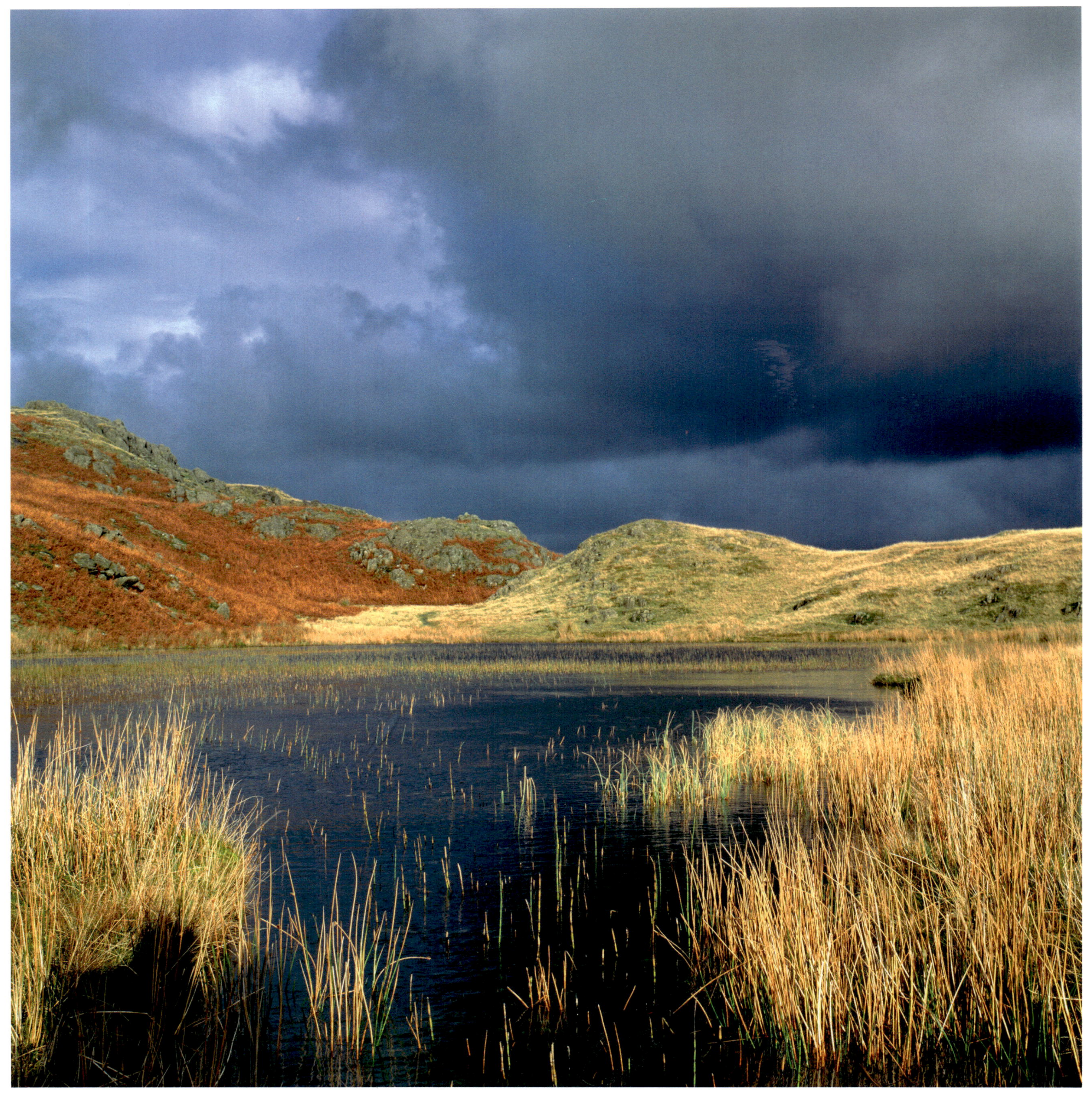

Stickle Tarn – Cumbria – England

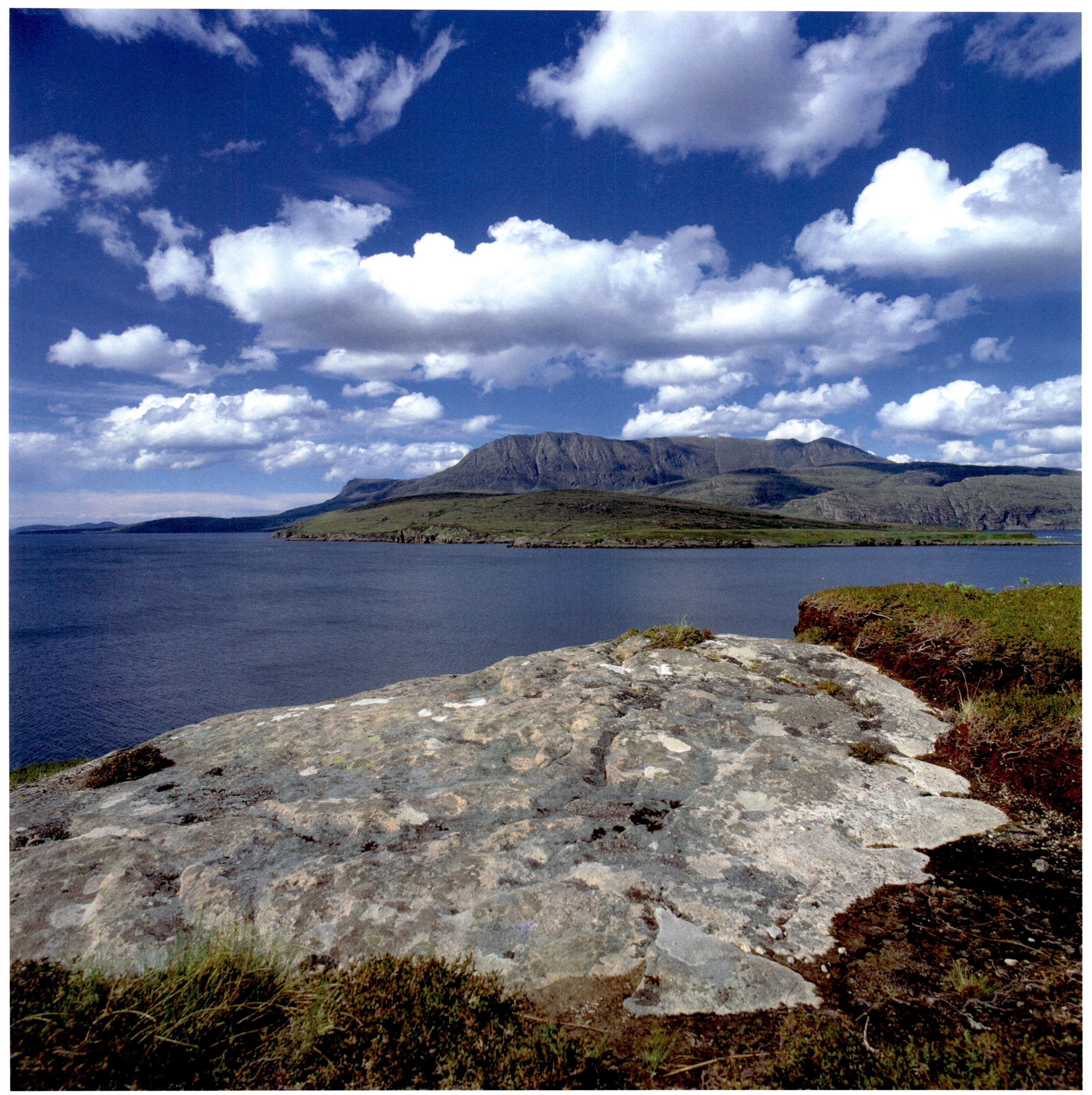

Ardmair Bay – Wester Ross – Scotland

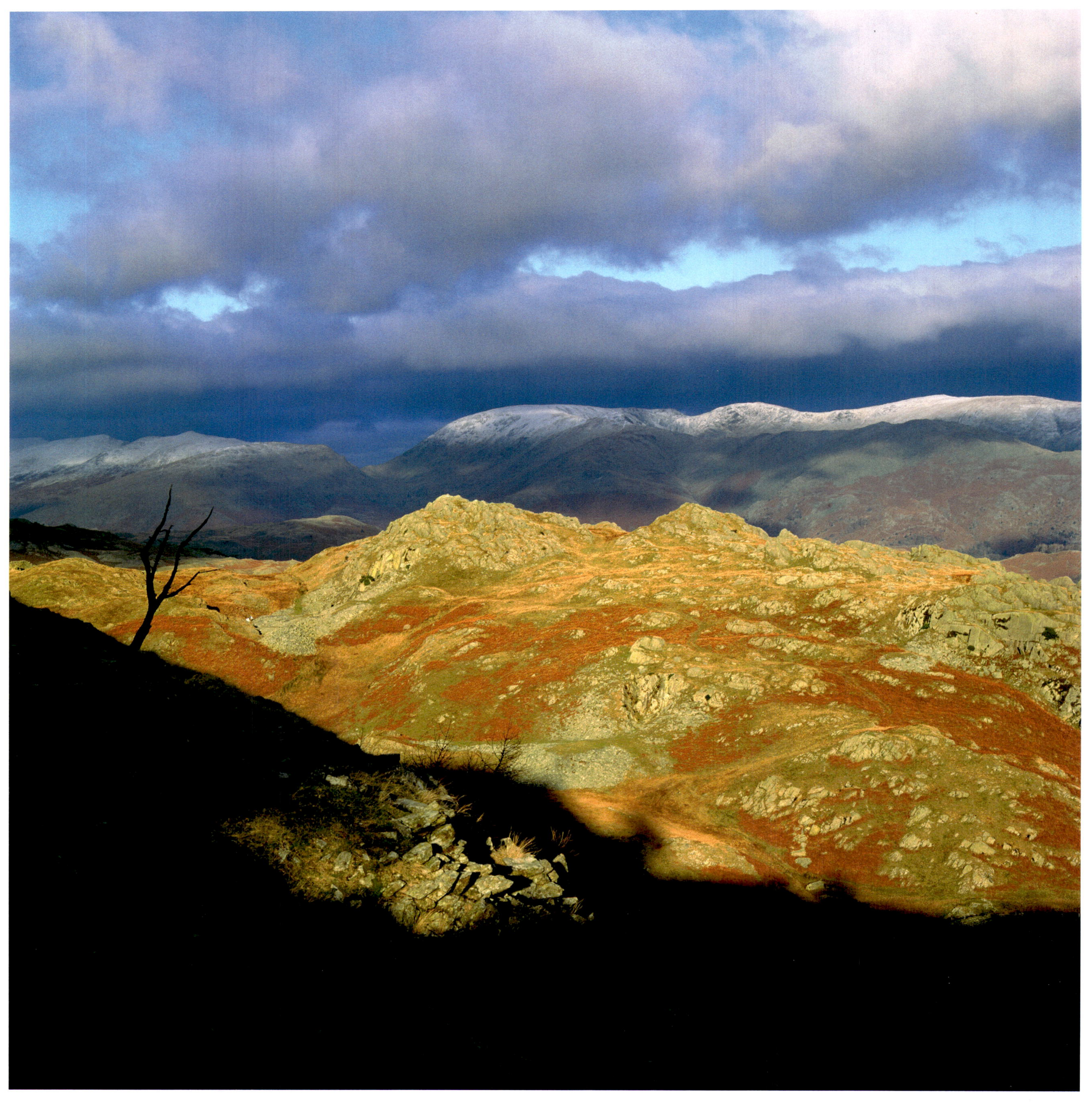

Wetherlam – Cumbria – England

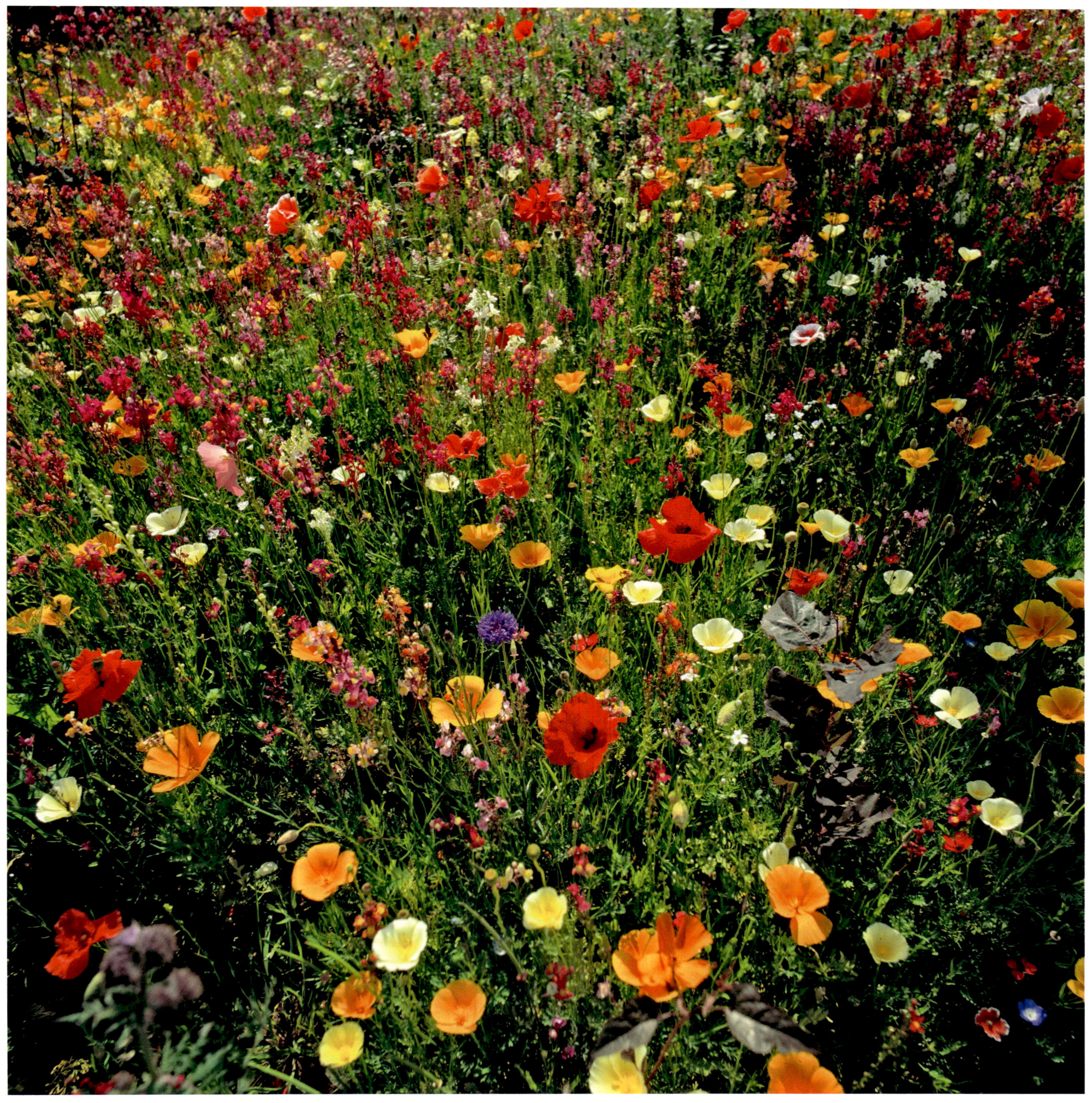

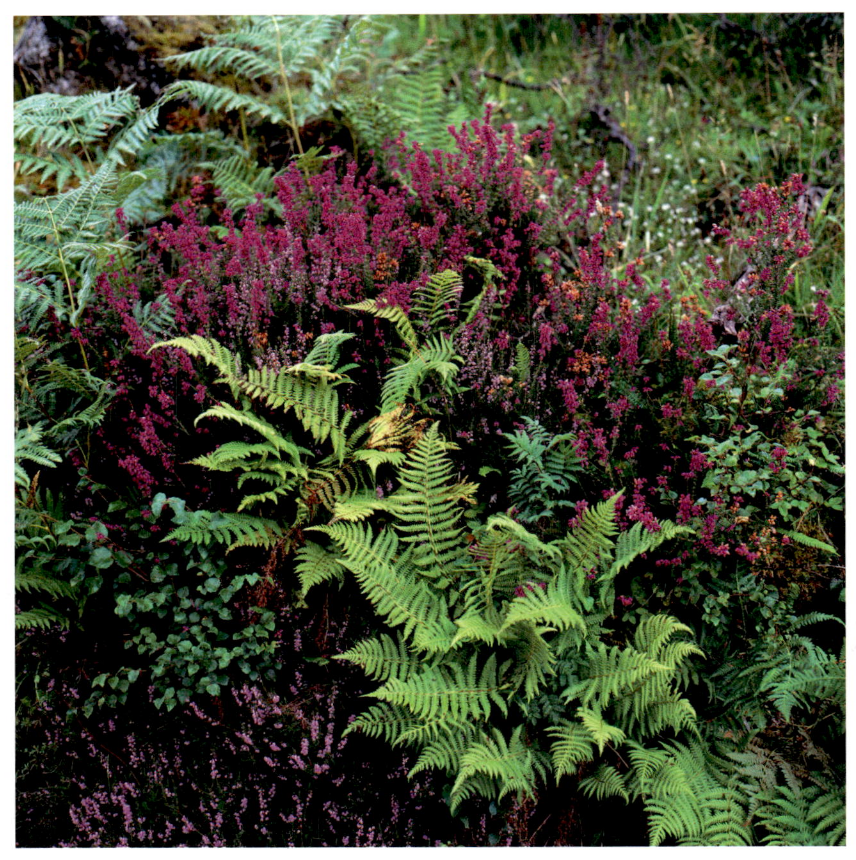

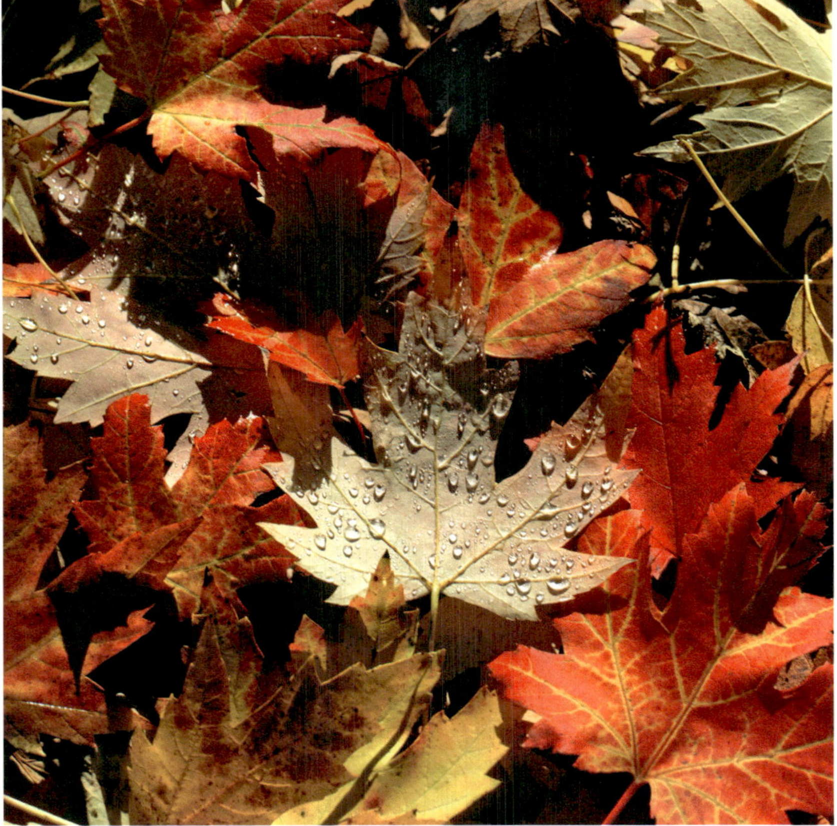

THE HASSELBLAD CAMERA SYSTEM

There is no way I want this book to be technical, so I will spare the reader any such detail, but I thought a quick explanation of the cameras and equipment I use would be helpful.

Before the second world war, Sweden didn't have a camera industry, but at the outbreak of hostilities that would soon change. In order to develop an aerial camera, the government commissioned a Swedish photographer – Victor Hasselblad. A factory was built, and, from scratch, the industry developed, but it was obvious after the war that demand for aerial cameras would not be huge, so Victor set about developing a 2¼ x 2¼ inch single lens reflex camera.

In 1948 he launched the first model at a press conference in New York. The camera system right up to the end of the century, and into the next, prided itself on designing parts that still fitted the earlier models, and the built-in obsolescence of many manufacturers was never present with the Hasselblad design.

The film size was 3½ times that of normal 35mm film and, consequently, the resulting picture quality proved the old adage of 'a good big 'un is always better than a good little 'un'. However, with the use of Zeiss lenses, the quality of the resulting photographs meant that the camera was the envy of every photographer, and the label of 'best camera in the world' was always associated with the name Hasselblad.

A great advantage of the system are the interchangeable magazines (backs). These magazines can be removed from the camera body at any point, no matter what frame you are at, as the film progresses through the camera. So, if you are half way through a colour film and want to take the same shot in monochrome, you simply insert a magazine slide between the back and the camera body, which then allows the magazine to be removed. A new magazine containing monochrome film can then be placed on the camera body and, when required, it is possible to revert to colour using the same process.

All the photographs in this book have been shot using Hasselblad cameras. For various reasons I have six Hasselblad bodies, together with a 30mm Distagon fisheye lens, 40mm Distagon wide angle lens, 80mm standard Planar lens, 120mm Makro Planar lens, 150mm short telephoto Sonnar lens, a 250mm Sonnar short telephoto lens and a 350mm Tele Tessar lens.

All the photographs were shot on film, Fuji Velvia 50, which has, for many years, been the benchmark film for colour transparency work and especially loved by landscape photographers. The film was, and is, so loved that when Fuji announced its demise in the early part of the 21st Century, photographers bought hundreds of rolls, to store in their freezer, so they would have plenty in stock for some time to come. Fuji did however (after furore from photographers) change their decision and re-instated the film in its sales catalogue.

I truly hope film doesn't die because it has characteristics that I believe can never be matched by digital photography. However, times change and things sometimes improve for the better, but I hope the photographs I have chosen for this book illustrate what this affinity to film means to many photographers.

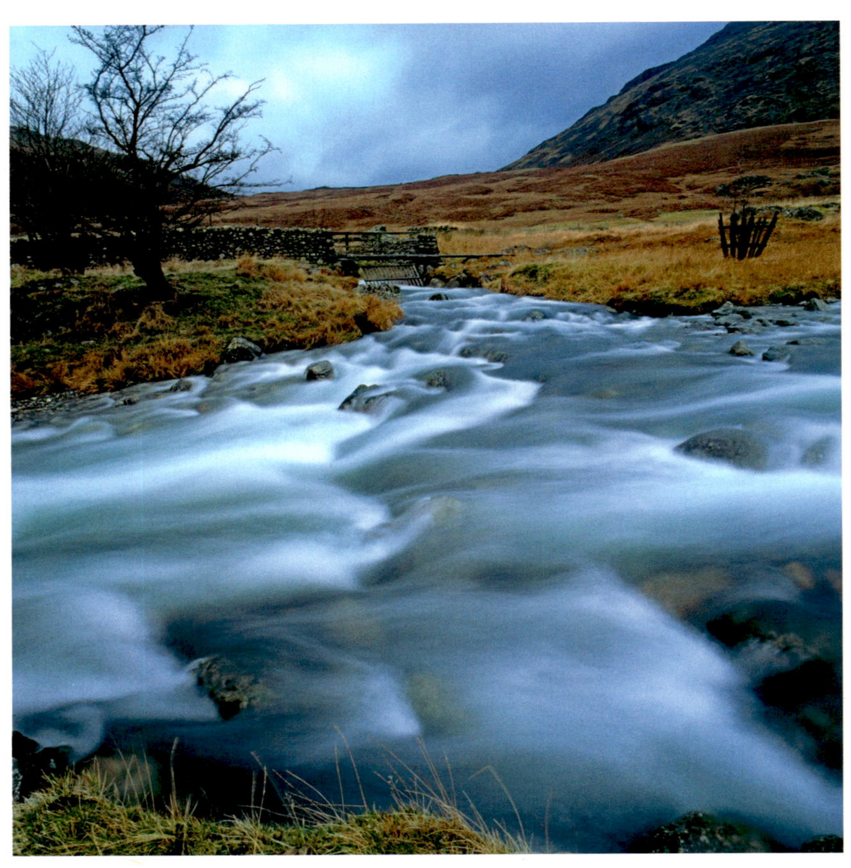

Cockley Beck – Cumbria – England

Clappersgate – Cumbria – England

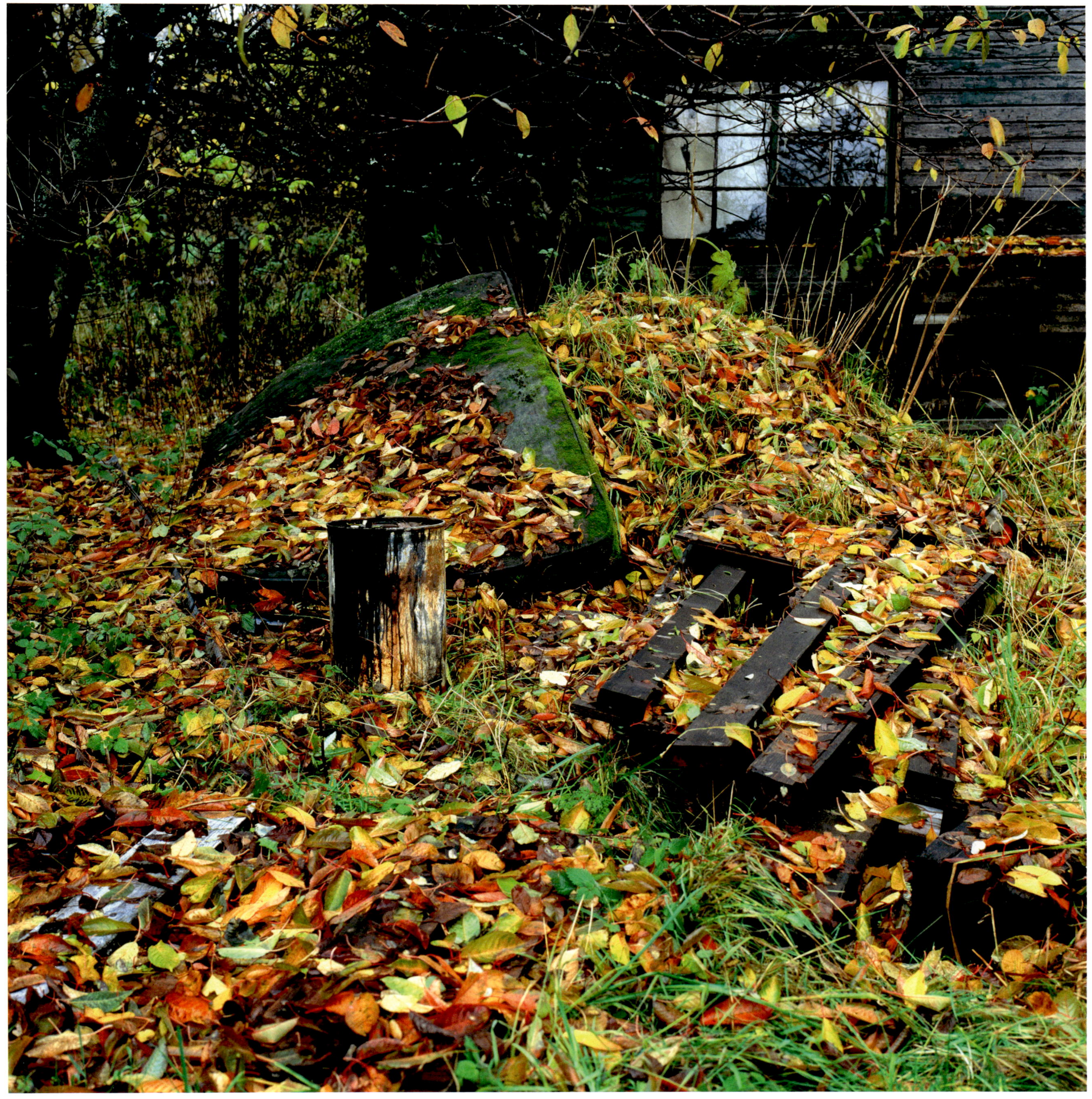

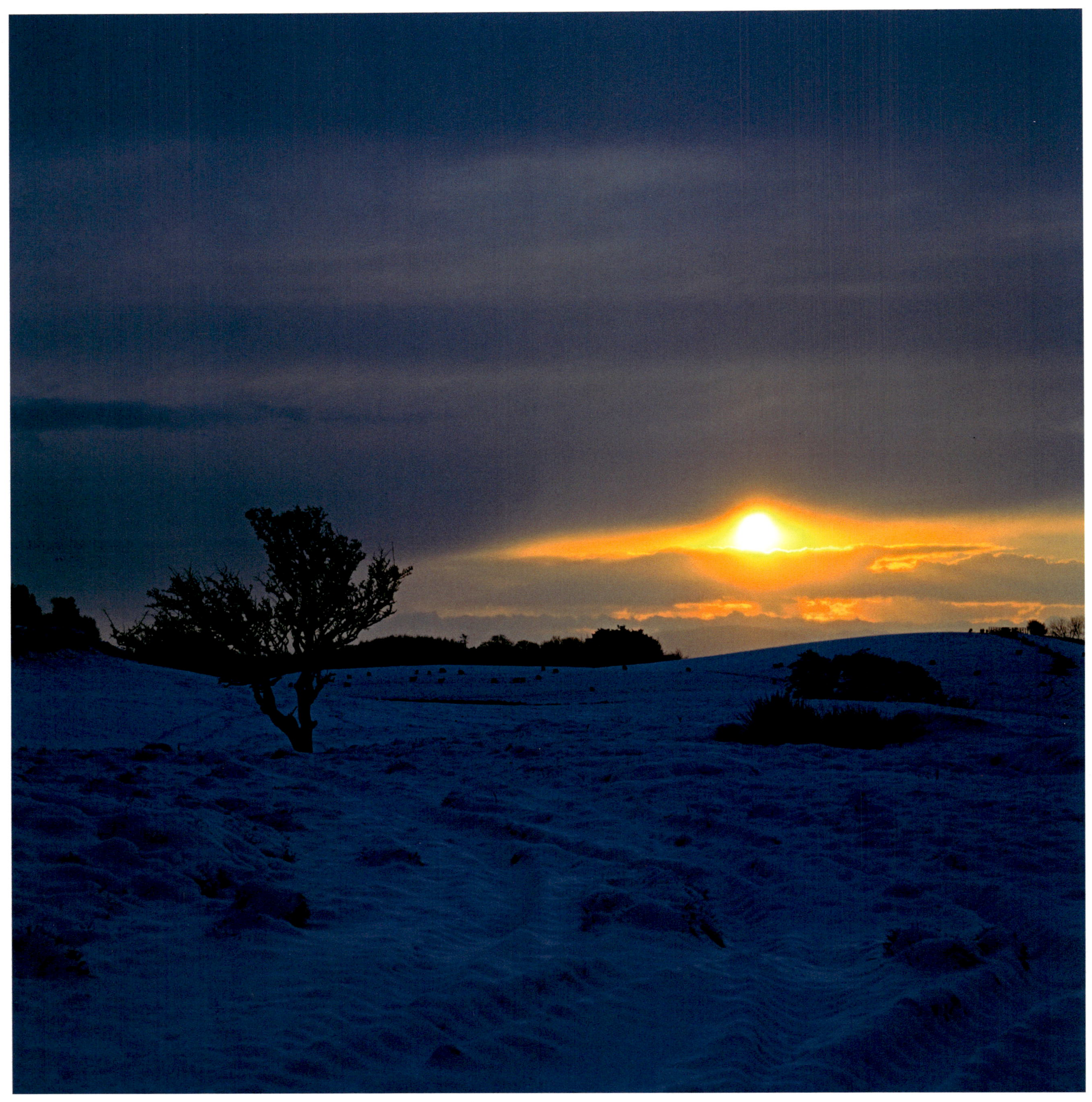

Broughton Mills – Cumbria – England

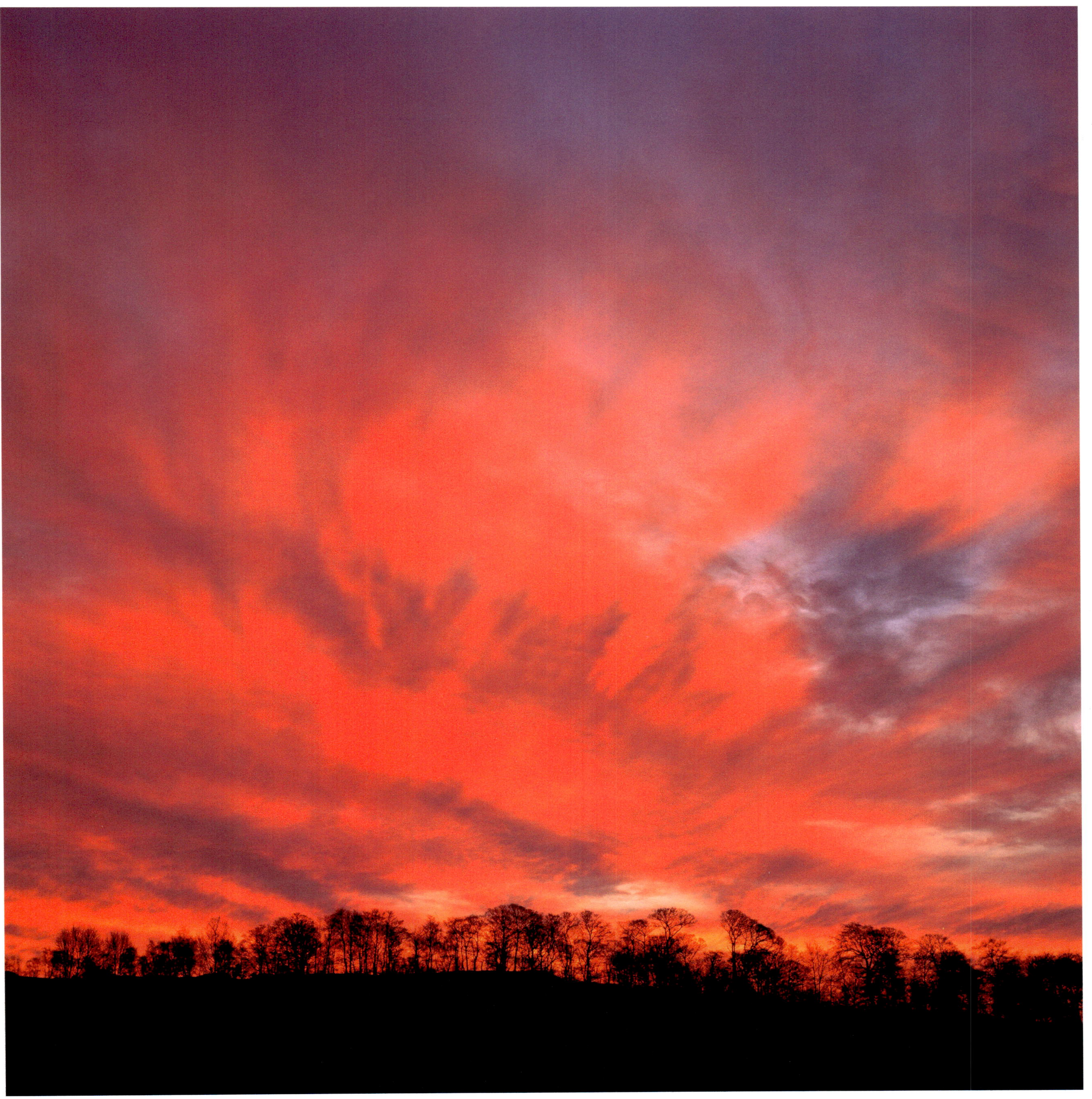

Hooton Roberts – South Yorkshire – England

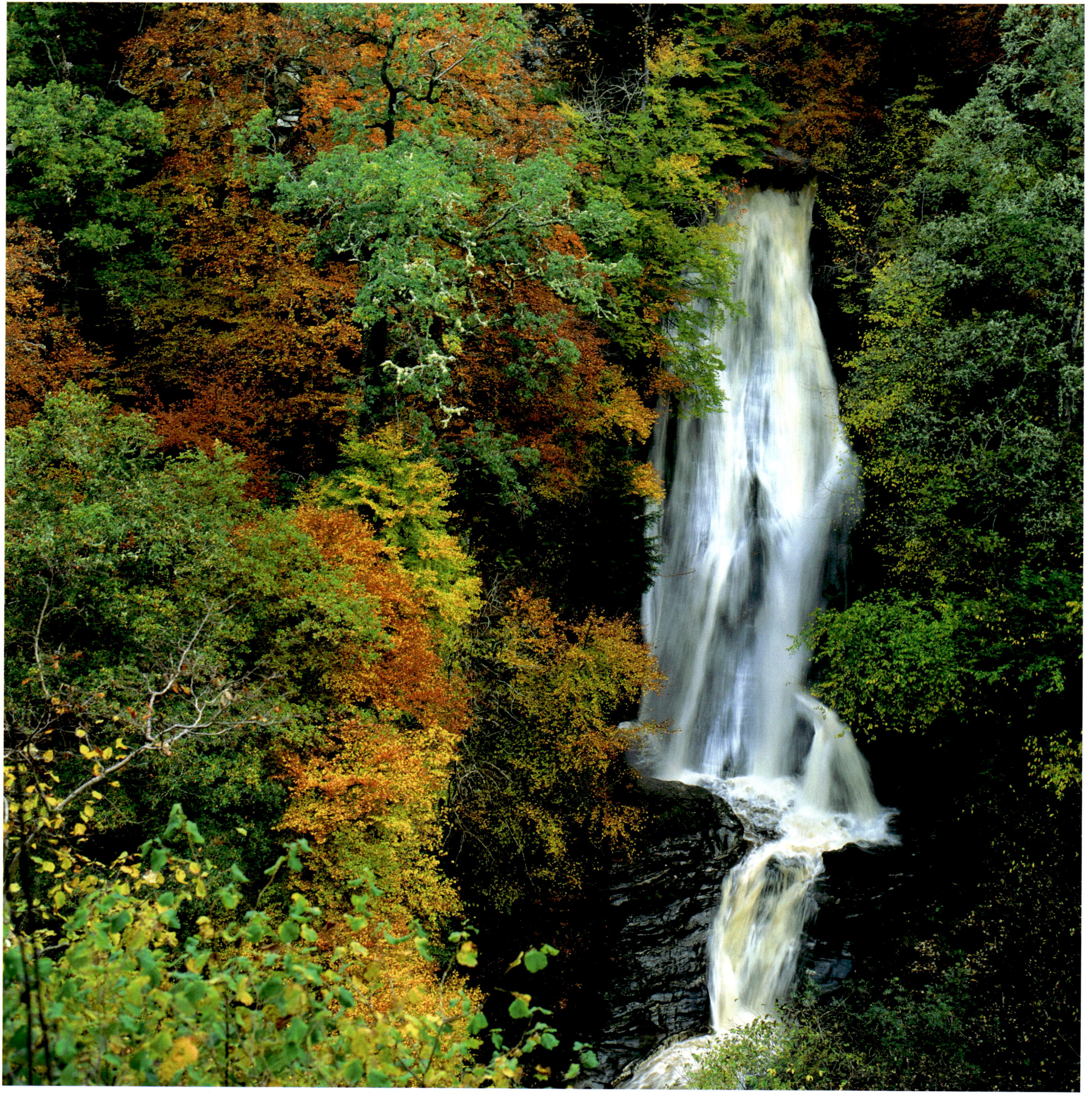

Falls of Acharn – Perthshire – Scotland

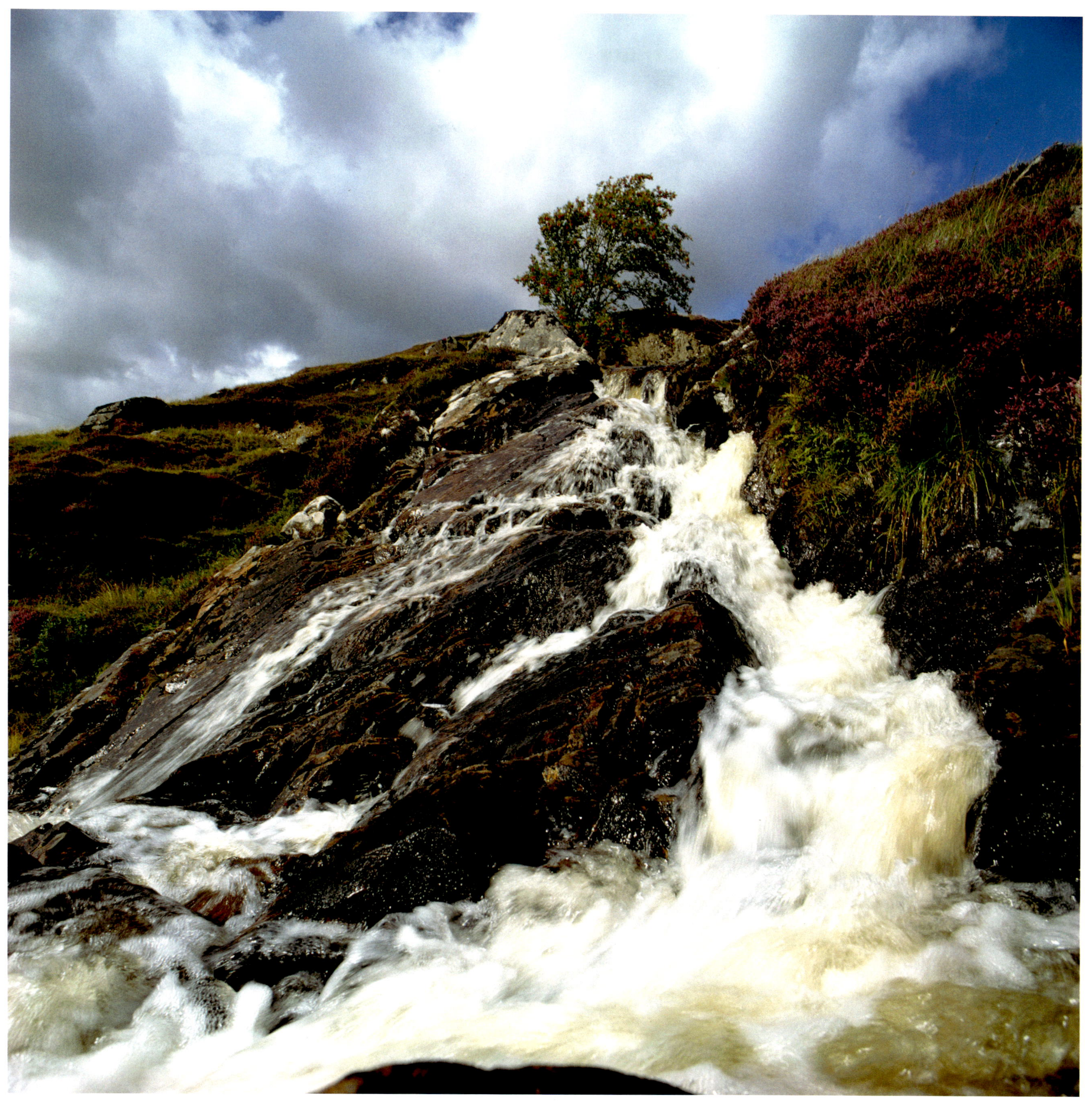

Glen Cassley – Sutherland – Scotland

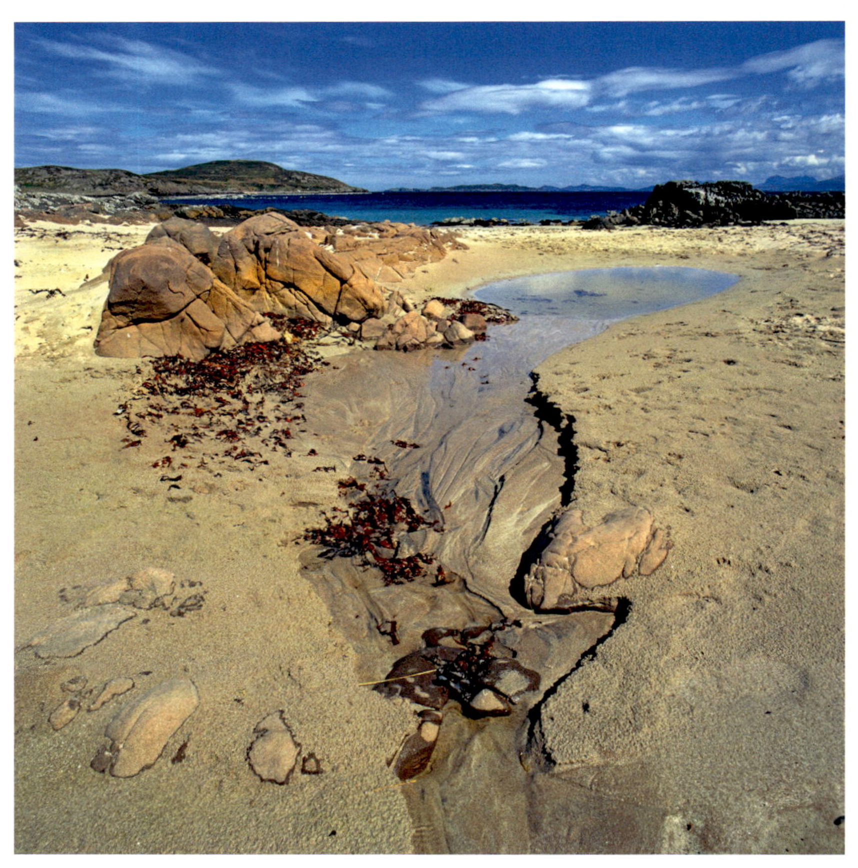

Mellon Udrigle – Wester Ross – Scotland

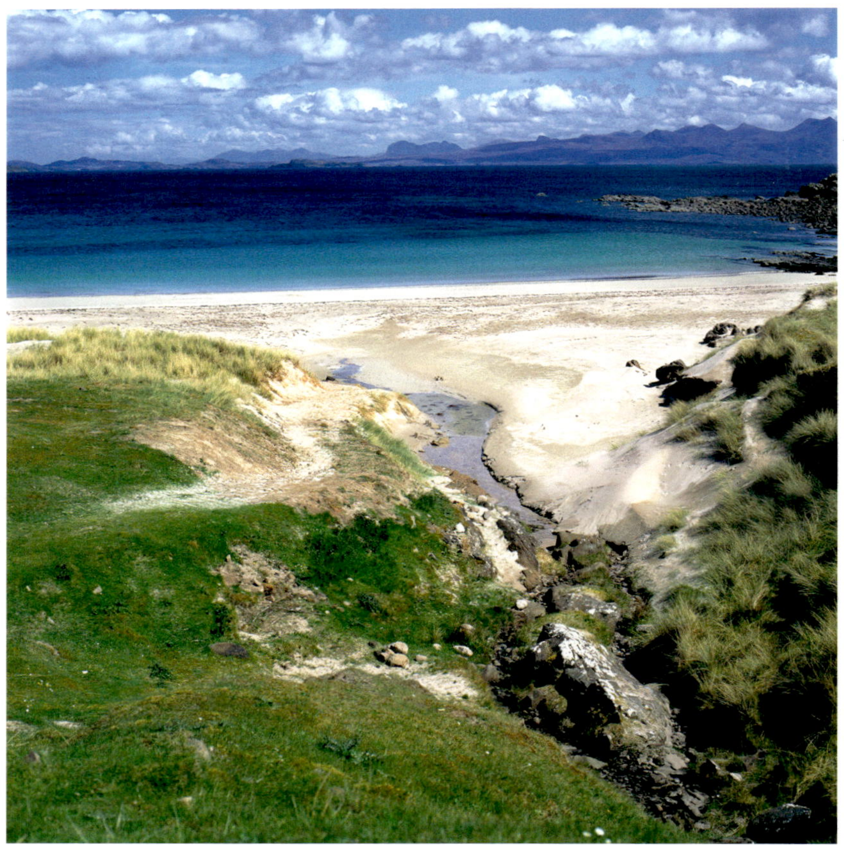

Mellon Udrigle – Wester Ross – Scotland

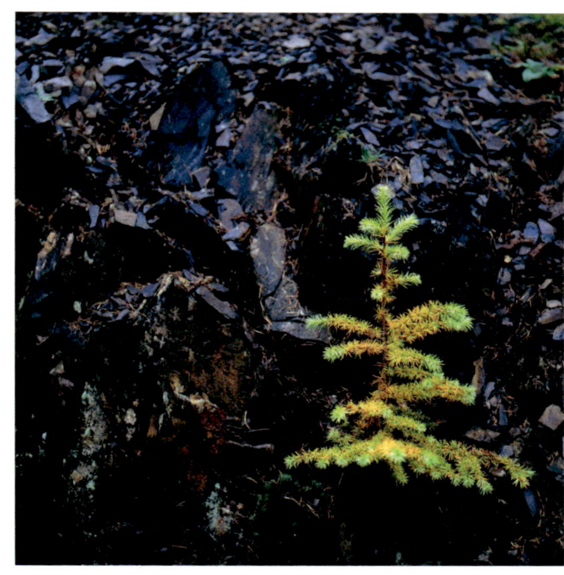

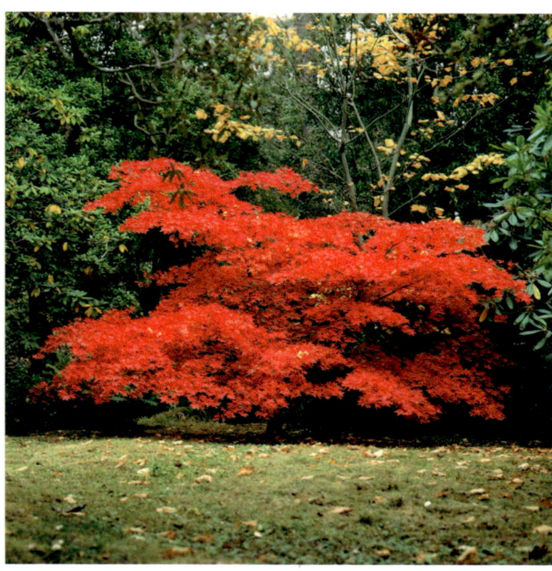

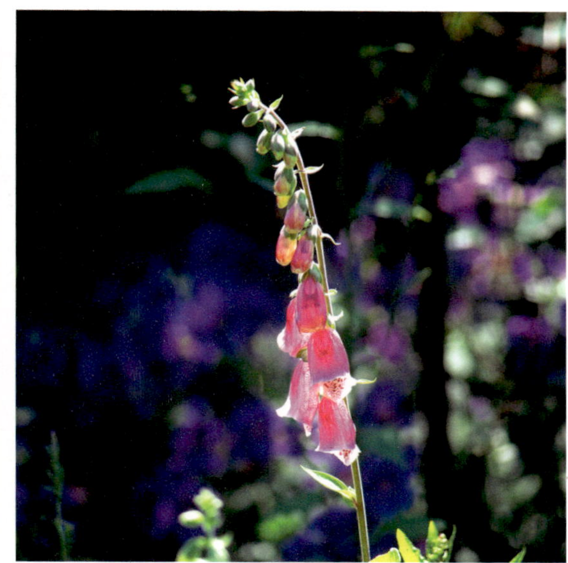

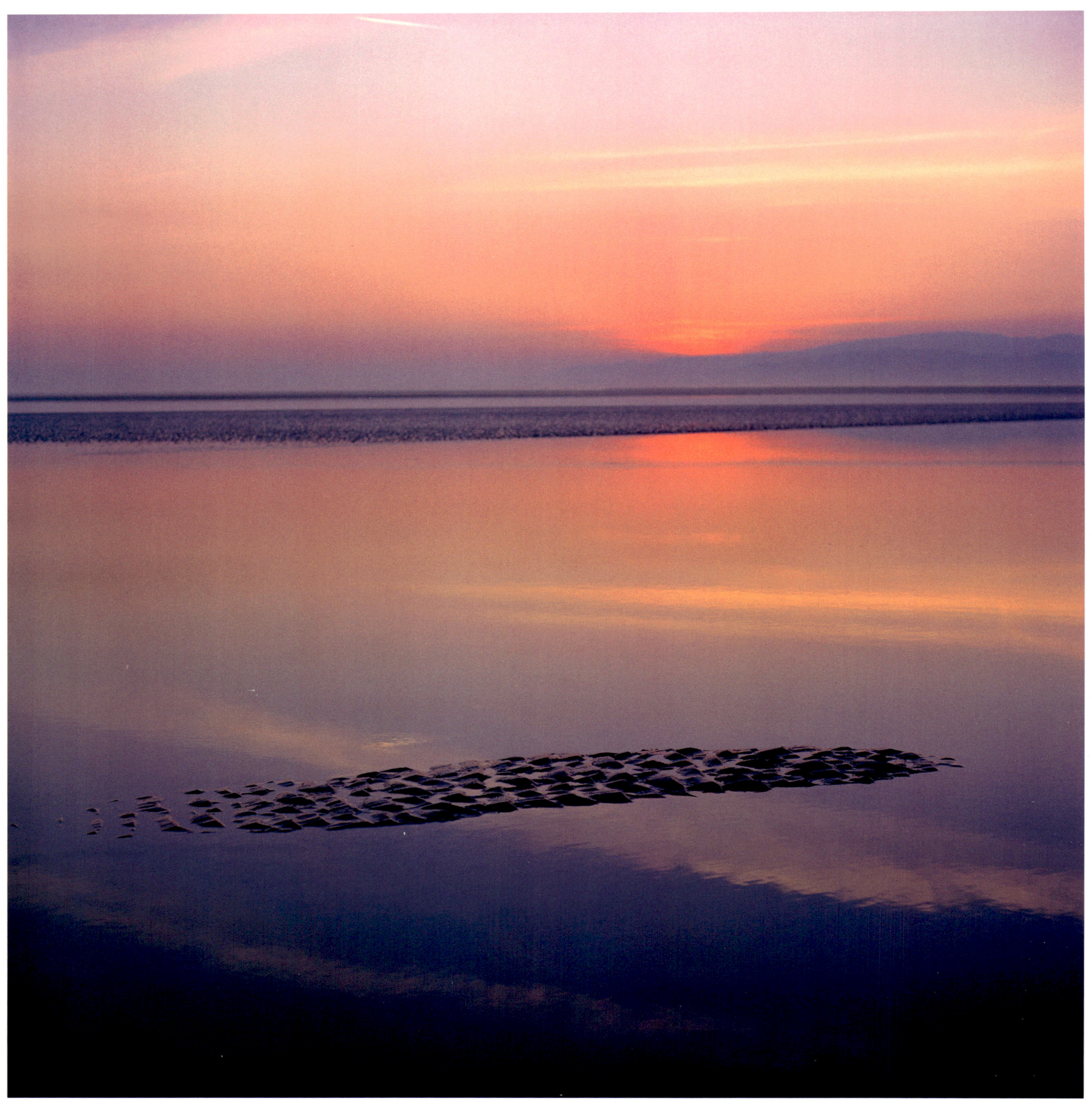

Duddon Estuary – Cumbria – England

SUBTLETY

Not too long ago, the majority of colour photographic printing was achieved using dyes. Now, with the development of technology, the majority of amateur photographers print their own work using inkjet printers.

I see a lot of this printing up and down the country and, for me, much of it is really over the top as far as colours are concerned. The use of really strong vibrant colours can kill a photograph and it's always pleasing to see colours that are a true representation of the scene.

I spoke to a well-known colour printer who agreed with me that subtlety has 'gone completely out of the window' in recent times. He said that ten years ago people would return photographs to him if they thought the colours were slightly out, but nowadays, when printing their own, they let the same shots 'slip through the net'.

The film I use (Velvia) is slightly rich in comparison to some of the other transparency films, but it has, for a long time, been a favourite of landscape photographers and, in many instances, does record colours quite accurately. The shot opposite and the following six illustrate my point.

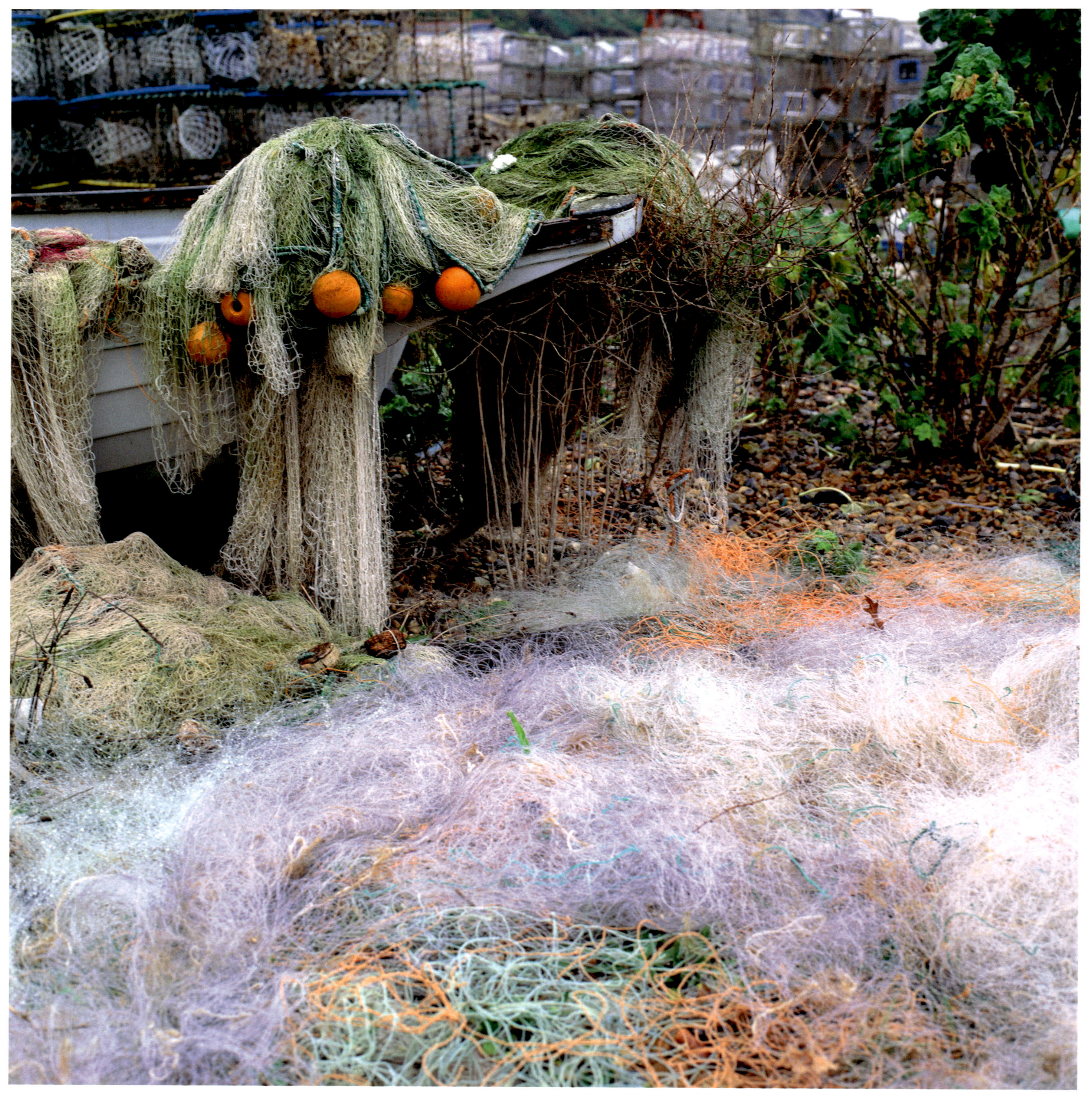

Hastings – Sussex – England

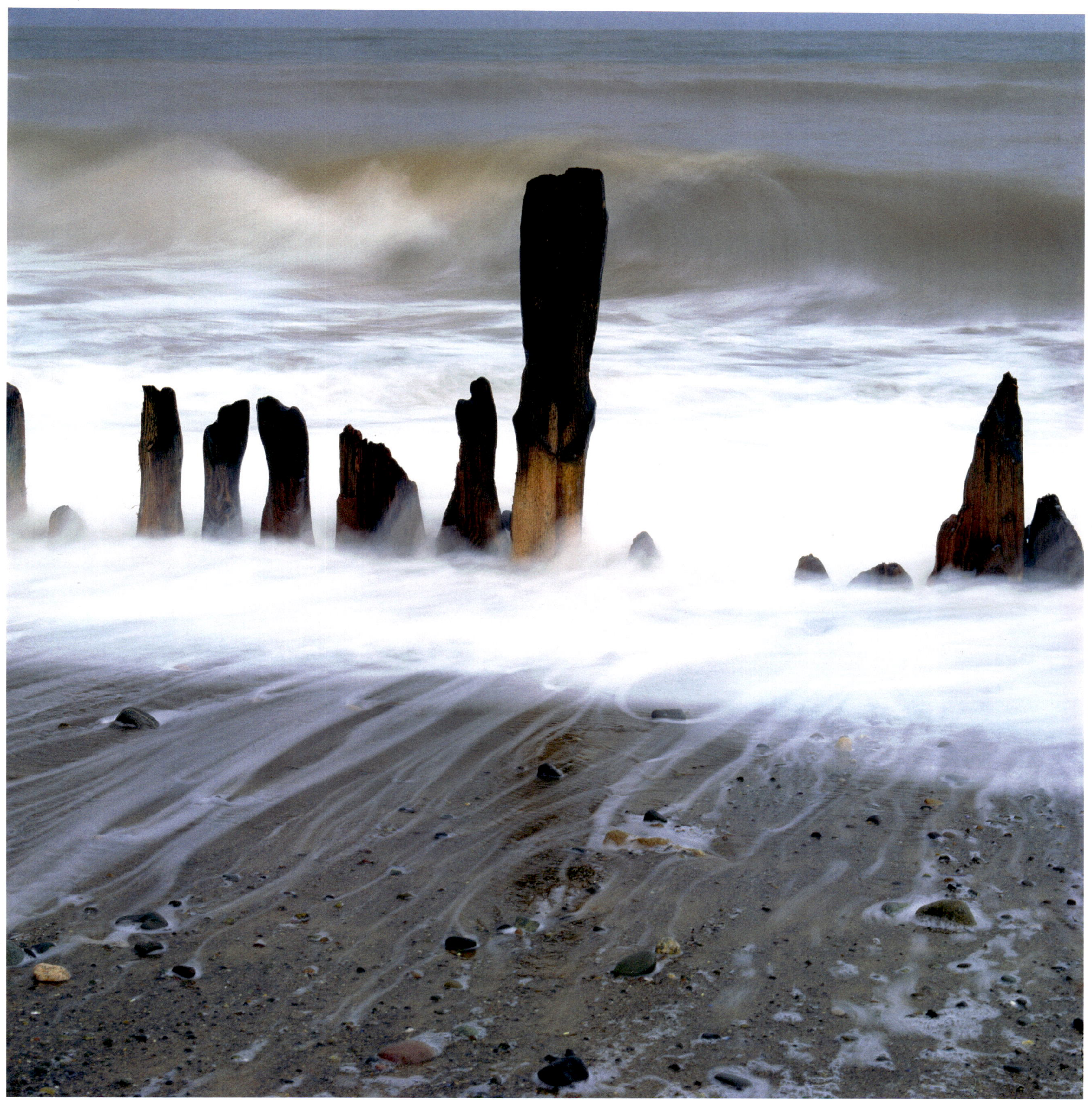

Walney Island – Cumbria – England

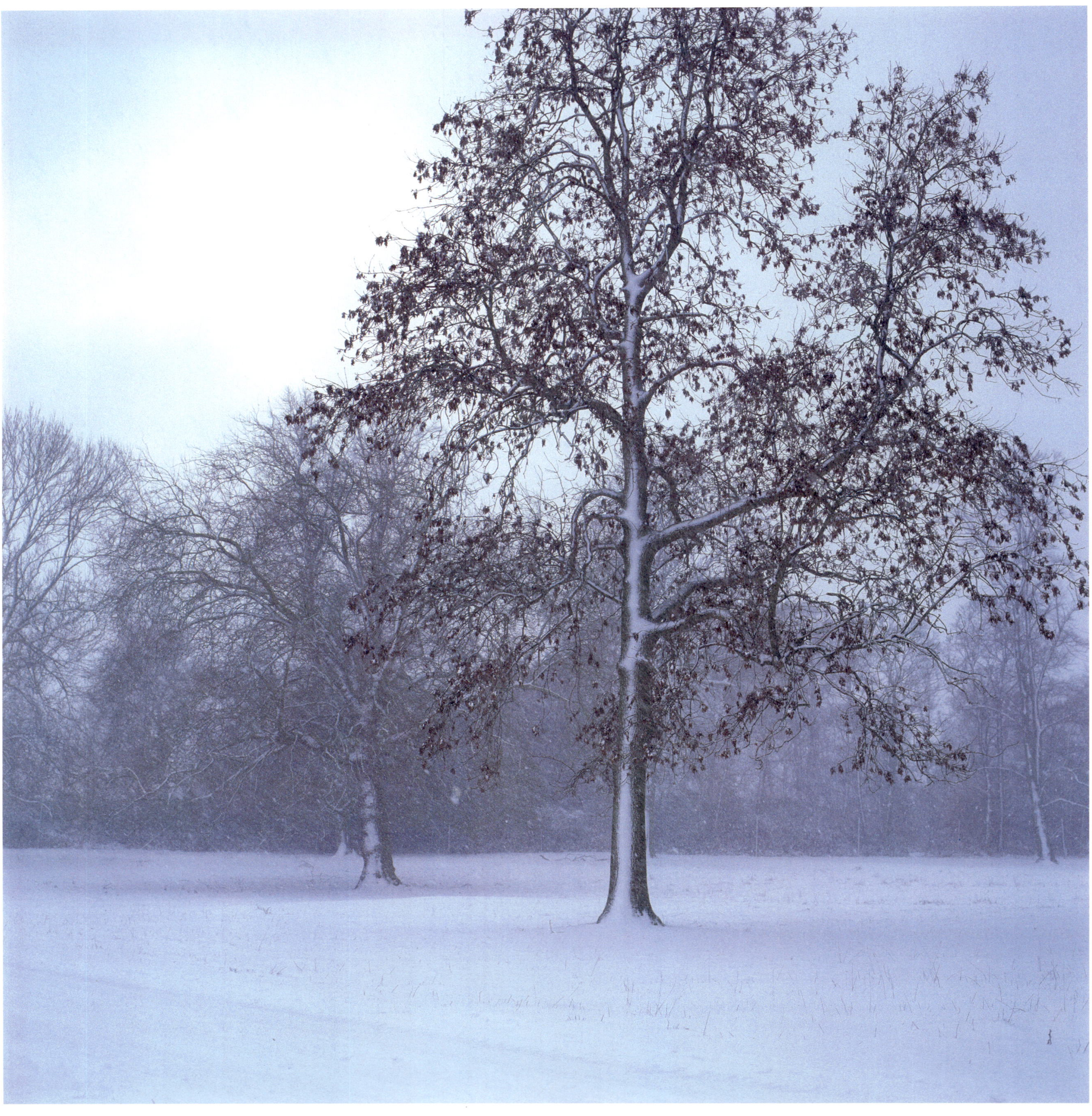

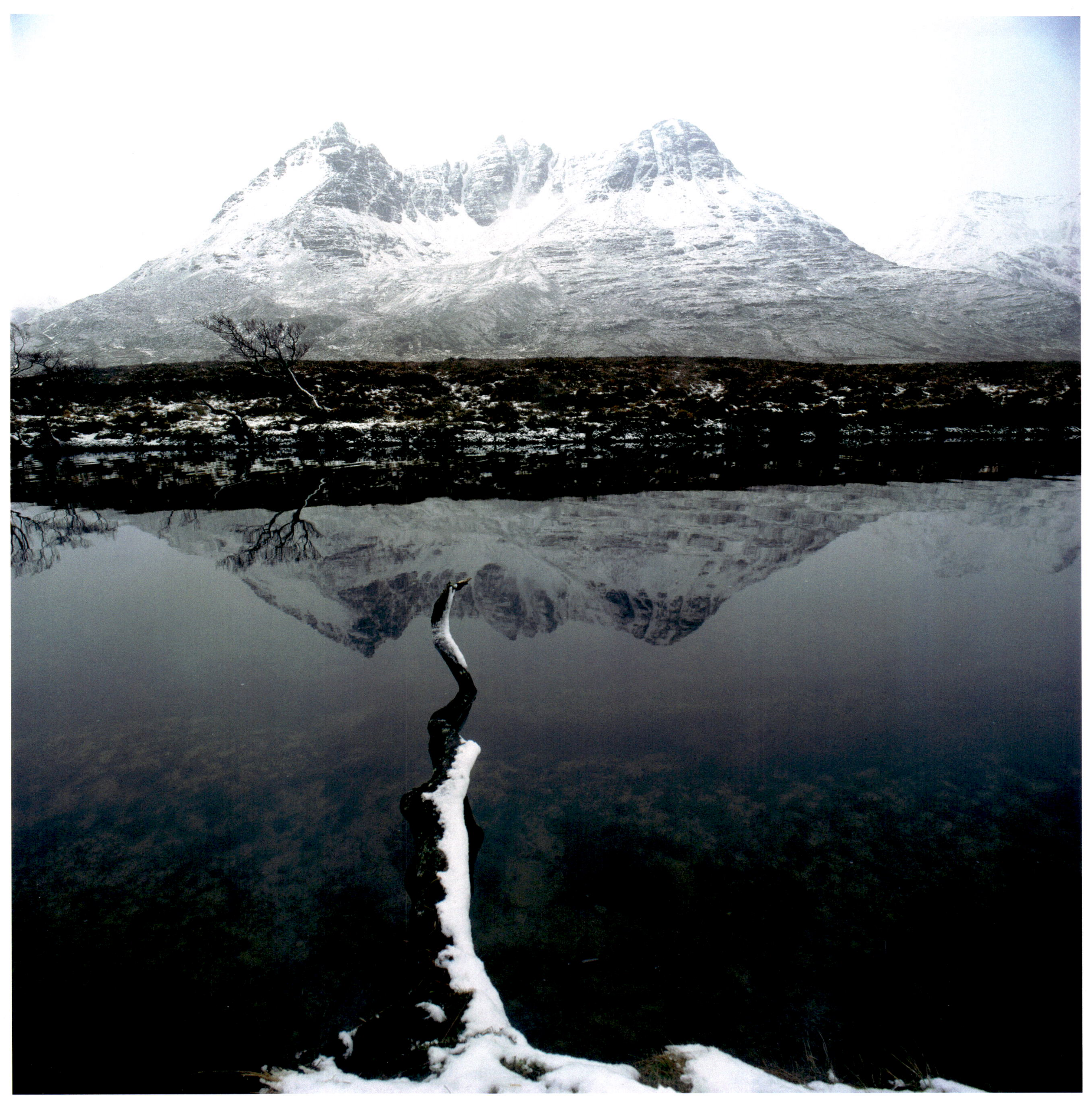

Loch na Sealga – Wester Ross – Scotland

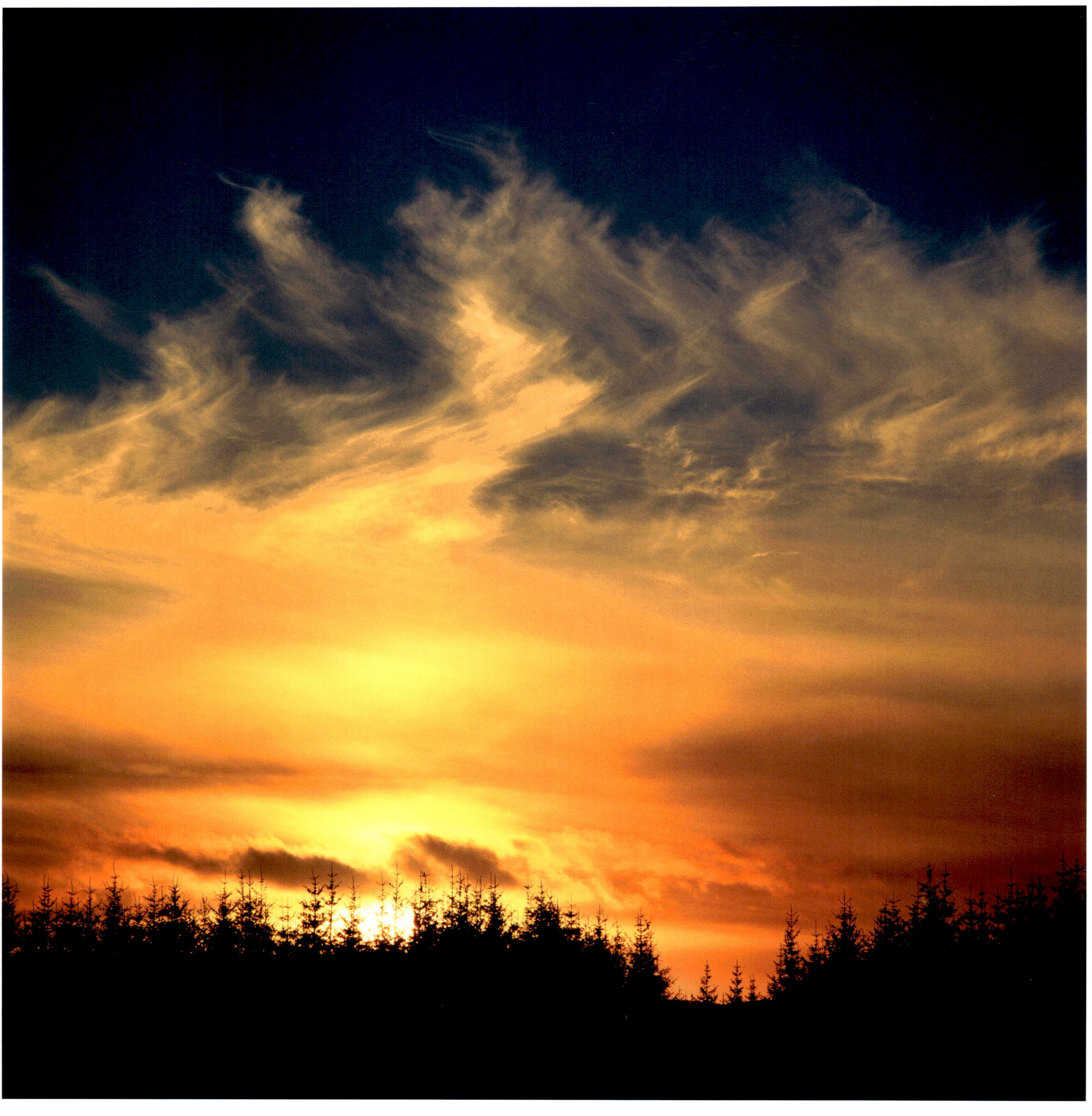

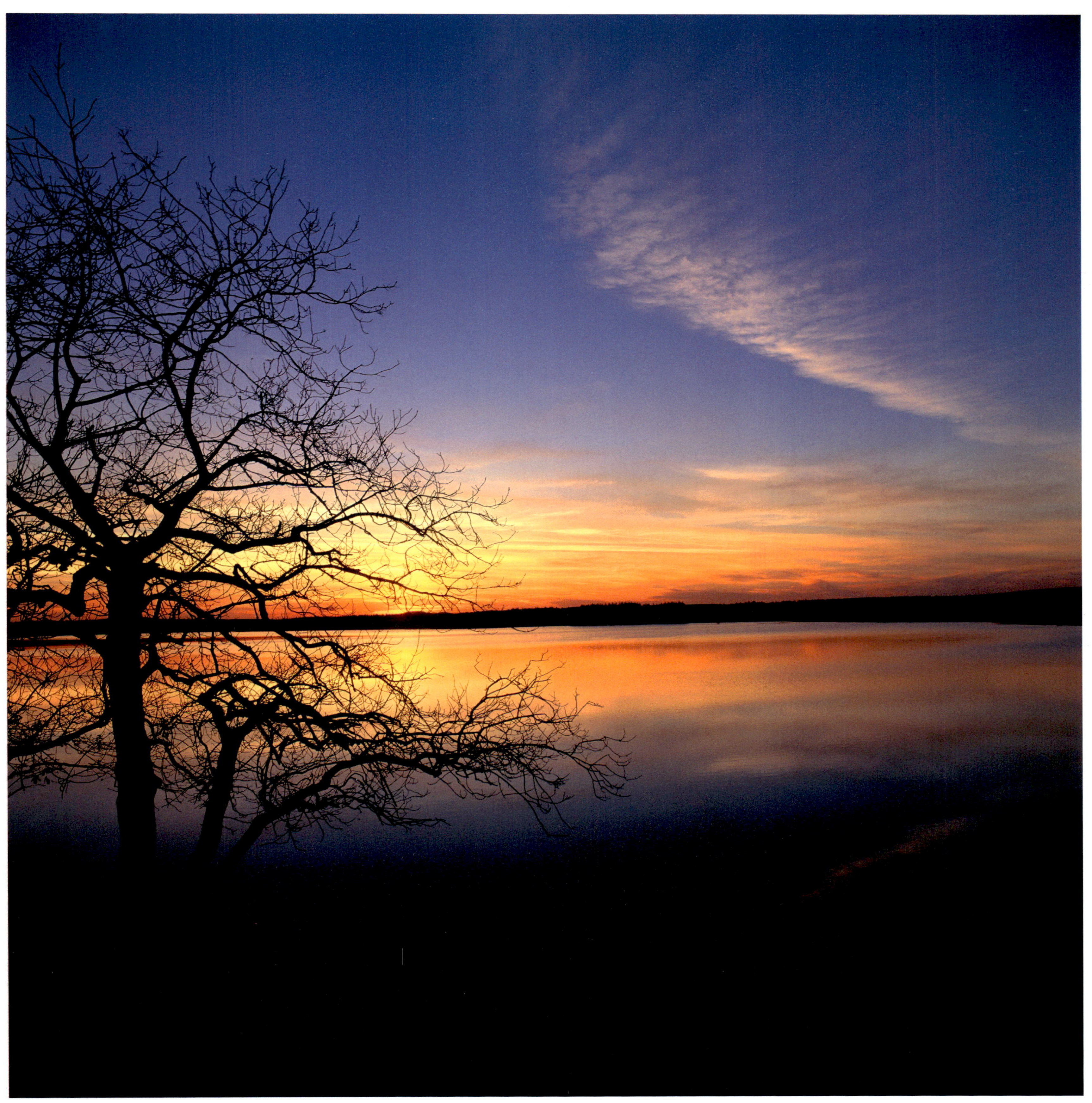

Loch Ronald – Dumfries and Galloway – Scotland

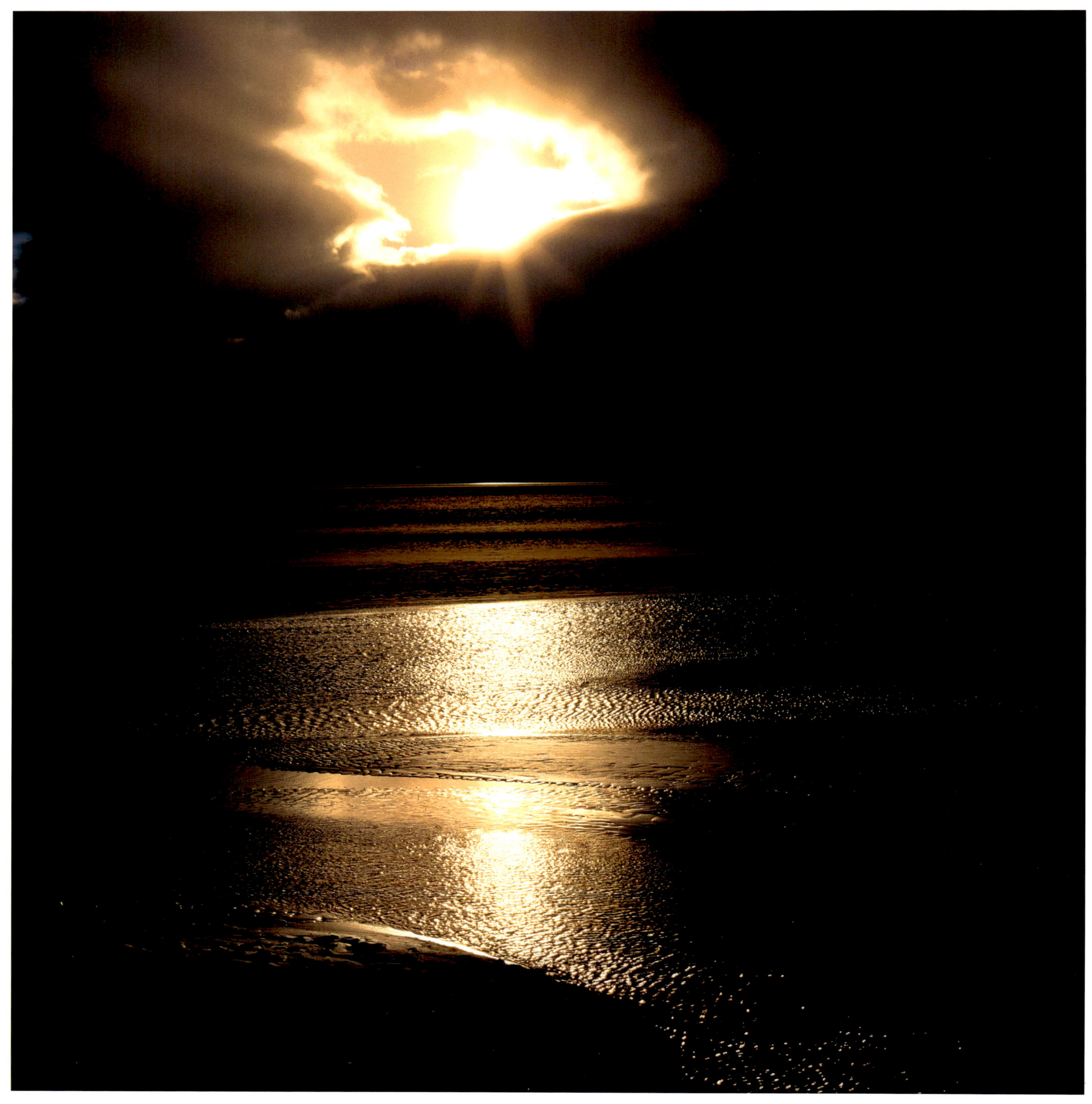

Foxfield – Cumbria – England

THE DUDDON ESTUARY

I first visited the Duddon Valley nearly sixty years ago.

Occasionally when I'm conducting my photographic workshops somewhere like Swaledale, somebody will comment, 'Oh I've already been to Swaledale'. So have I, scores of times over many years. Yet you always see it in a different light and I'm still taking photographs of the same places fifty years later. '*Been* there before' doesn't mean you have '*seen* it all before'.

I have some friends who live by the Duddon Estuary and I've been in the fortuitous position to house-sit for them when they have gone on holiday, sometimes for as long as three months. Whilst there I will often walk down to the estuary to sit and wait for 'something to happen'. Sometimes it does, sometimes it doesn't, but as a photographer, and especially one with patience, there's always chance that nature will throw up some form of display for you.

The shot opposite and the following seven were all taken within 'spitting distance' of one another in this beautiful little spot.

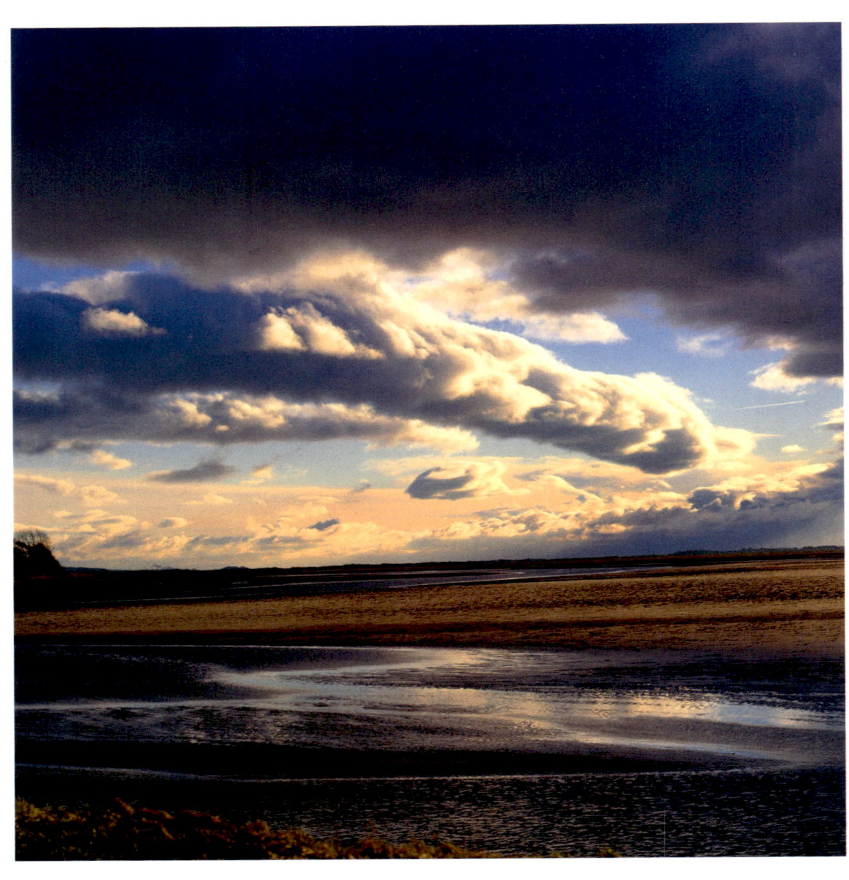
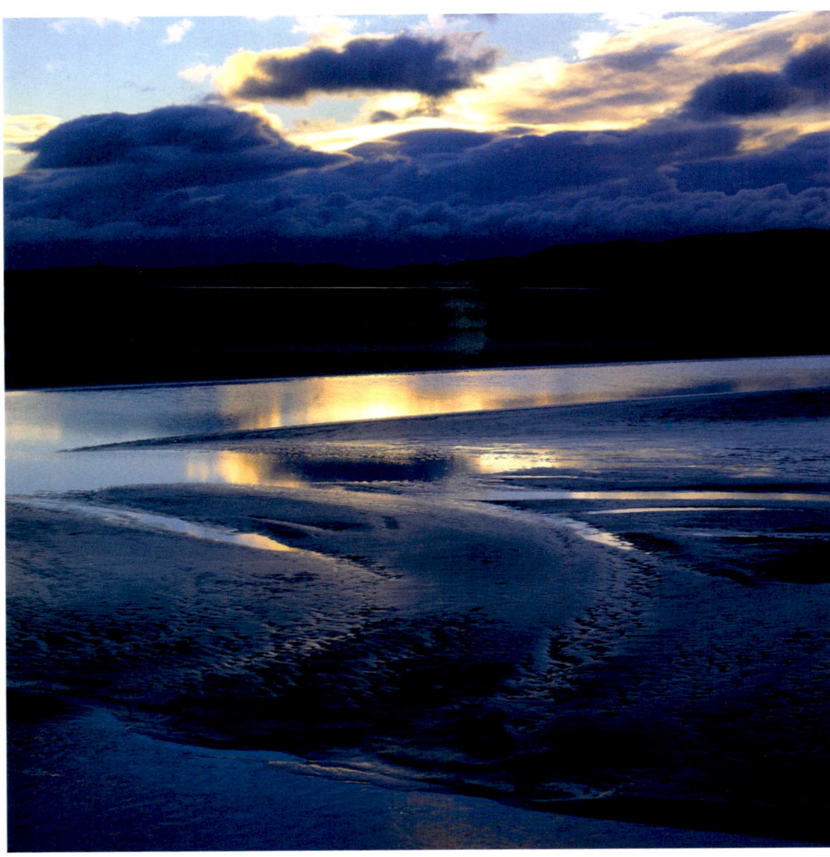
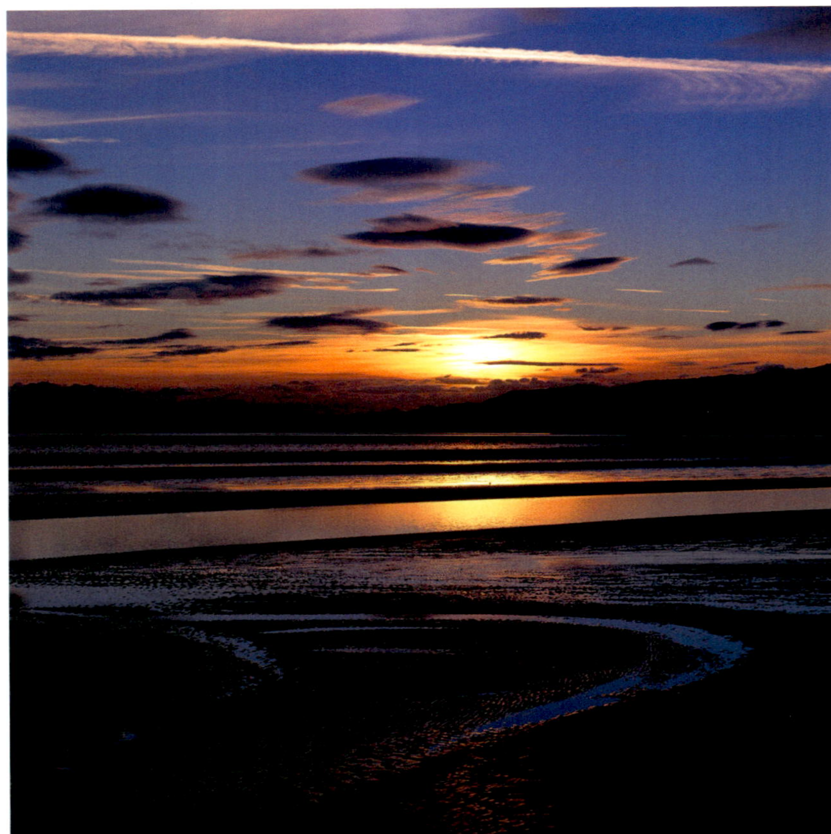
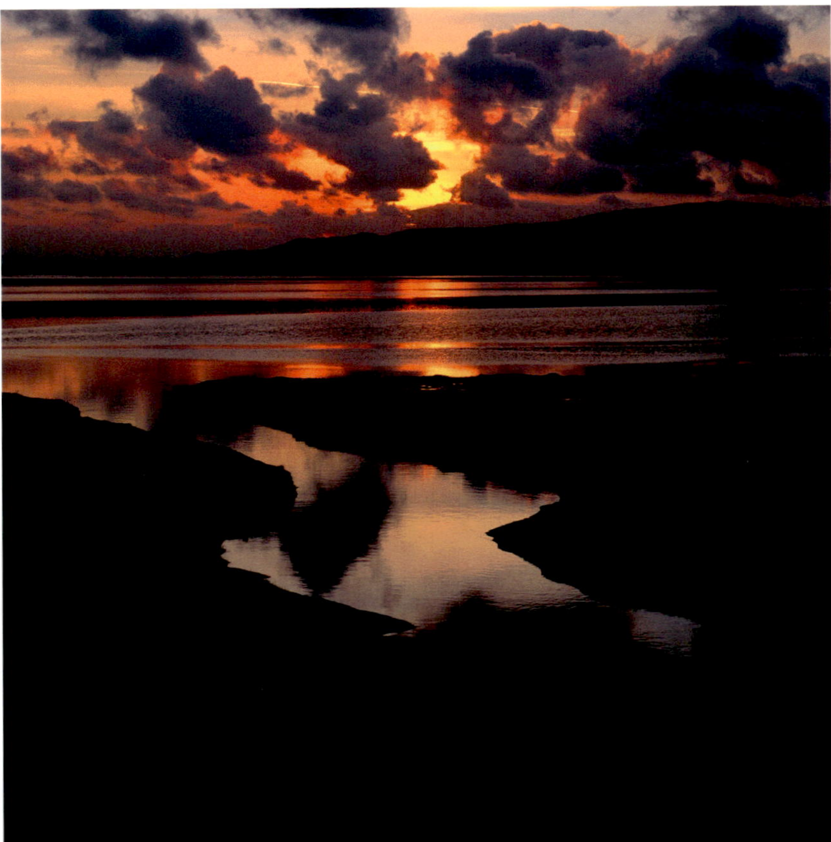

Foxfield – Cumbria – England

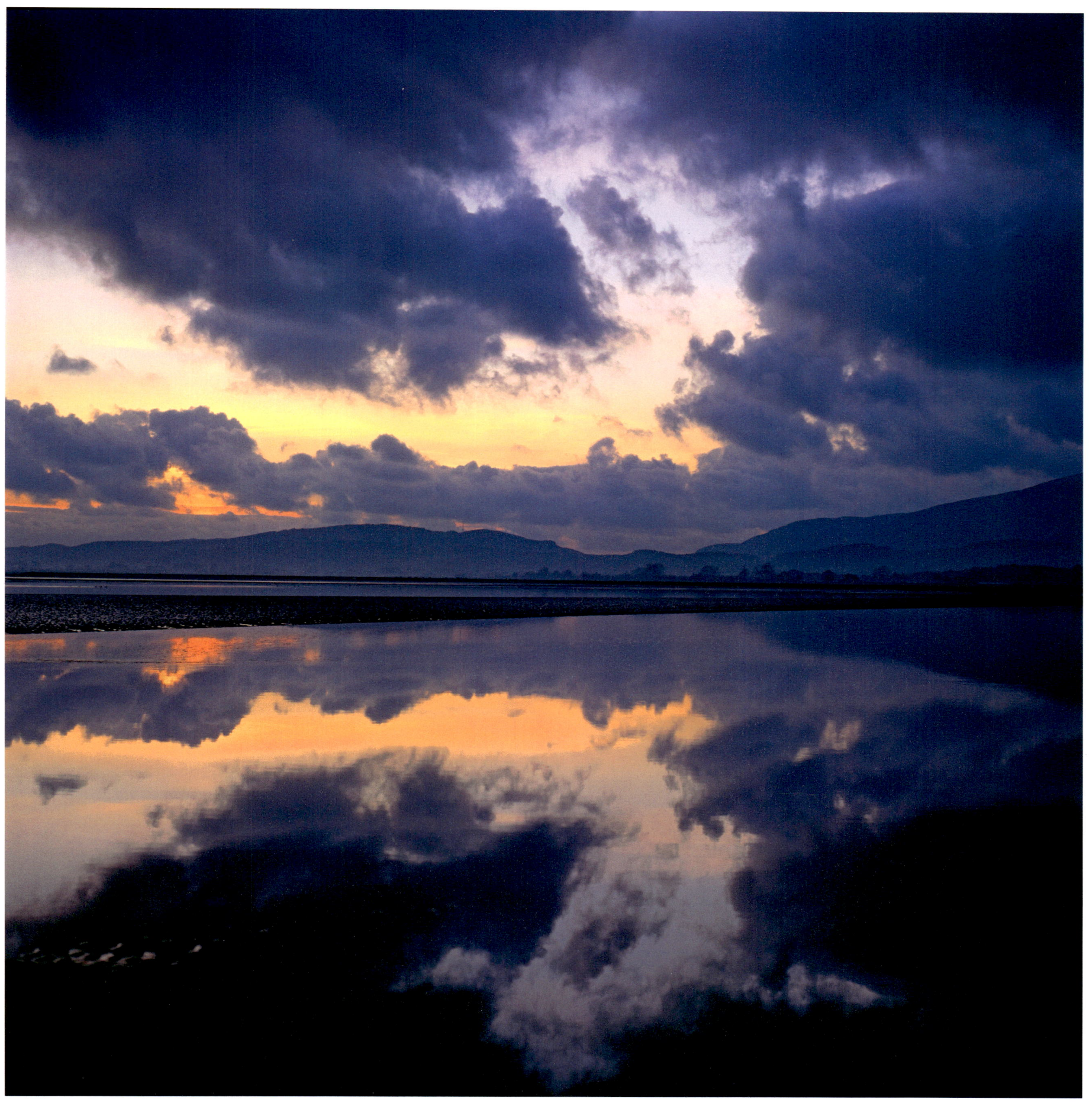

Foxfield – Cumbria – England

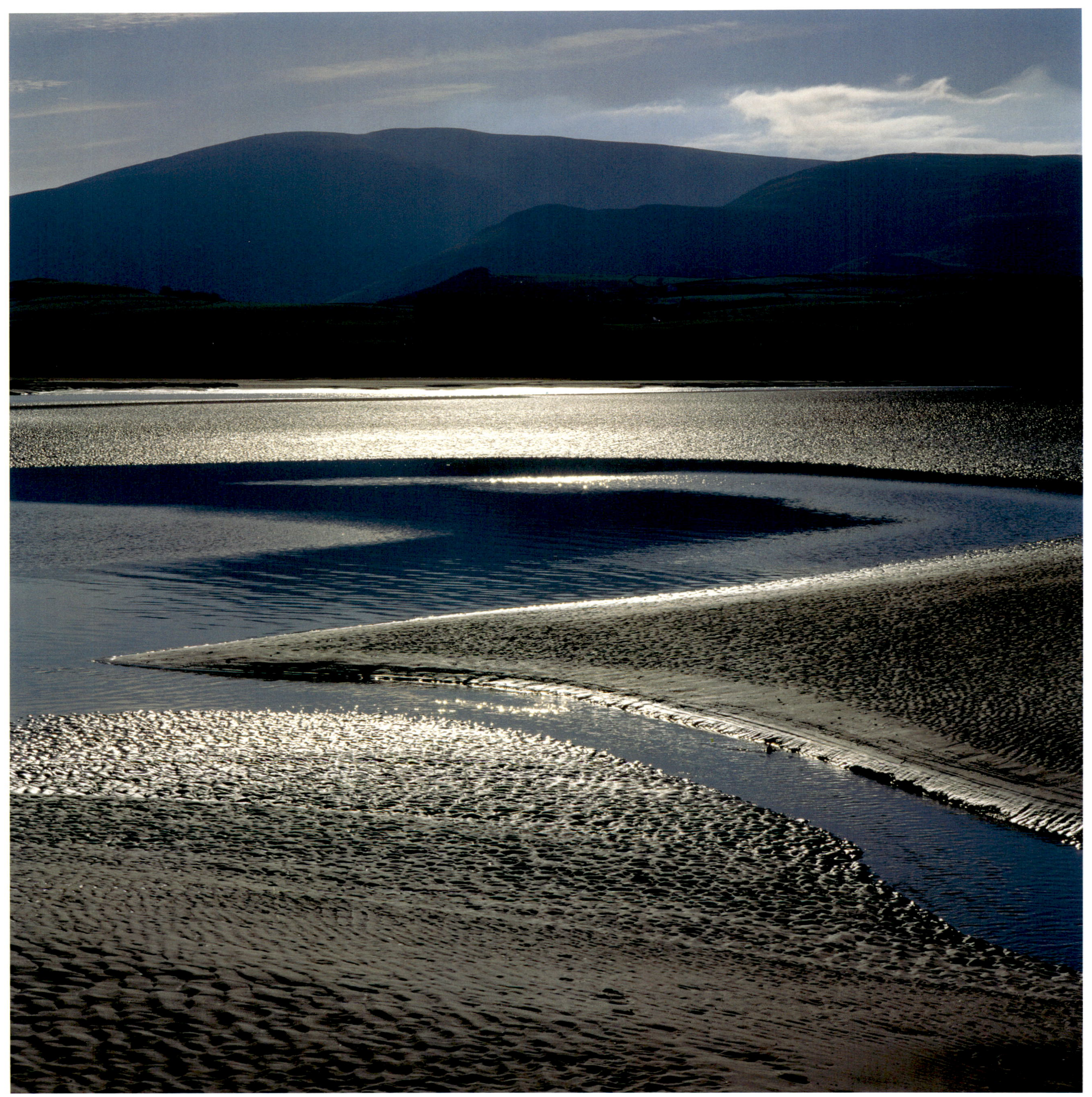

Foxfield (2 p.m.) – Cumbria – England

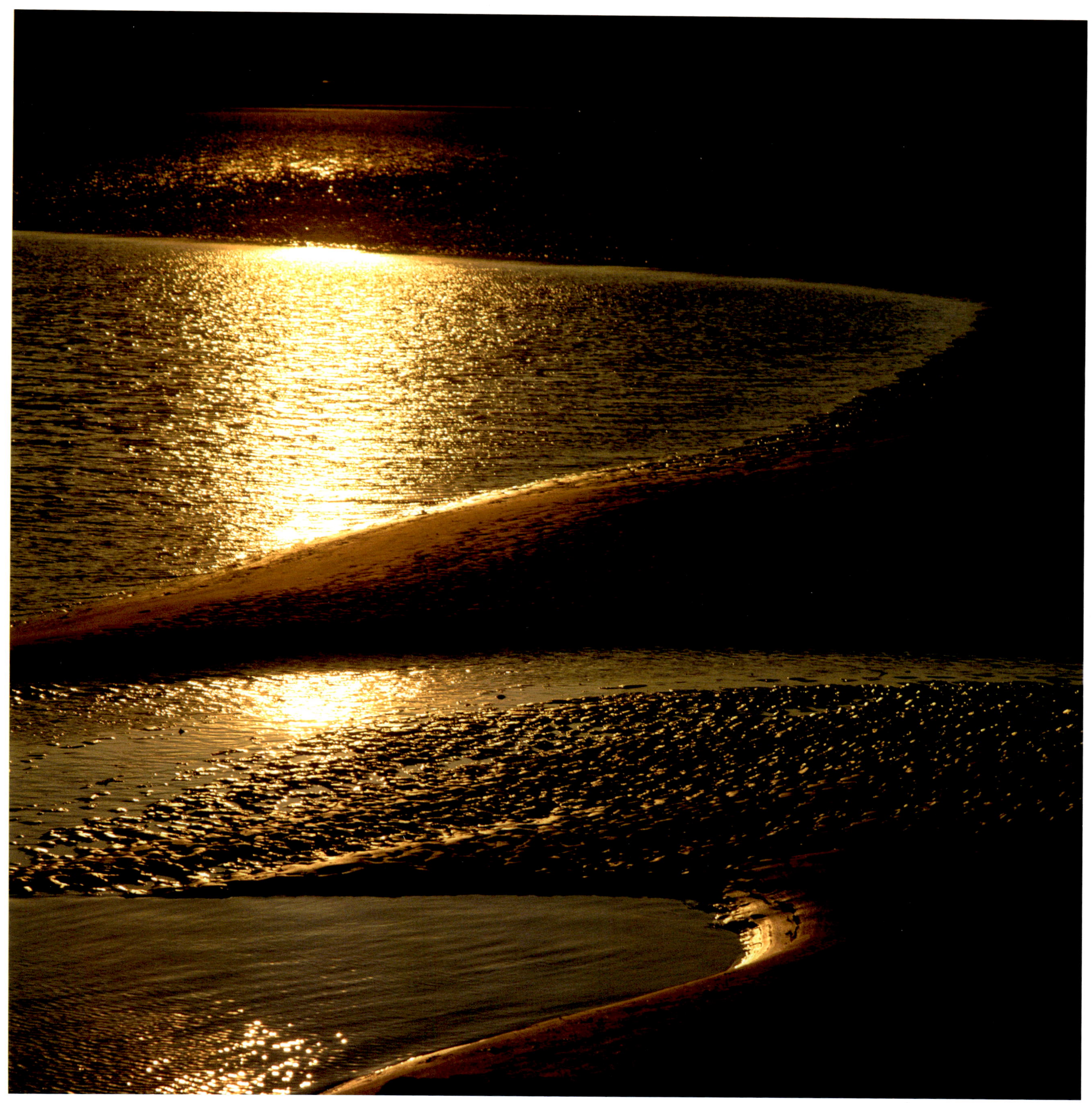

Foxfield (4 p.m.) – Cumbria – England

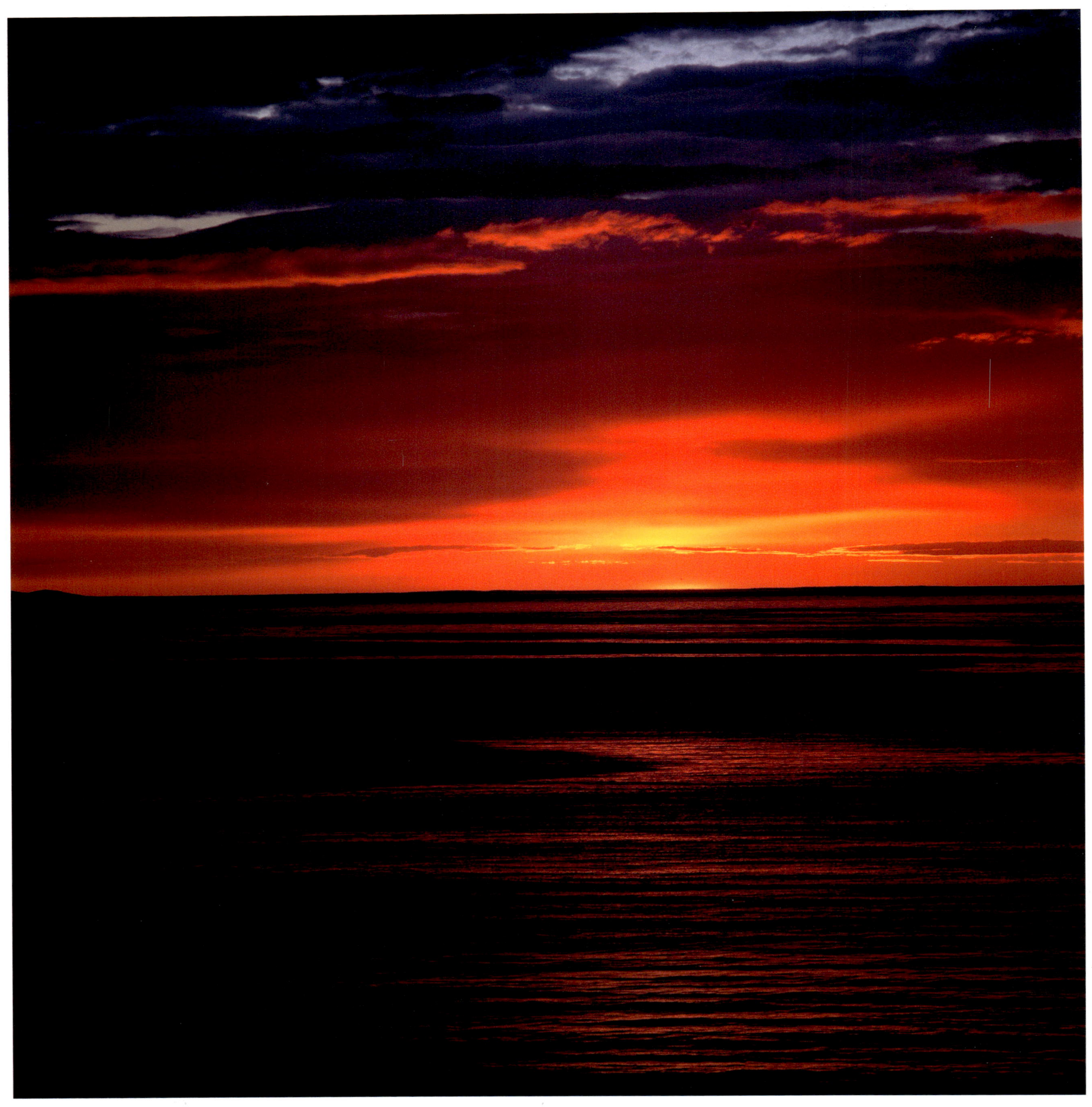

Mellon Charles – Wester Ross – Scotland

TECHNOLOGY

Technology! A costly business. It seems that as soon as you buy anything to do with technology these days, it's old hat the very day after. Unfortunately, photography has also become part of the technological era. No sooner does a model appear, its successor follows a short time later.

Although this technology is supposed to make life easier for us all, it actually consumes much of our time. Research shows that many people spend eight hours a day using computers, watching television and playing on phones and, for me this illustrates the old quote about life 'not being a rehearsal'. My time is precious to me and the last thing I want is to be indoors when I could be out photographing.

This was all brought home to me when visiting a family who were 'walking' through a virtual woodland in a darkened corner of their living room. I couldn't help but think that it would be far better for them all to walk through a real woodland, hearing and smelling the reality of it all. It would certainly be a healthier option.

In photographic terms, therefore, capturing an image in the camera when out on location is all-important to me. Then for someone to admire your work, in the knowledge that no manipulation has been carried out, is very gratifying.

These kinds of experiences are so awe-inspiring that I just want to see more and more of them. The only time I won't be able to do so is when my legs have given up the ghost. Hopefully, by that time, technology will have developed motorised limbs to help me out.

Men for the sake of getting a living forget to live.
MARGARET FULLER

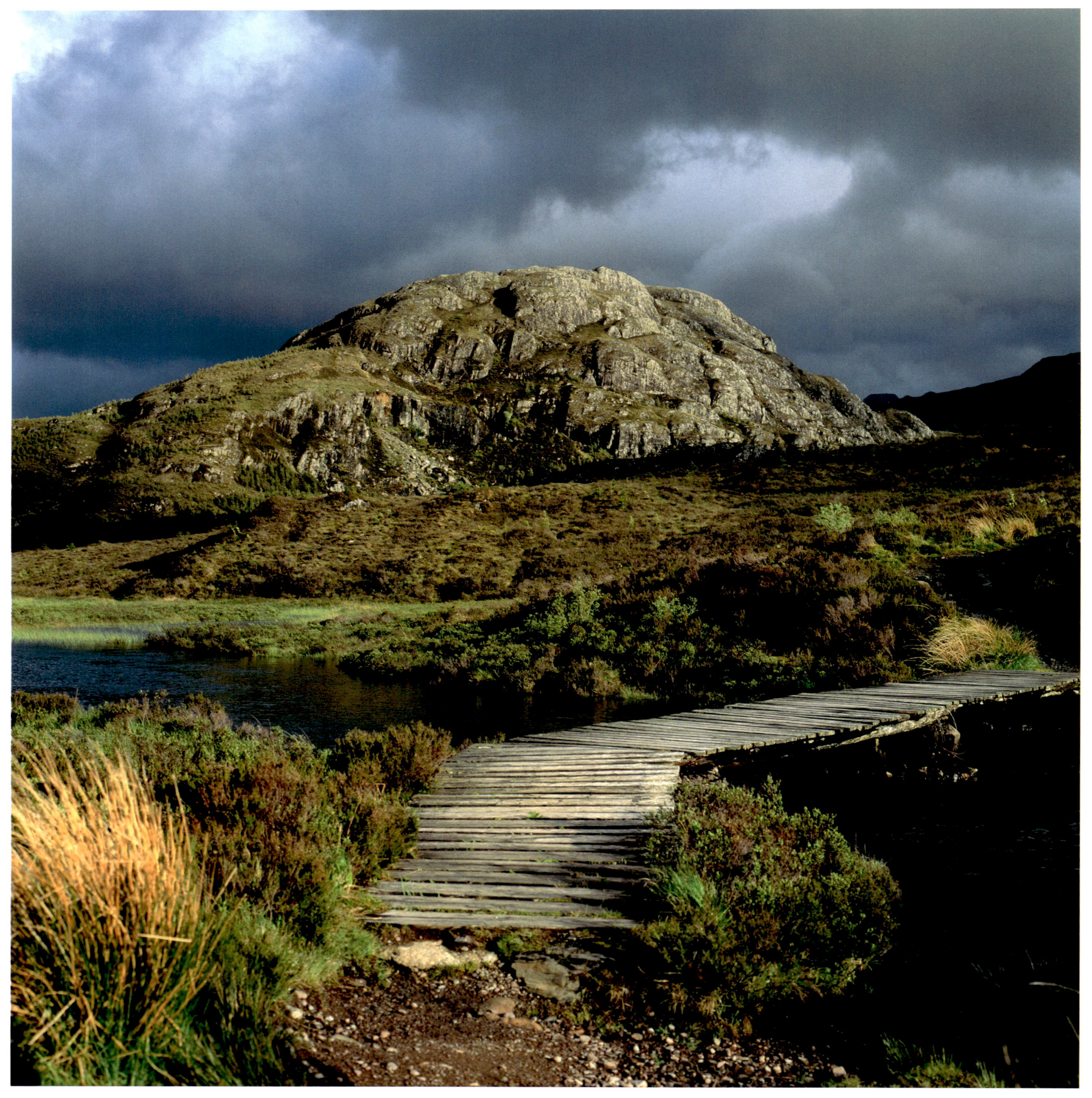

Am Feur Loch – Wester Ross – Scotland

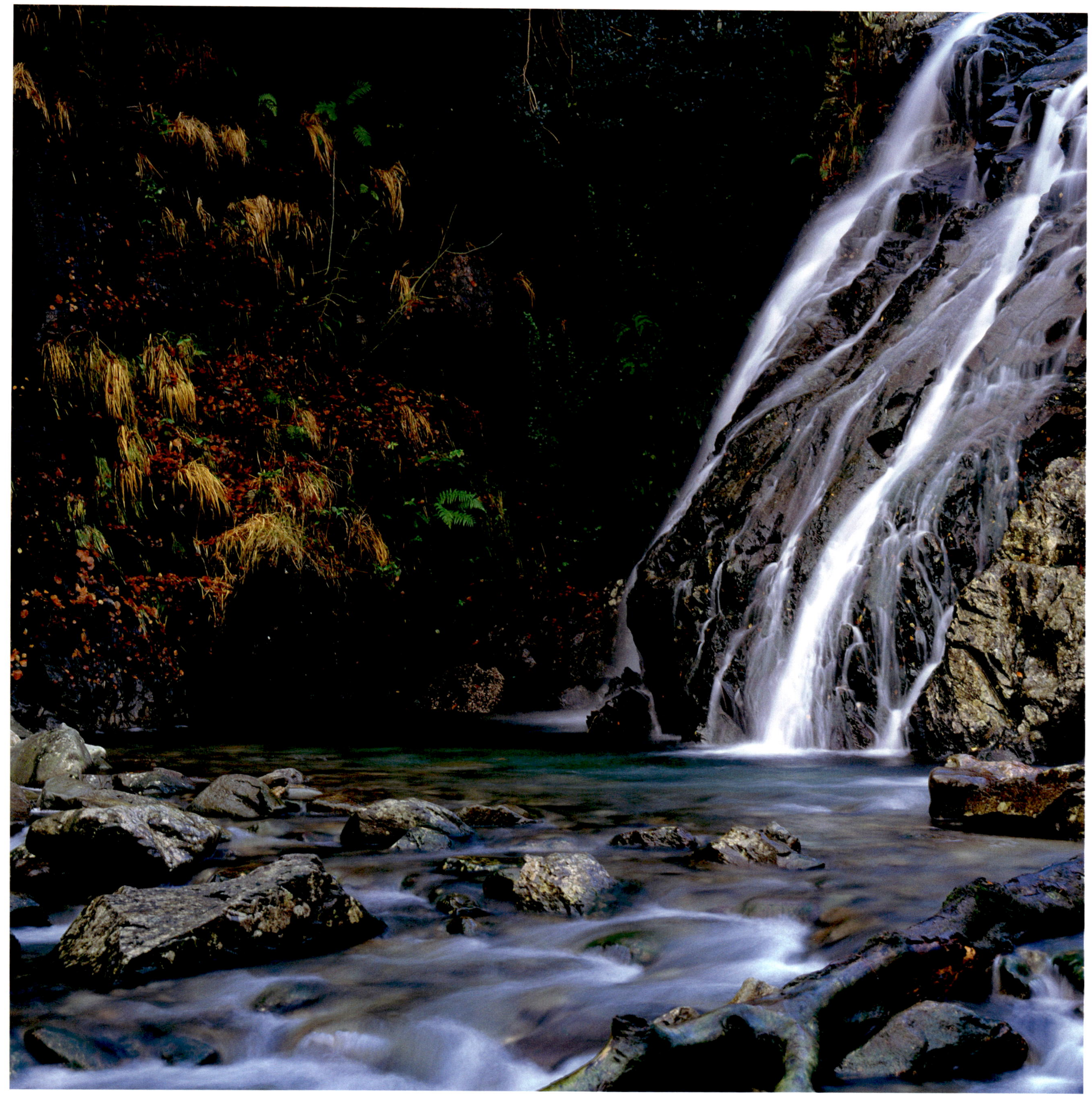

Church Beck – Cumbria – England

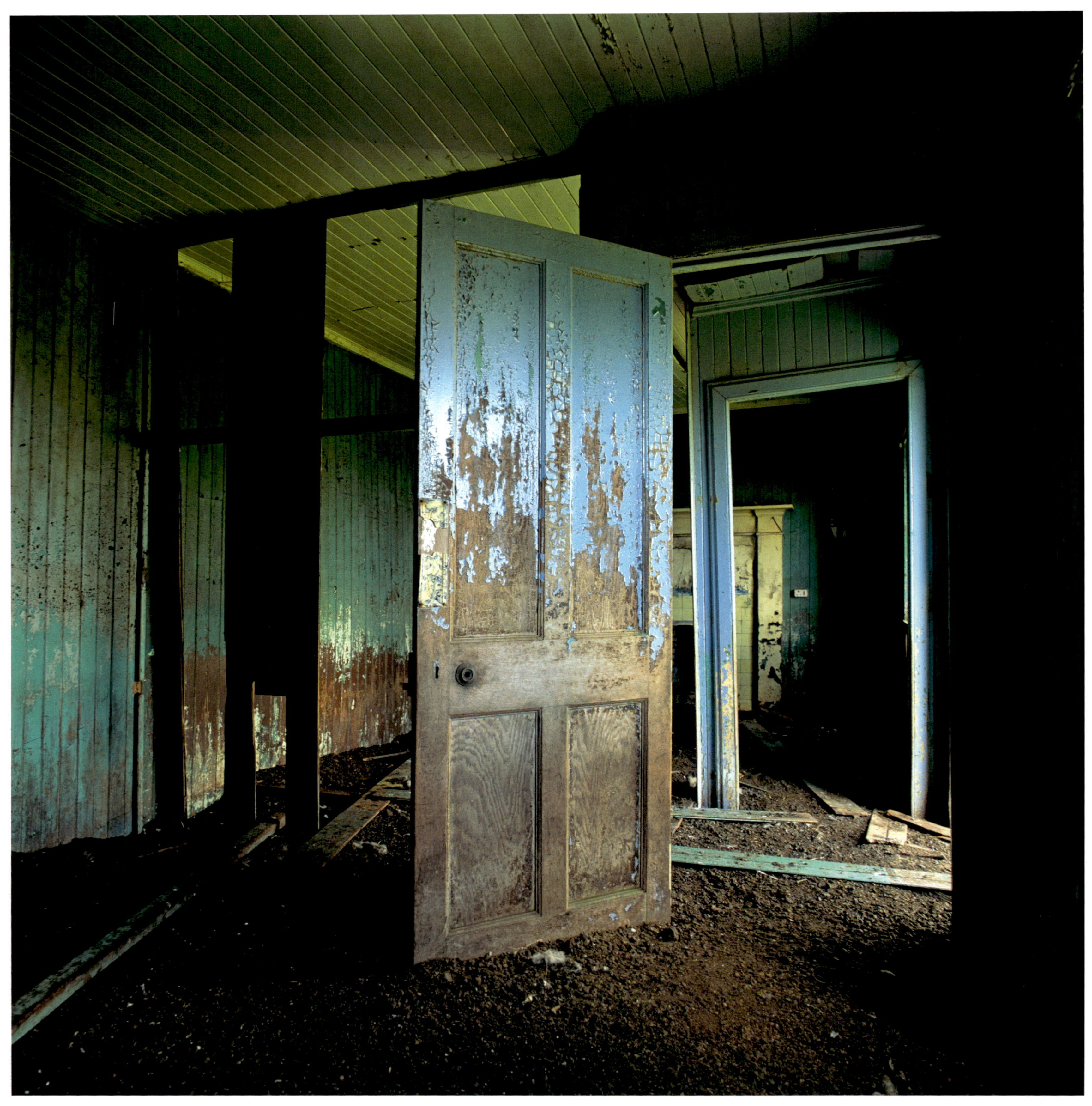

Melvaig – Wester Ross – Scotland

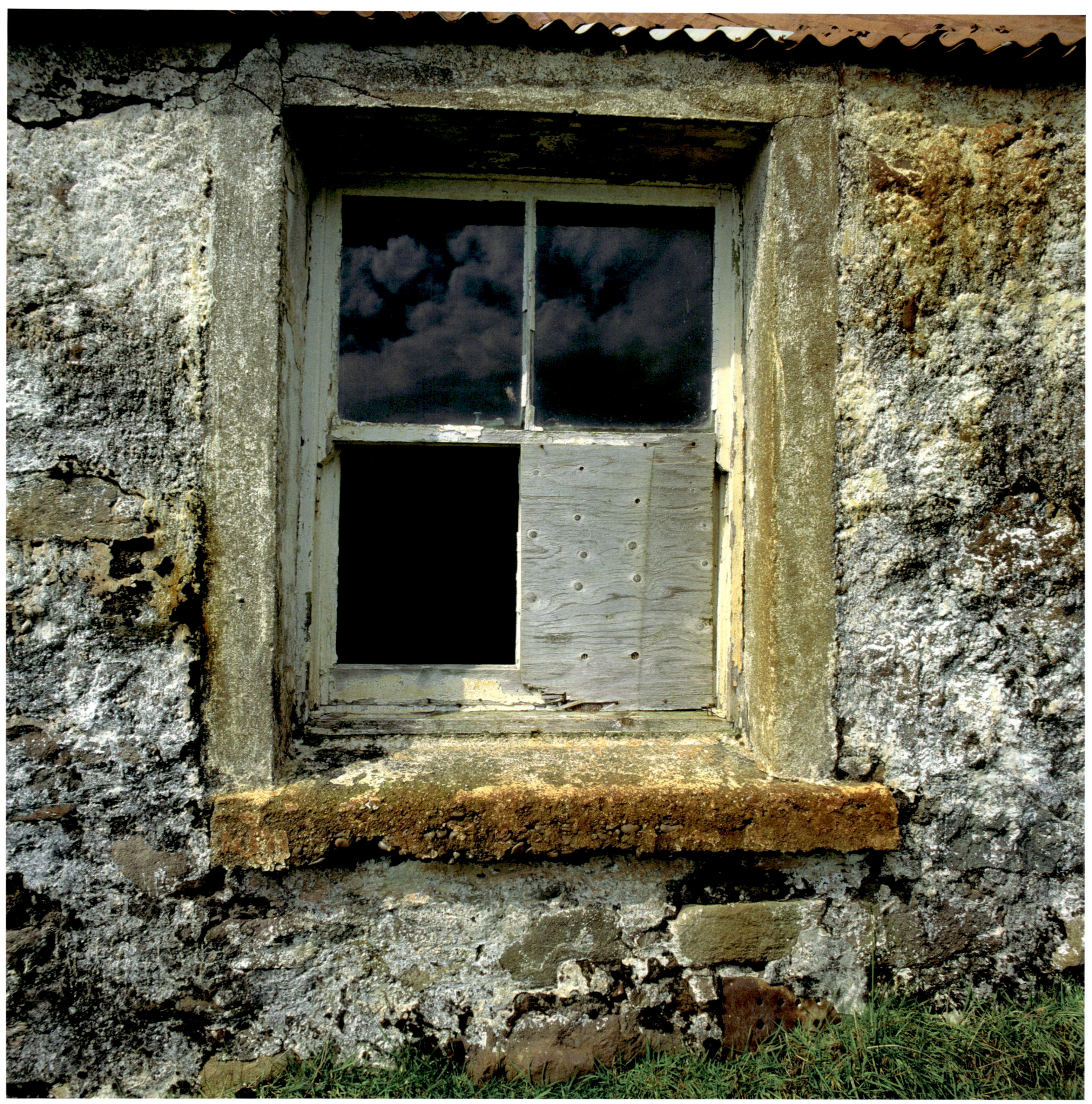

Melvaig – Wester Ross – Scotland

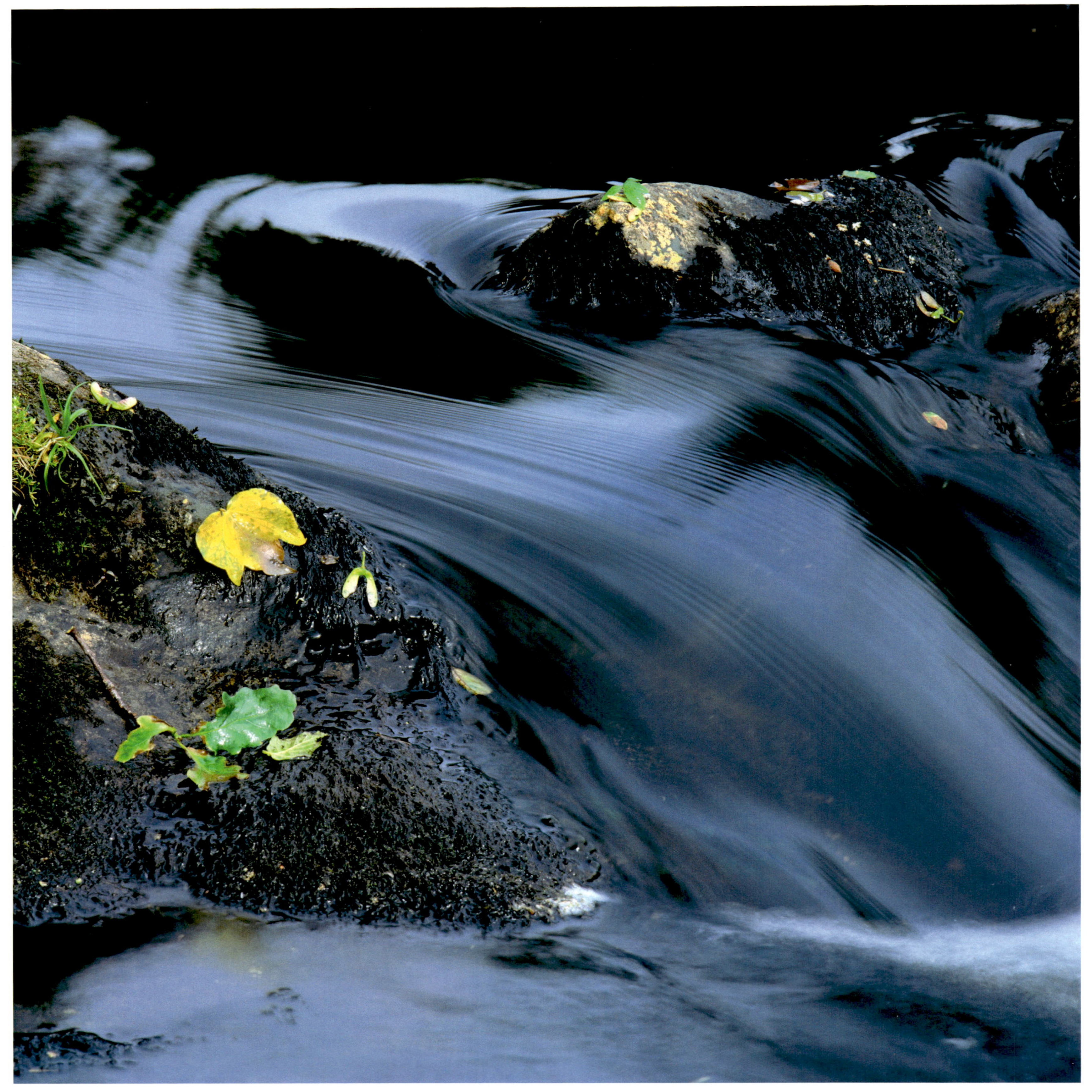

Logan Beck – Cumbria – England

I have two doctors – my right and my left leg.
G. M. TREVELYAN

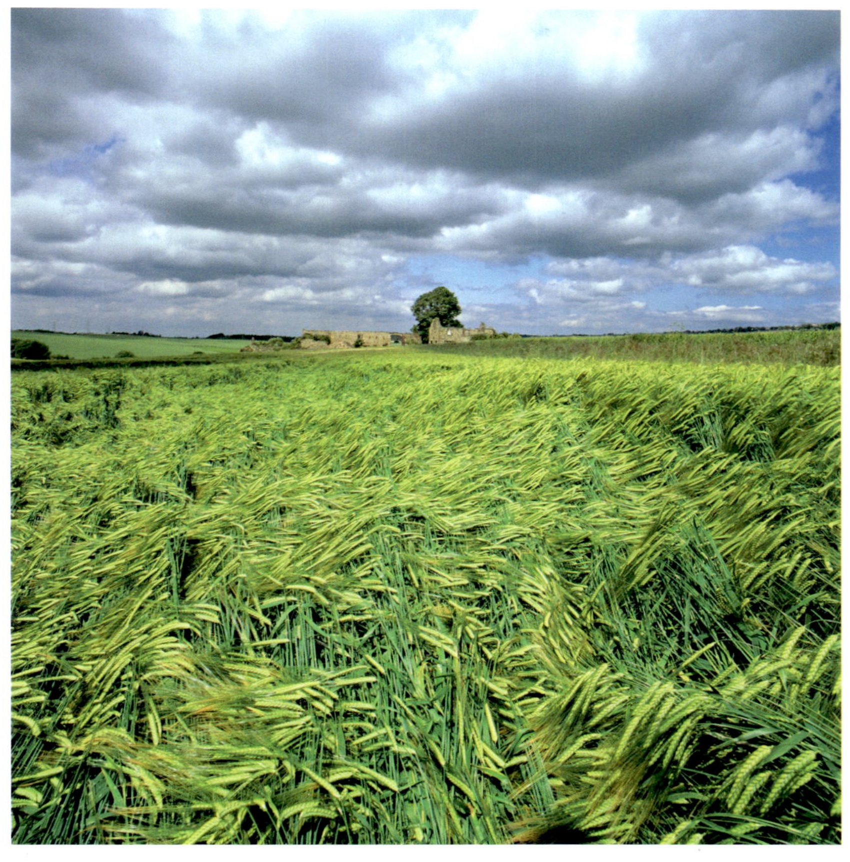

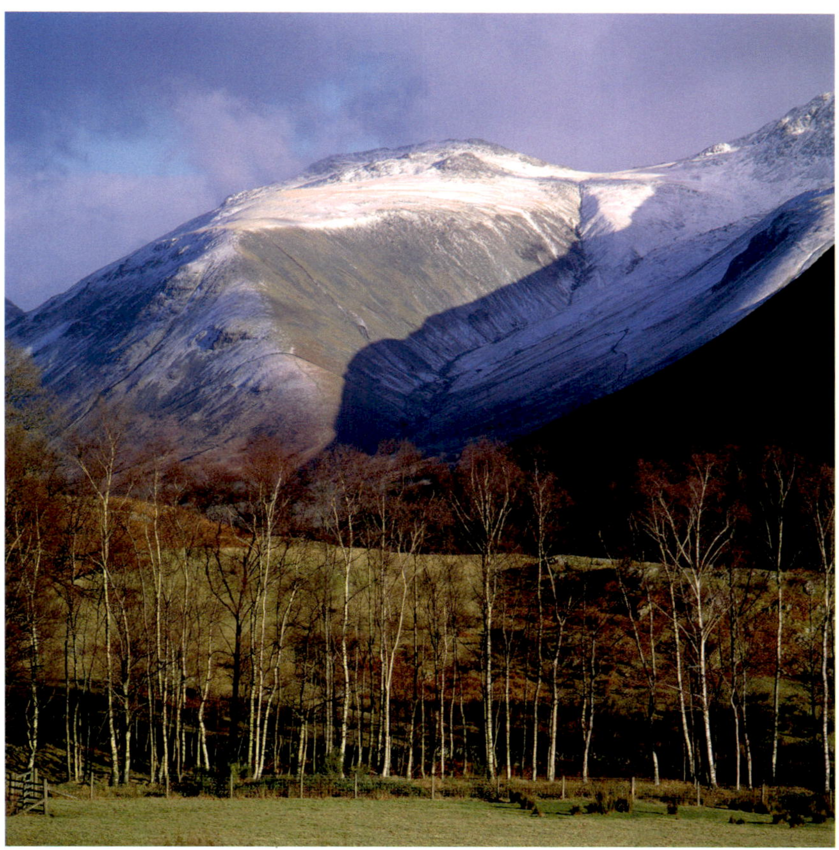

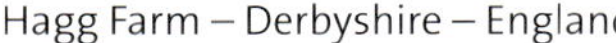

Hagg Farm – Derbyshire – England

Wasdale – Cumbria – England

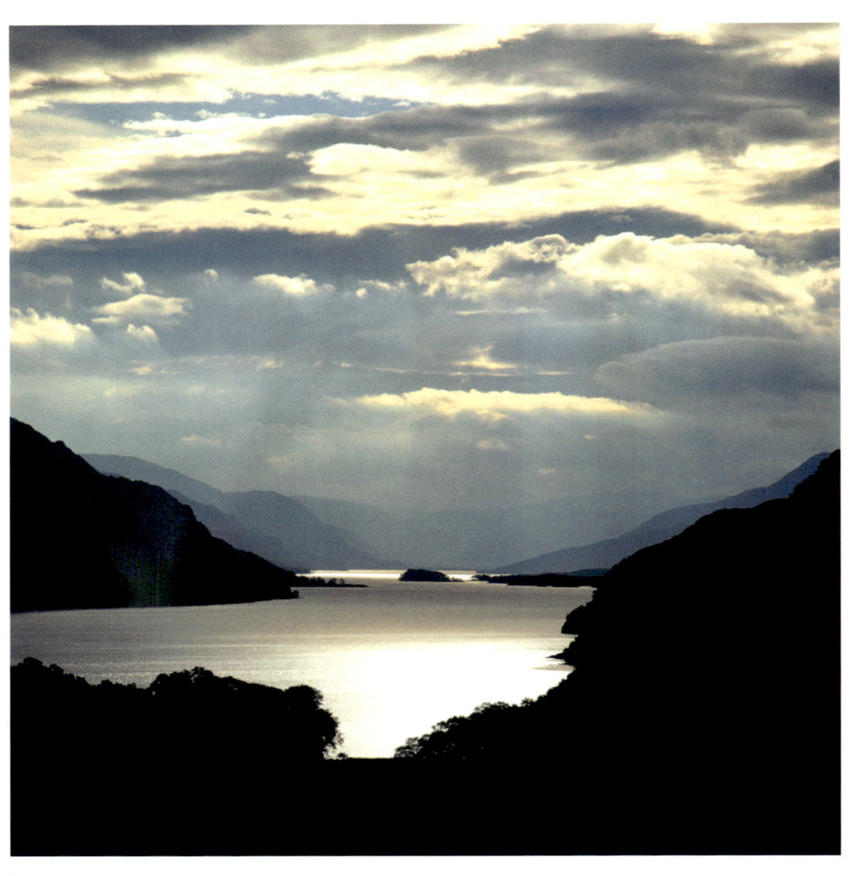

Loch Maree (morning) – Wester Ross – Scotland

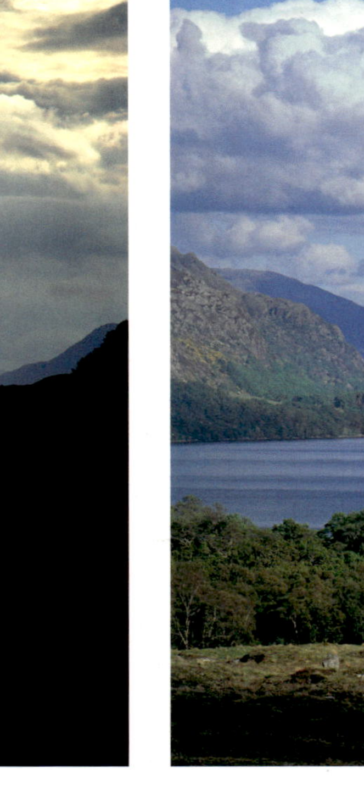

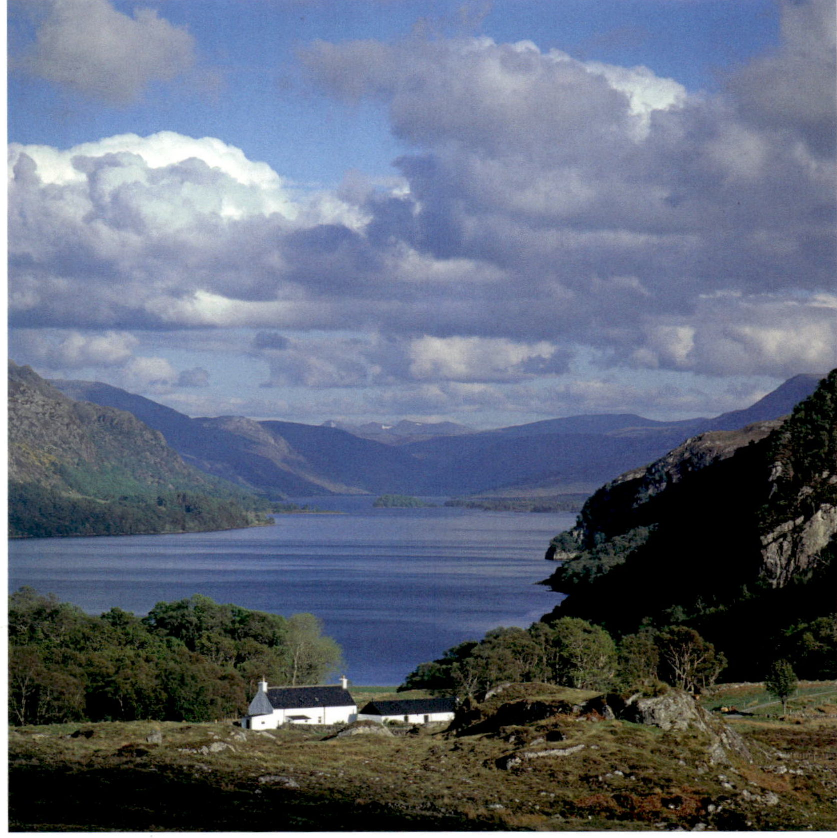

Loch Maree (afternoon) – Wester Ross – Scotland

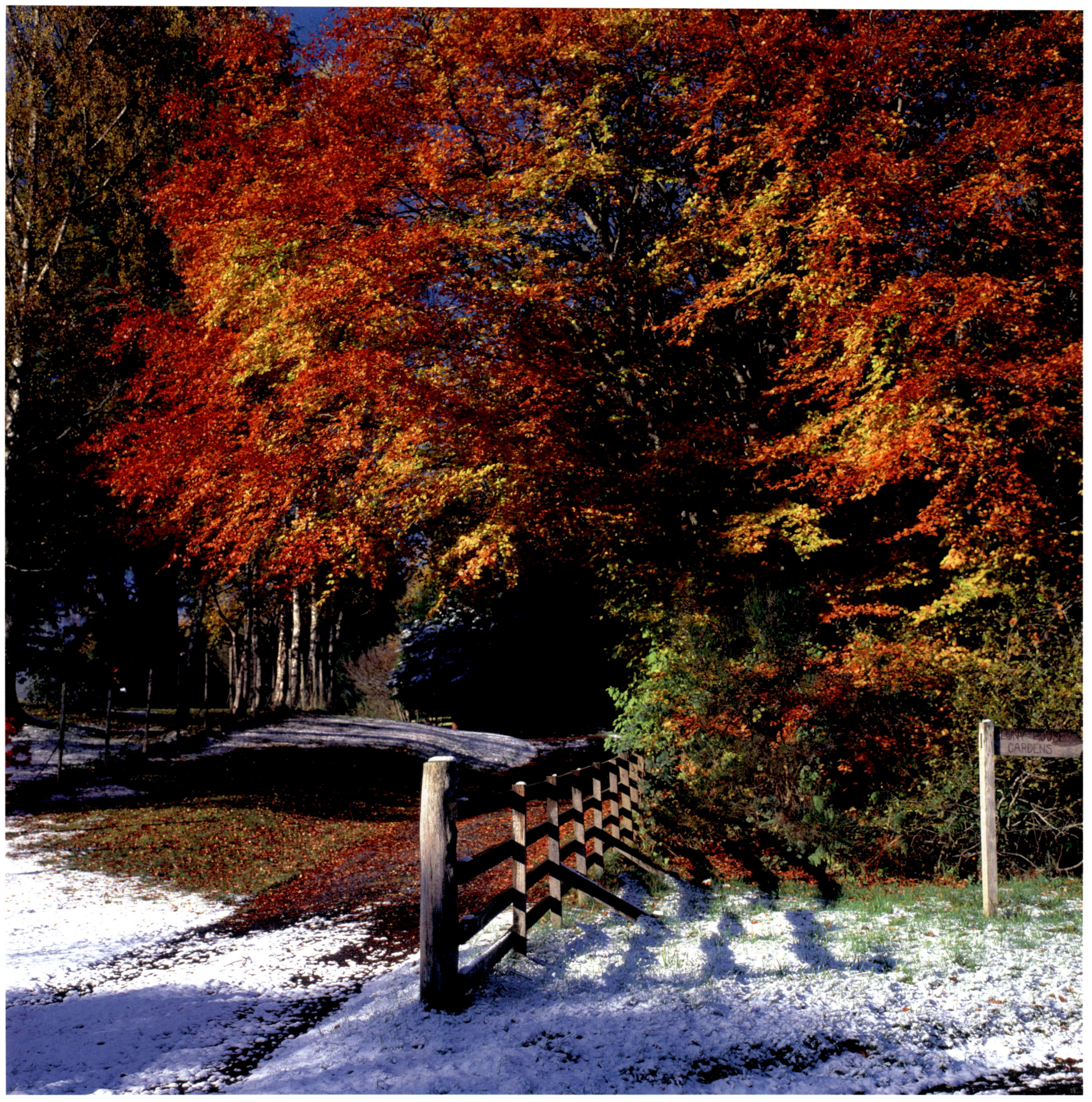

Tayside – Perthshire – Scotland

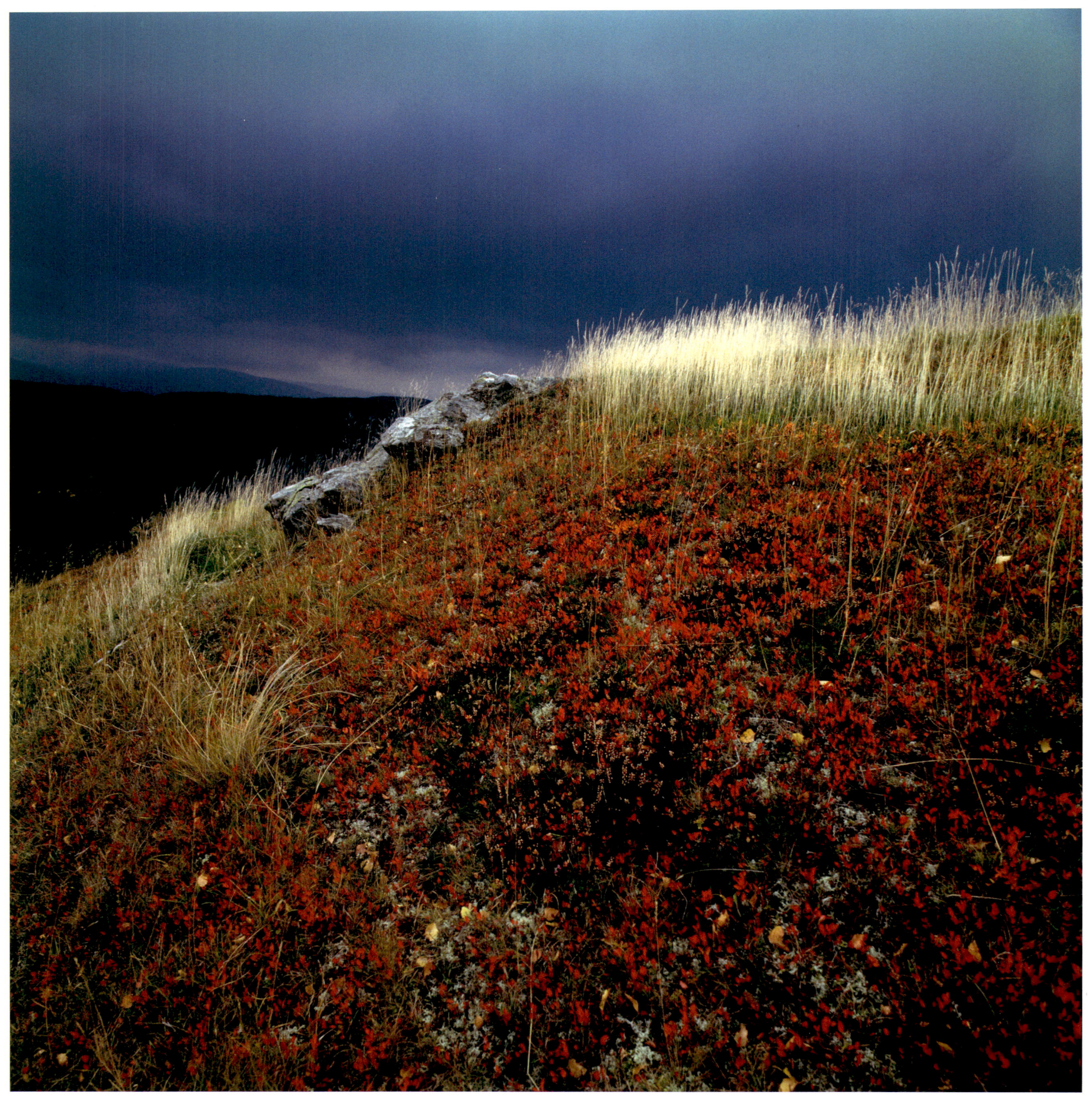

Above Loch Tay – Perthshire – Scotland

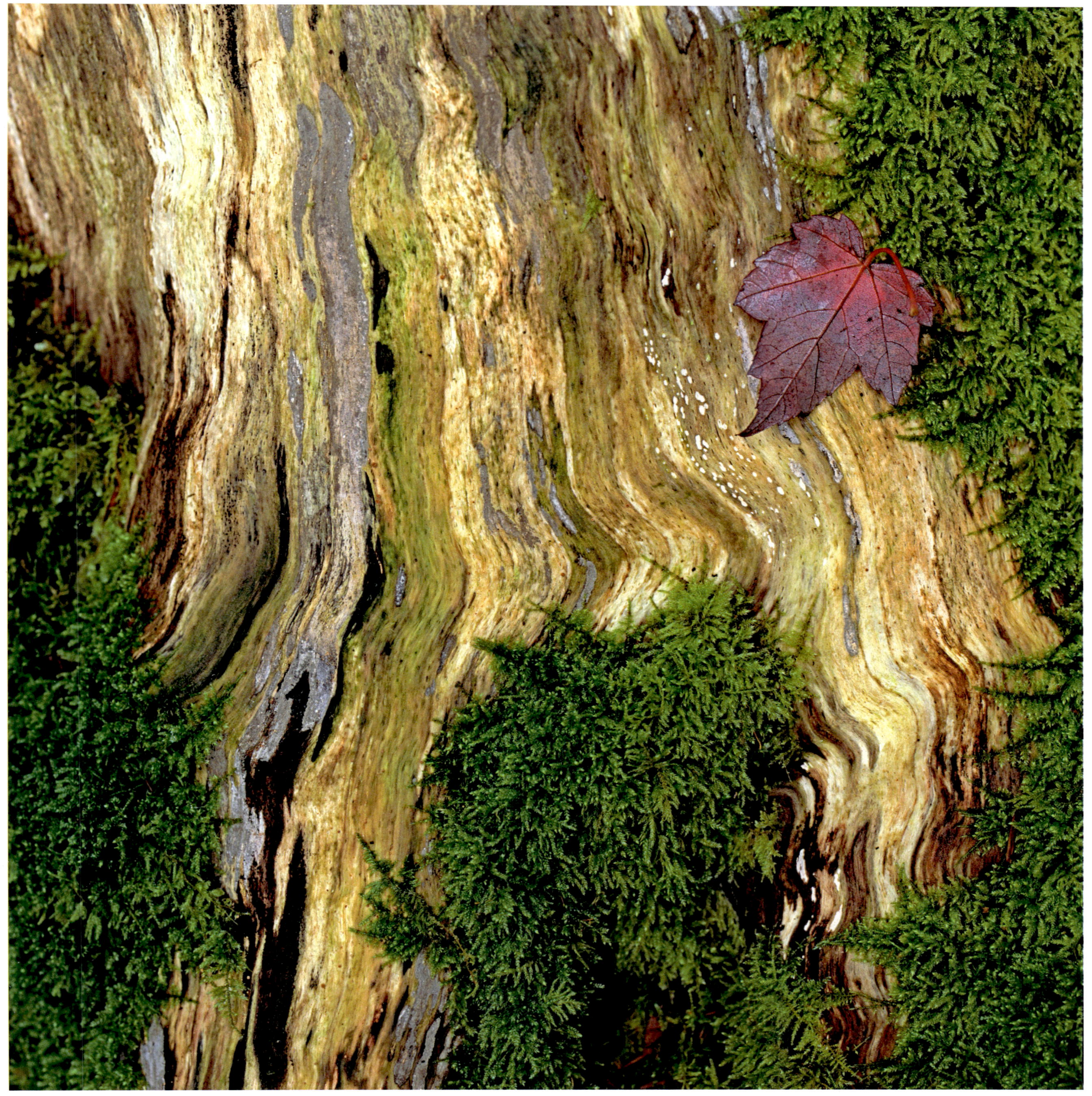

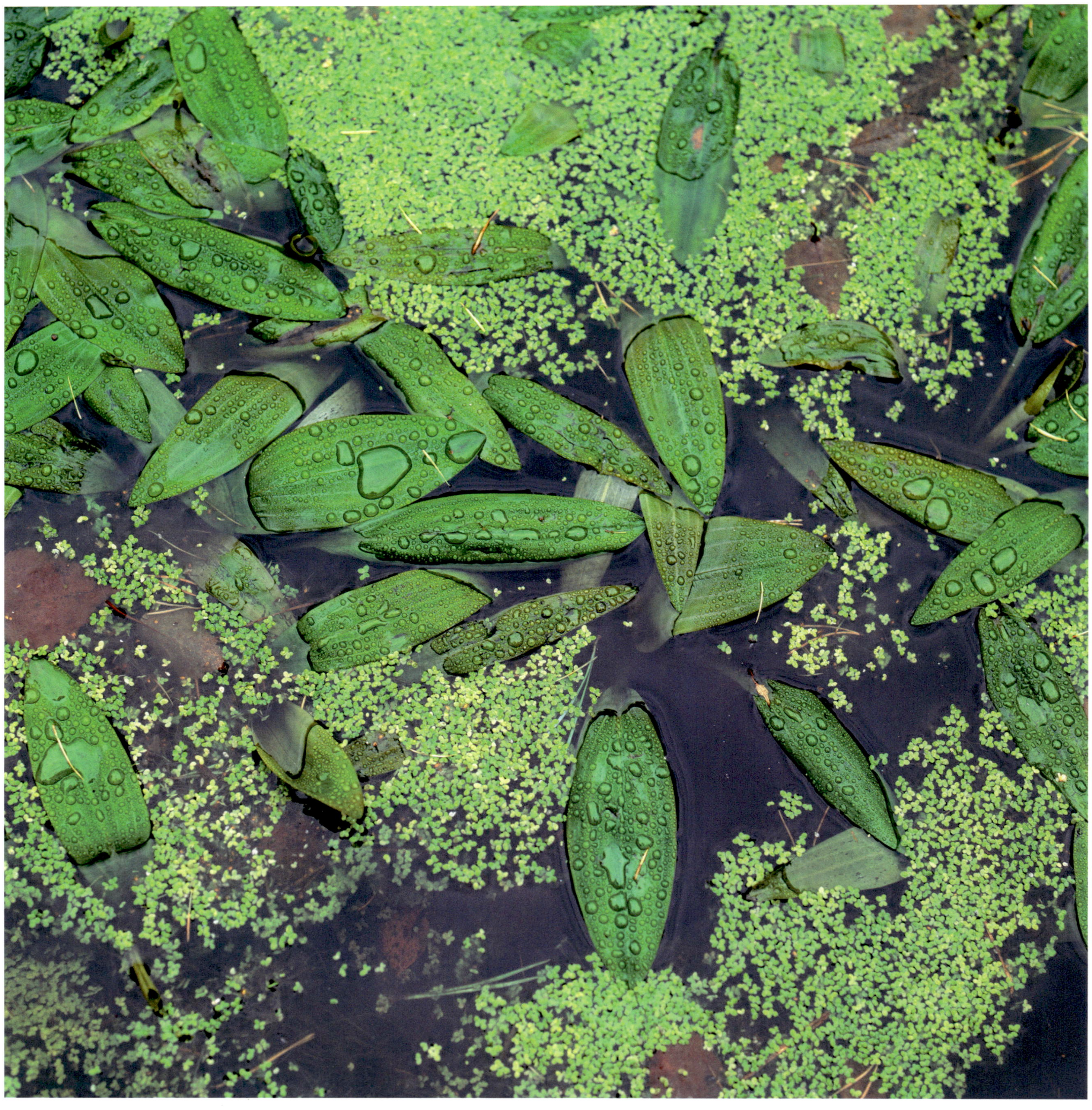

INCLEMENT WEATHER

I'm often asked when arranging photographic tutorials 'what happens if it rains?', to which my usual reply is 'we'll get great photographs'.

Luckily, over the years, I've had few inclement days on my arranged workshops. However, I did have one that could not be re-arranged and the forecast was for torrential downpours. The forecast was totally accurate and it rained almost horizontally for the whole of the day and we were literally drenched to the skin by the end of the session!

However, the shot opposite and the following three overleaf (the three overleaf were taken at Fountains Abbey, north Yorkshire) show just what can be achieved:

- As we rounded a corner we were met by sensational light on a well, making the whole scene seem as if lit by some form of artificial lighting.
- The shot of the logs shows incredible colour saturation.
- The tree stump (when shown on a projector especially) simply glows as if the subject has been gloss varnished.

The moral is of course don't let bad weather put you off.

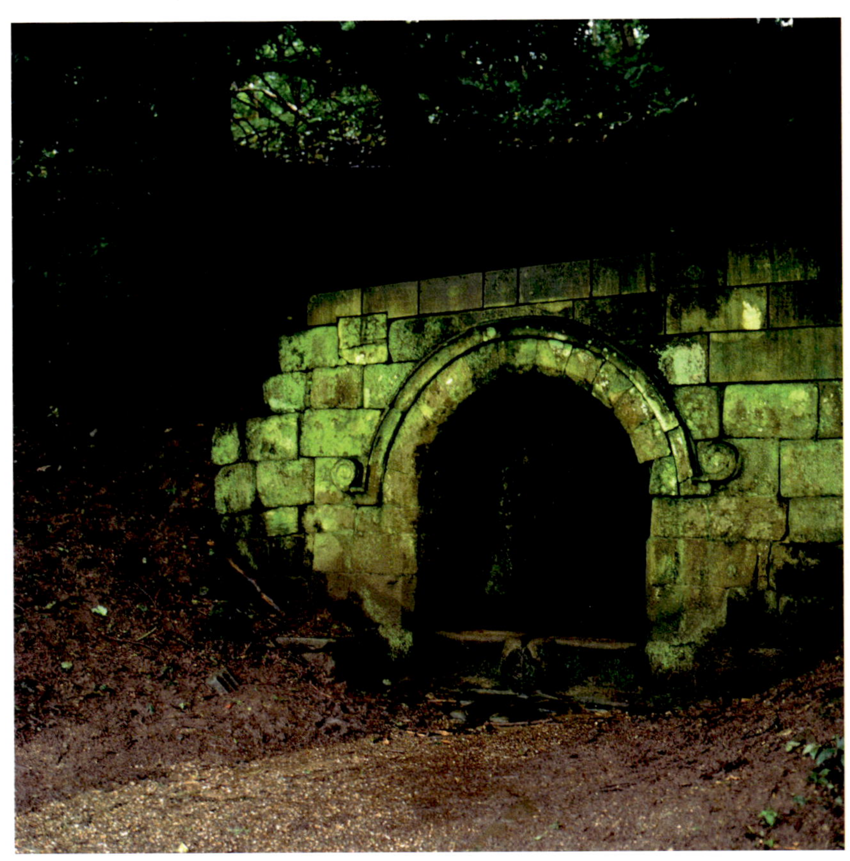

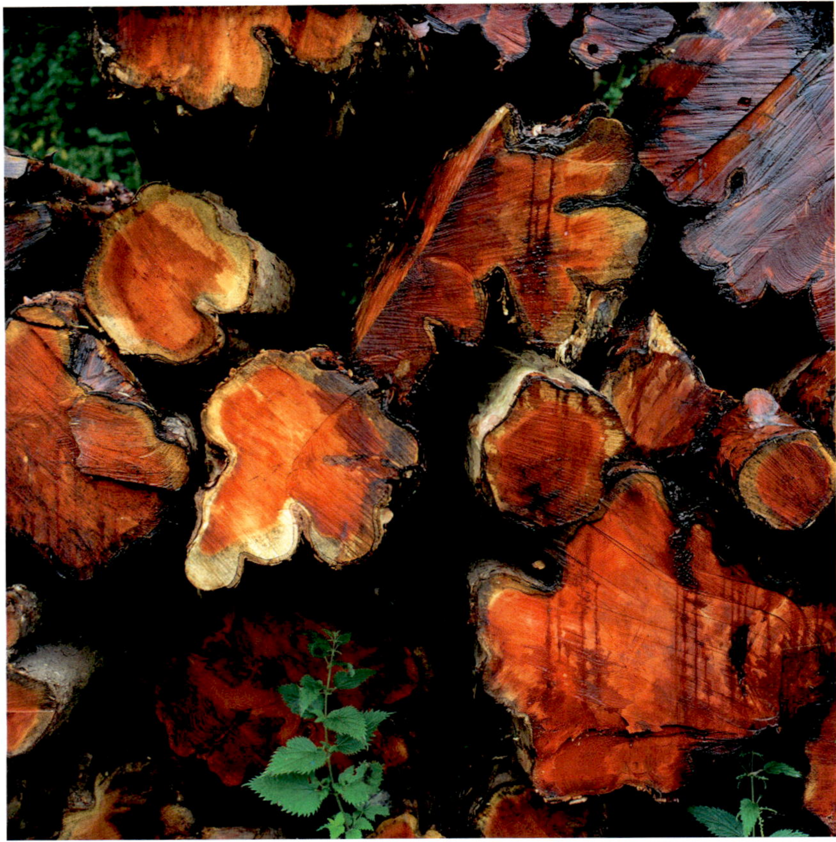

Fountains Abbey – North Yorkshire – England

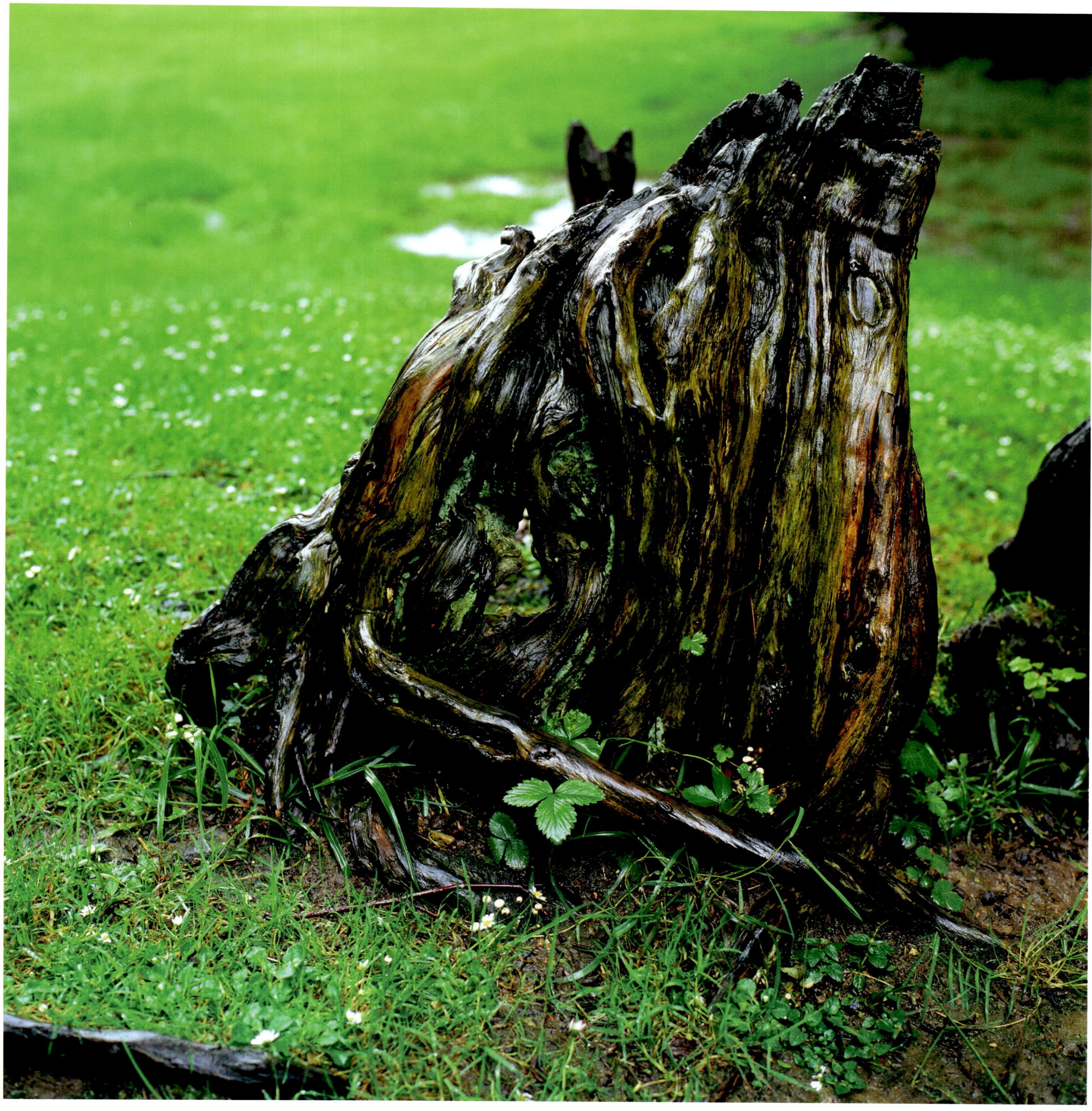

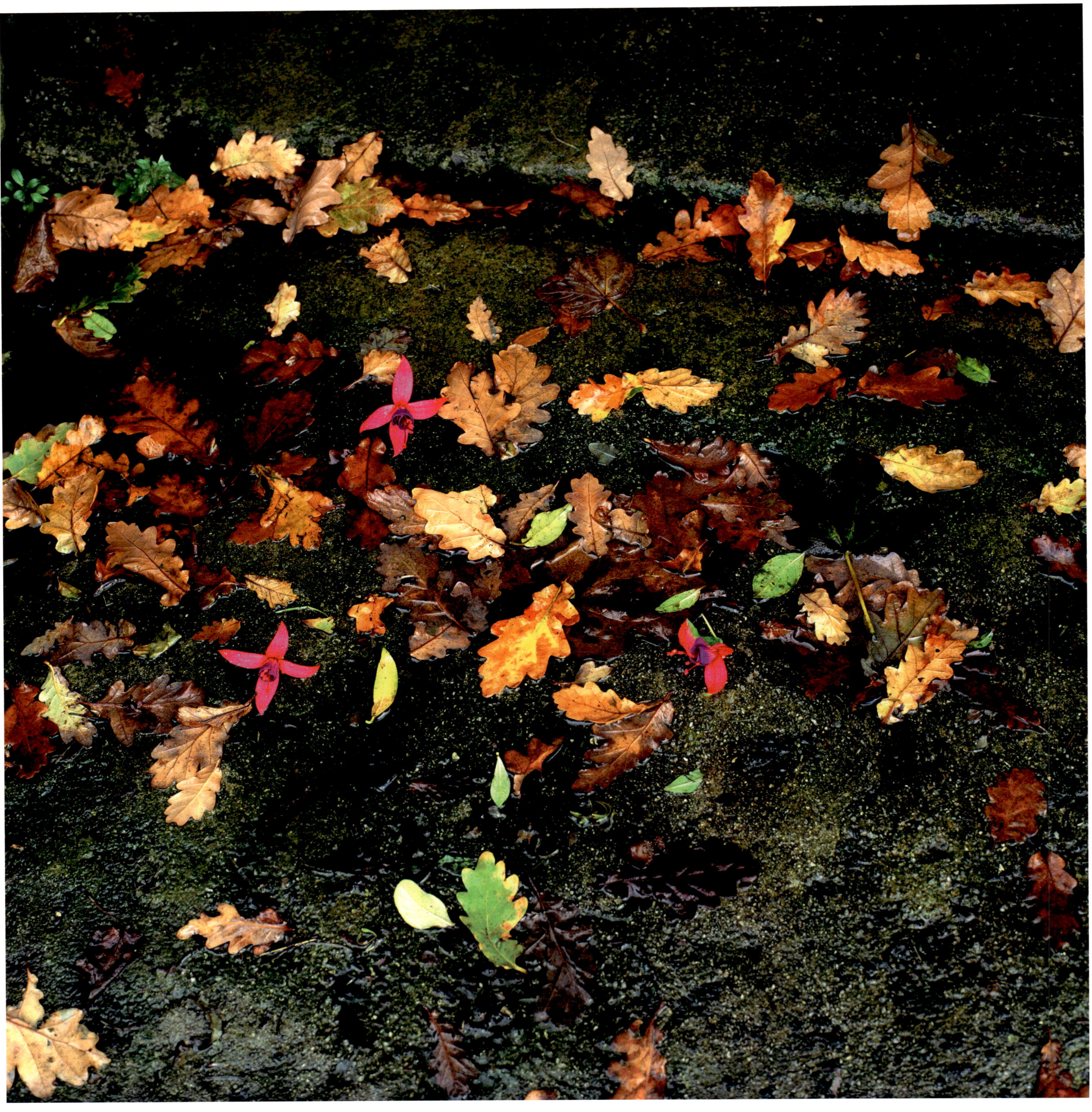

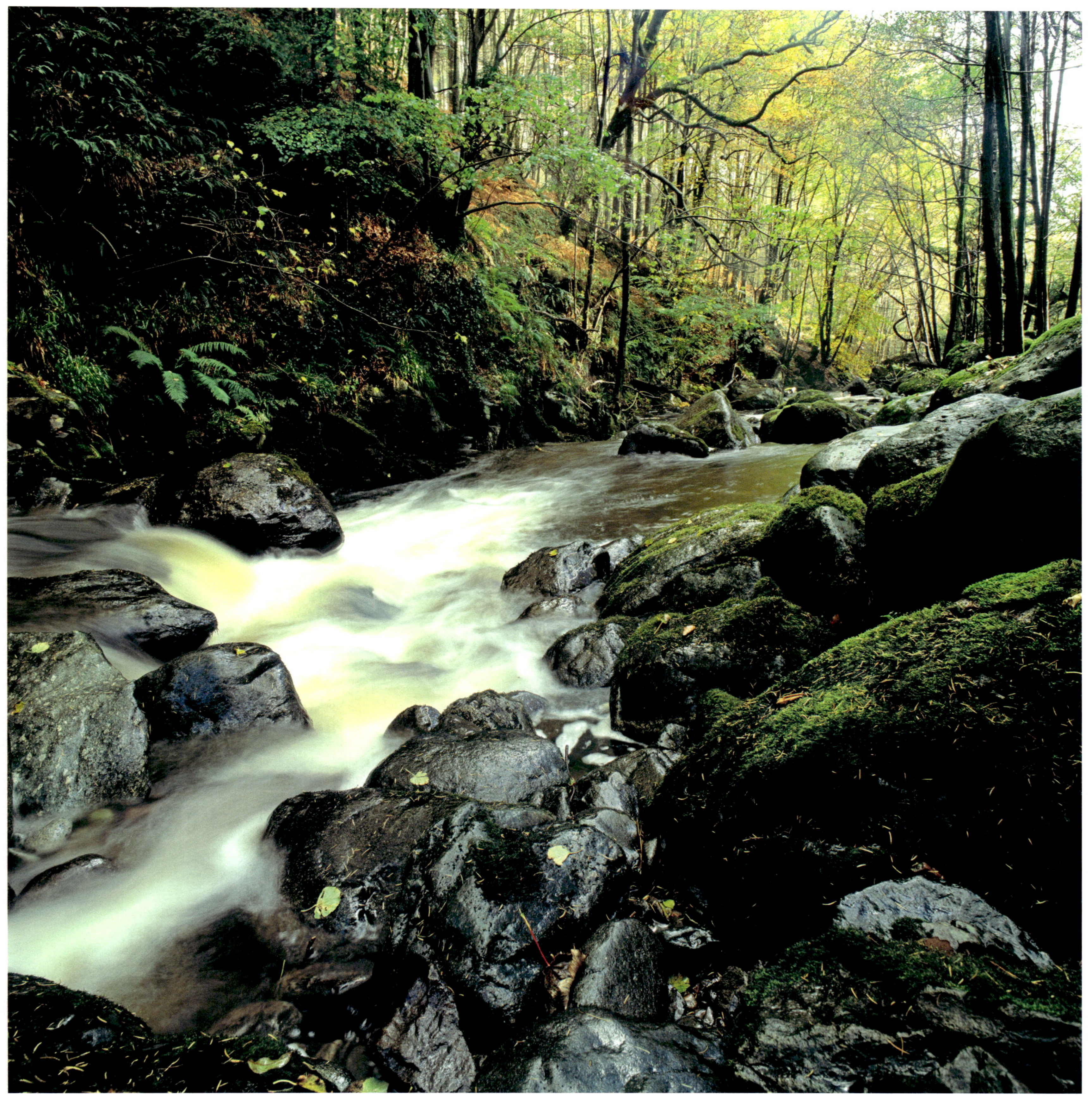

Logan Beck – Cumbria – England

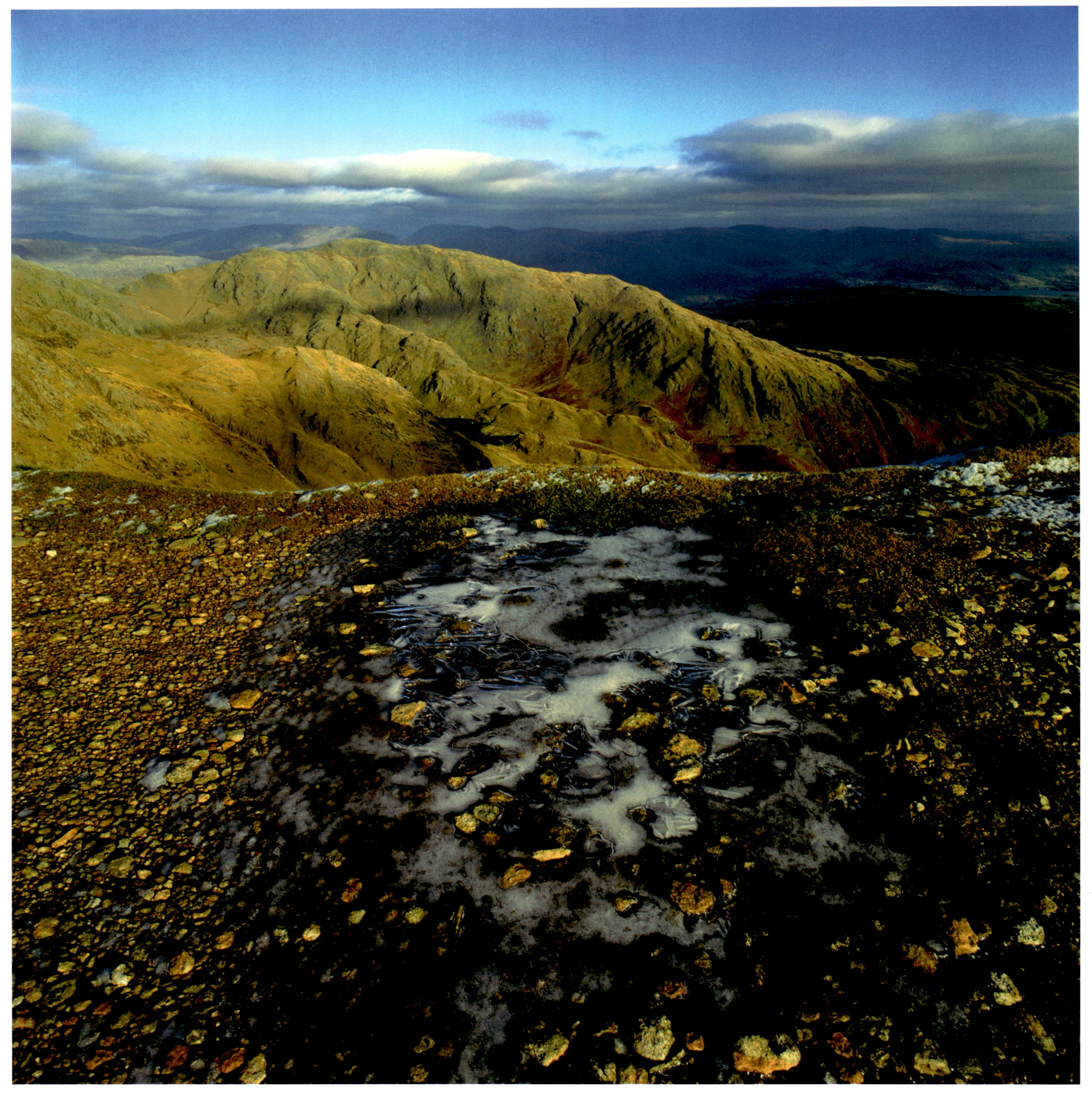

Swirl How – Cumbria – England

I haven't got any special religion this morning. My God is the God of Walkers, walk hard enough, you probably don't need any other God.

BRUCE CHATWIN

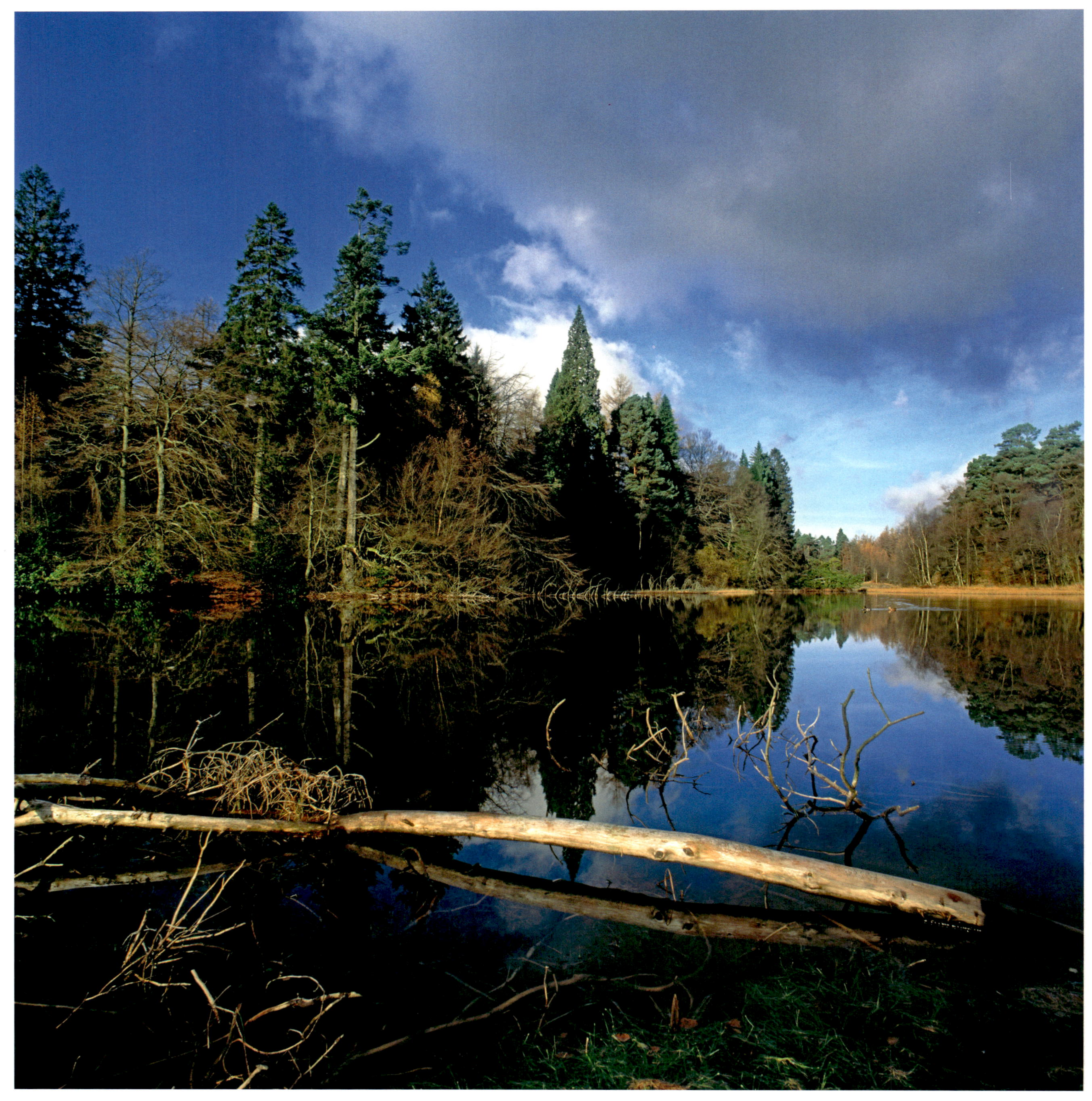

Tarn Hows – Cumbria – England

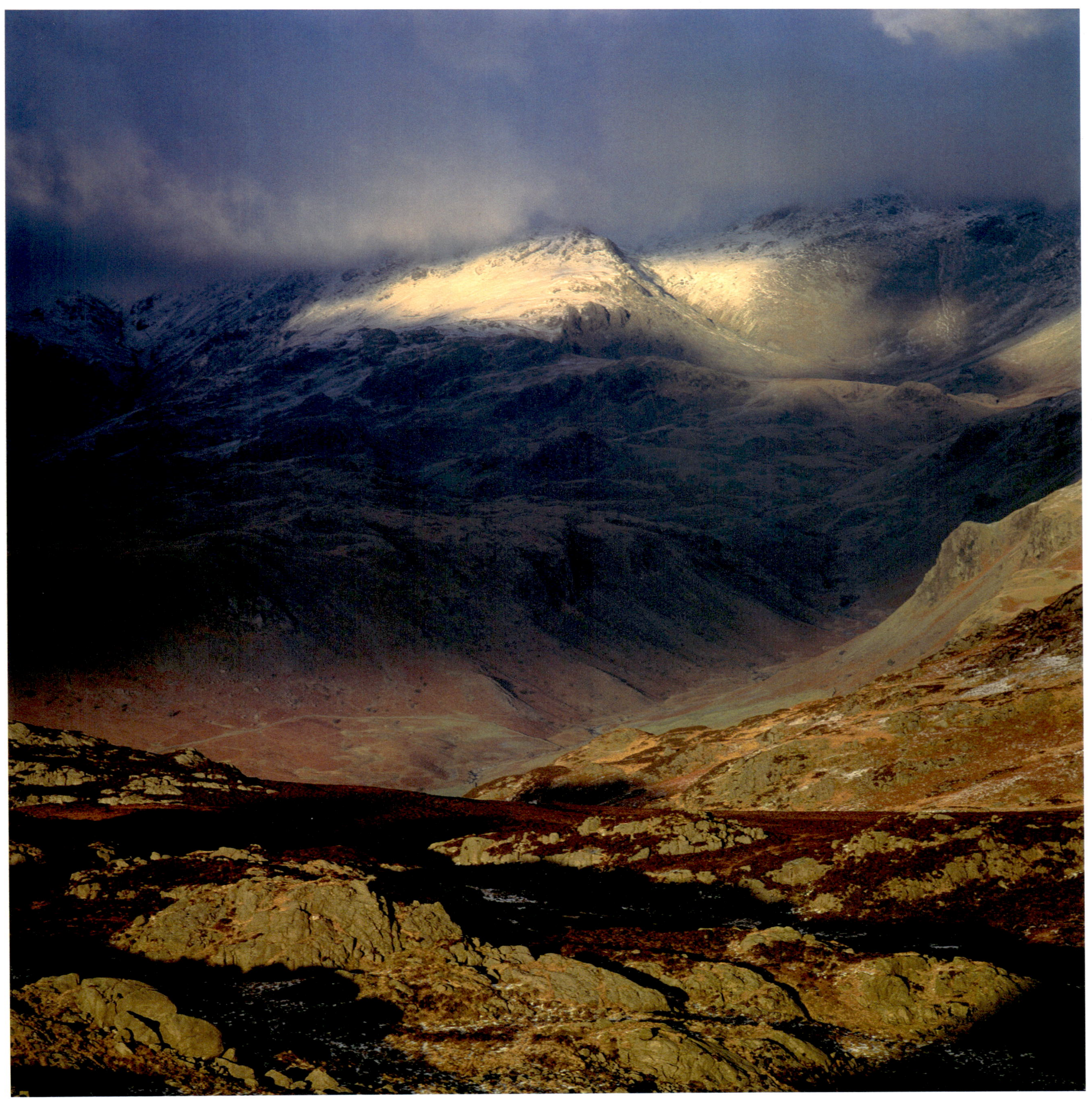

Eskdale – Cumbria – England

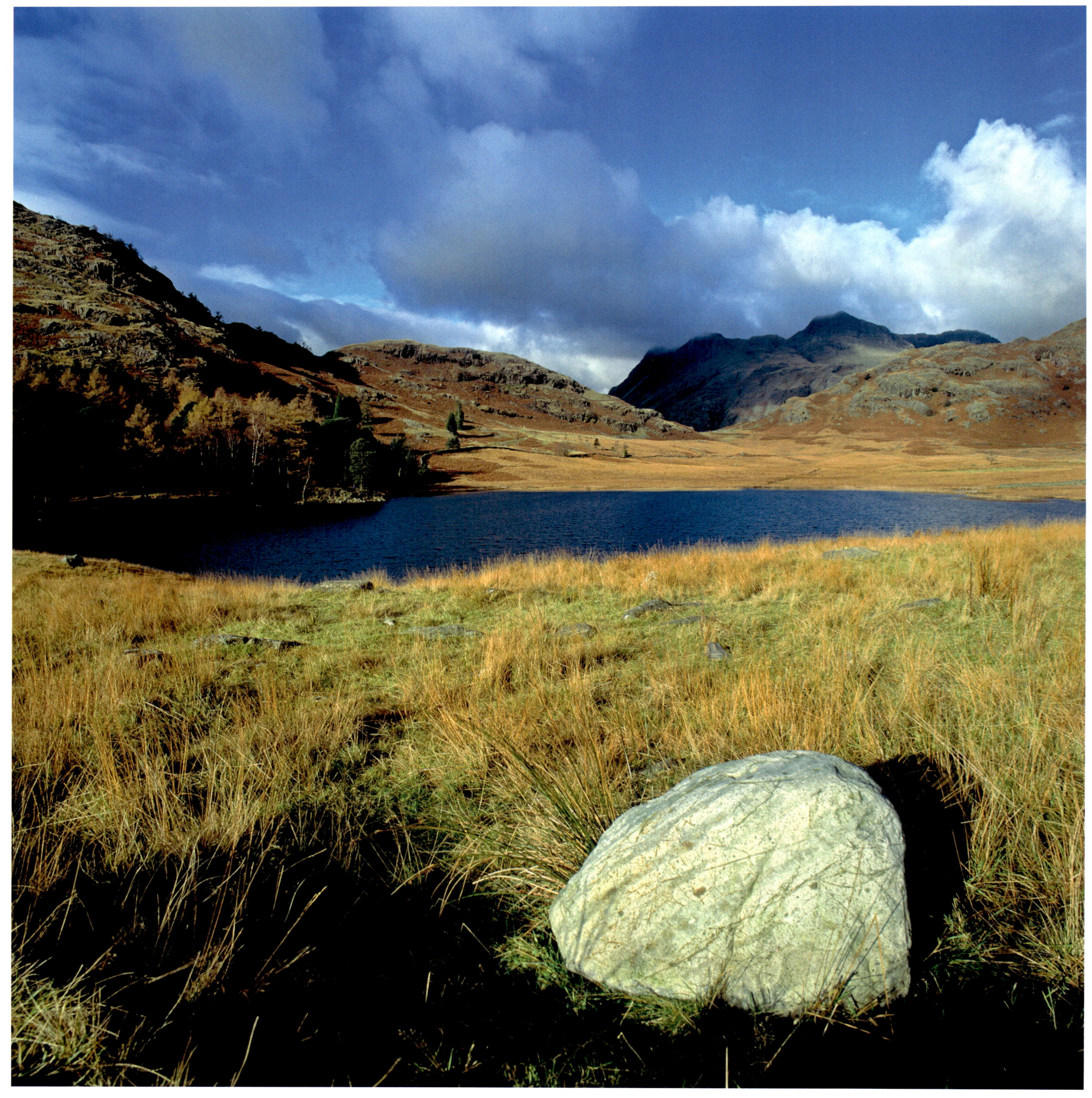

Blea Tarn – Cumbria – England

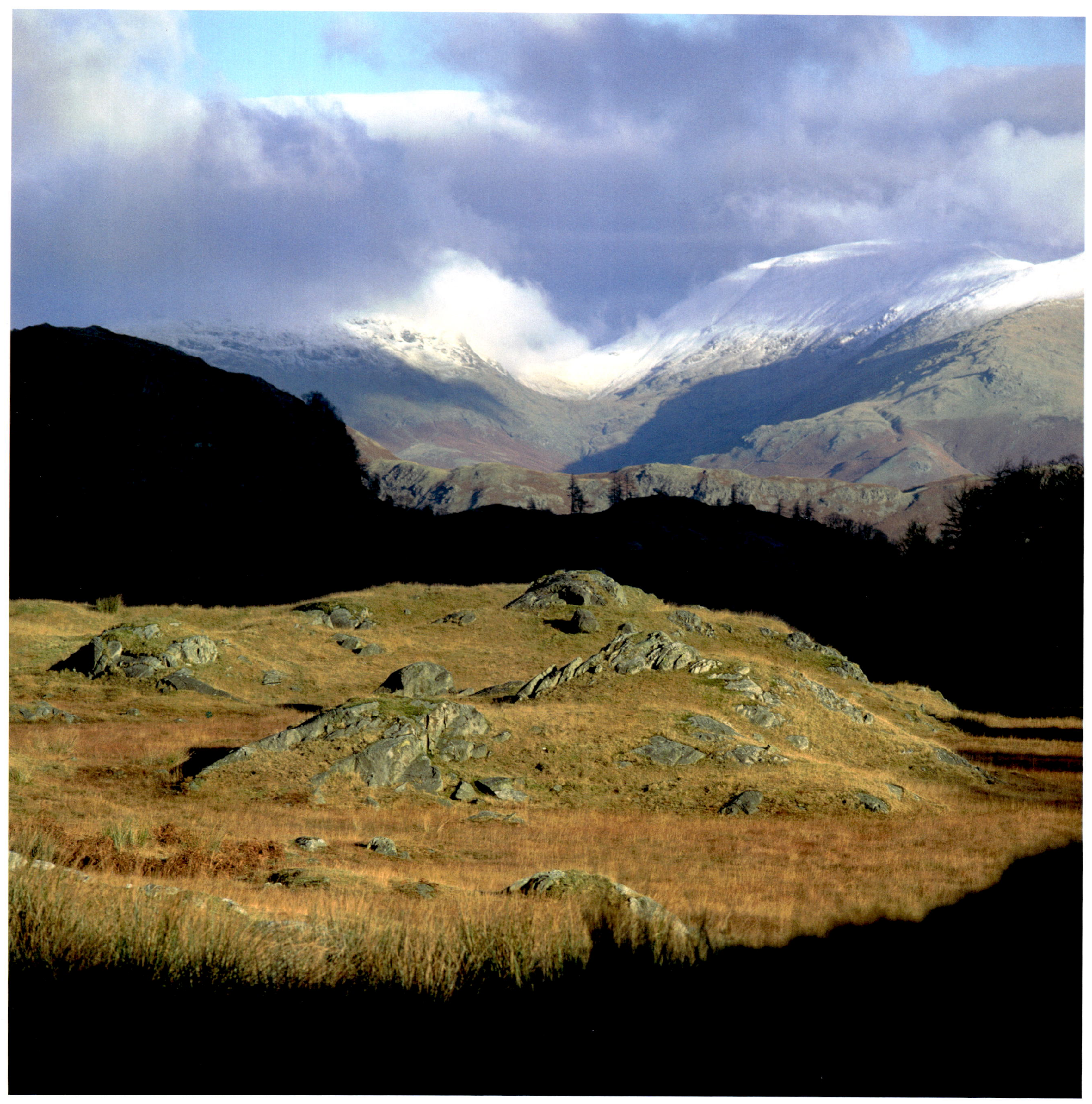

Little Langdale – Cumbria – England

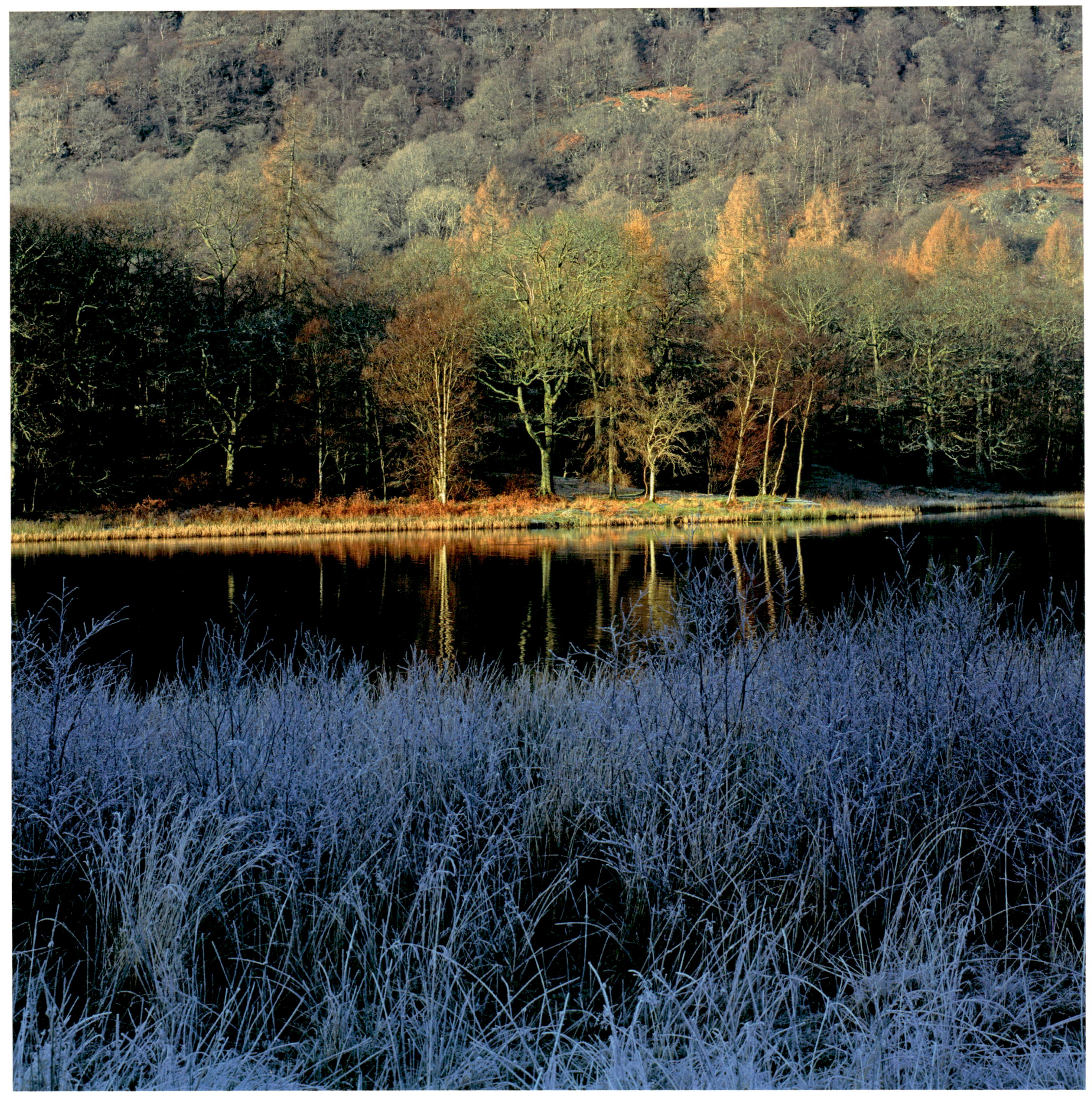

Yew Tree Tarn – Cumbria – England

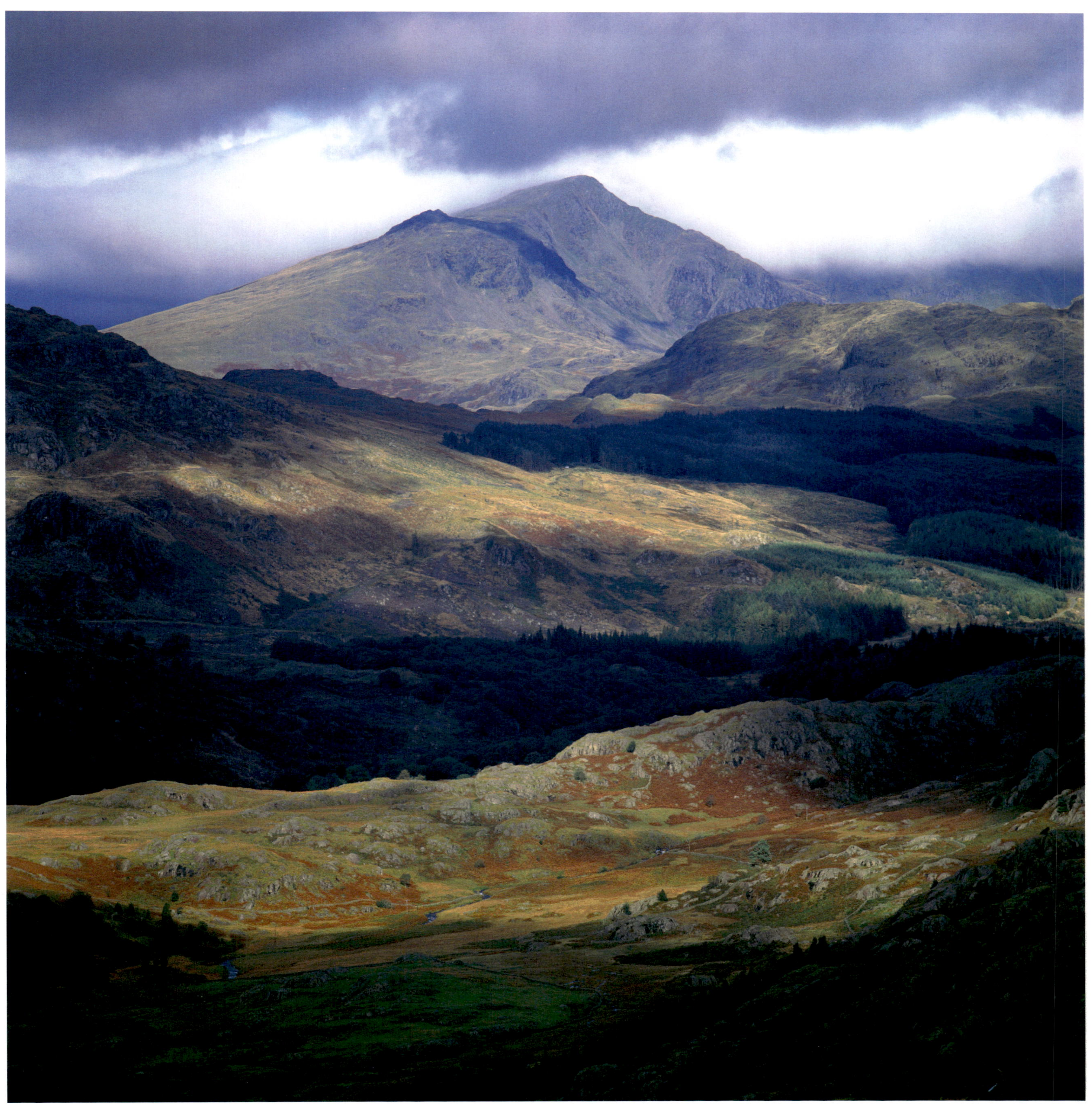

Duddon Valley – Cumbria – England

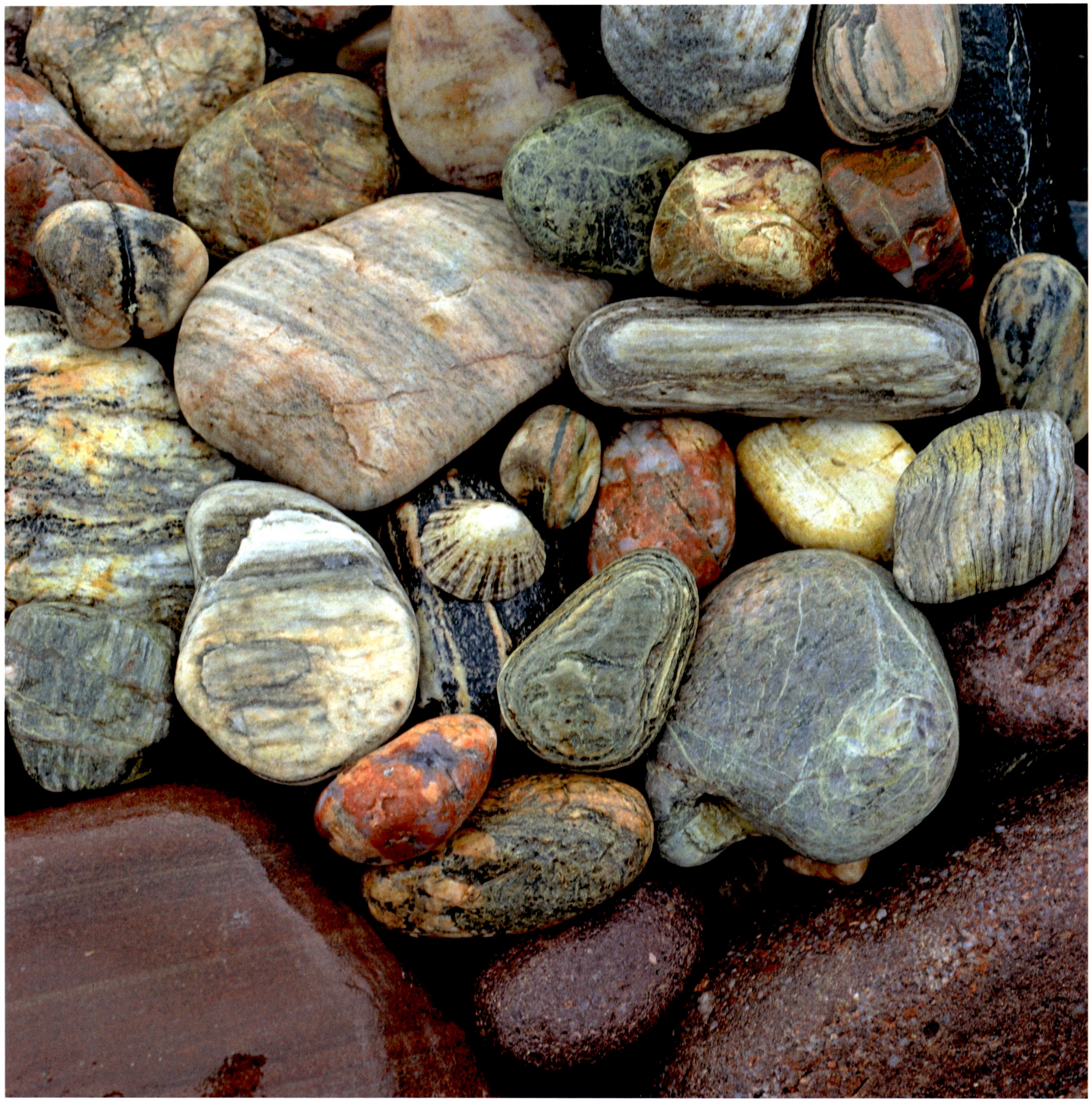

MELVAIG BEACH

When I take people to this location the look of disappointment on their faces is always apparent, because on your approach you are met by a fairly ordinary, dull, grey beach, especially when the sun isn't shining. Yet, once there, as you look down, there appears a beauty that is hard to describe.

To me, each pebble seems to be a masterpiece in design. However, I had one member of a group who struggled to see the photographs that lay before her and, while four of us continued to photograph, she decided to sit it out and have a coffee, giving the pebbles a miss.

A week or two after our return to England, we all met up and looked at one another's photographs. Upon seeing the shots that others had captured, she booked the same holiday for the following year and, that time, got some great photographs. Nature's colours are really at their best in this very special place.

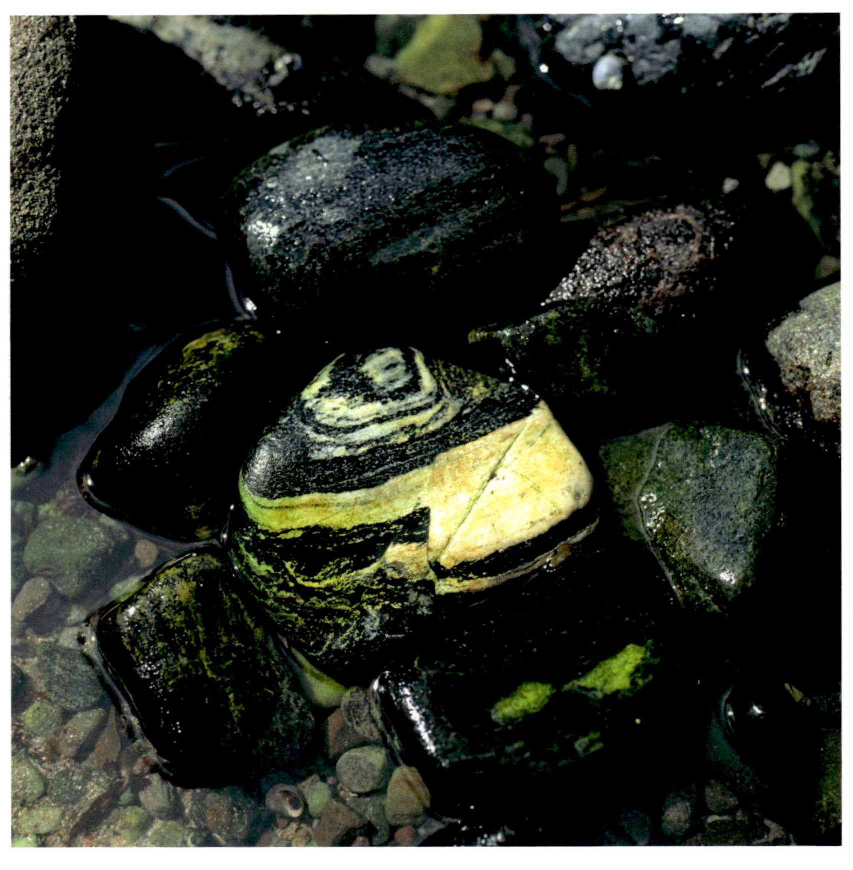

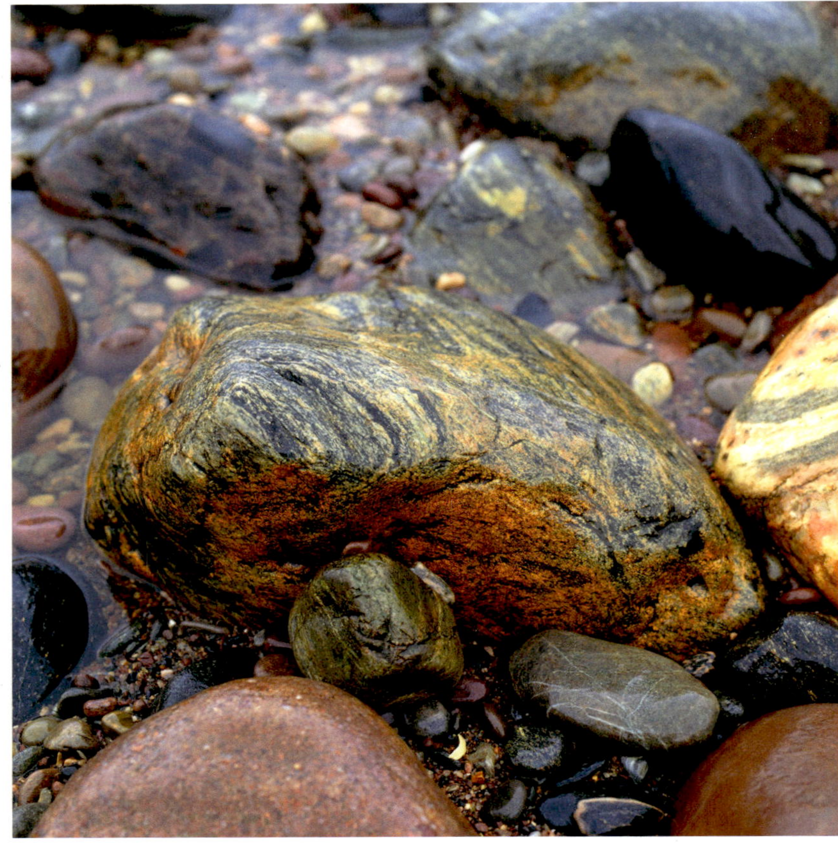

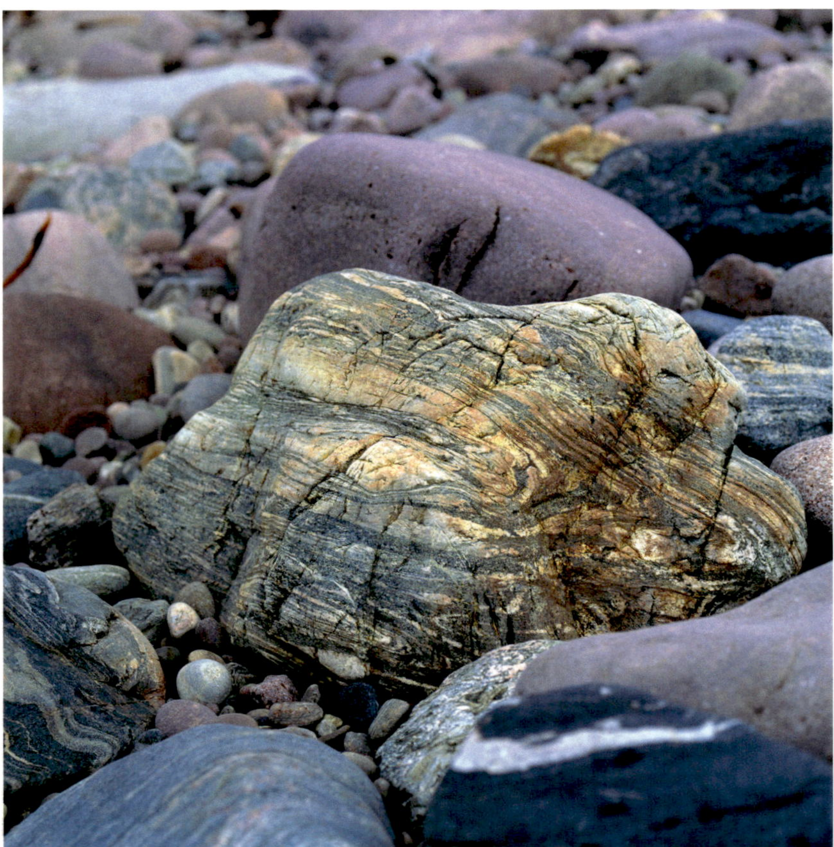

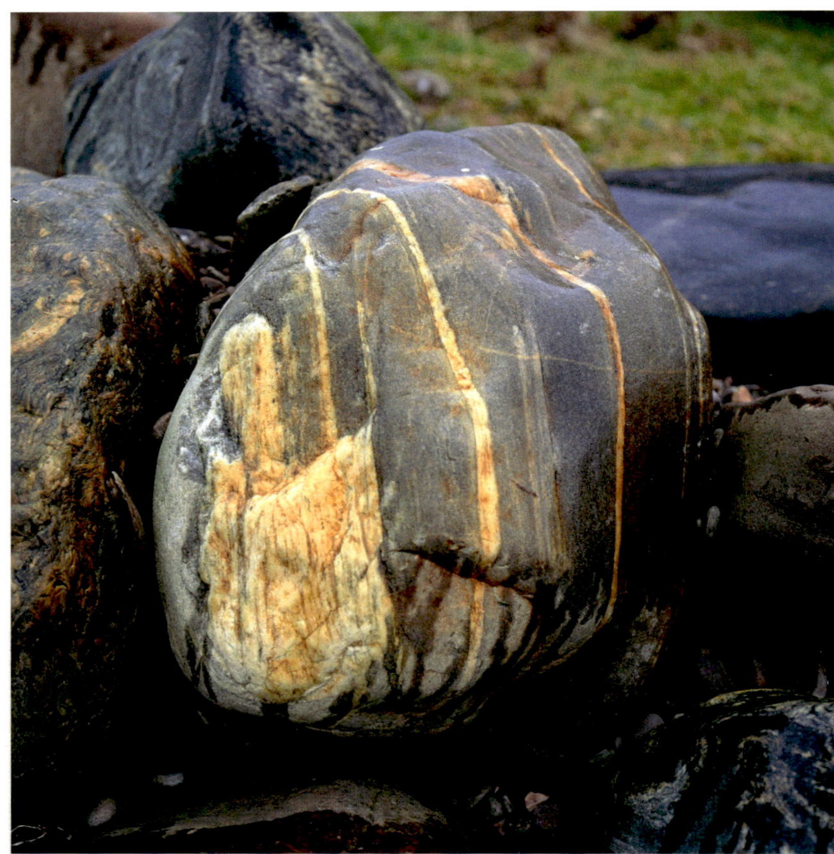

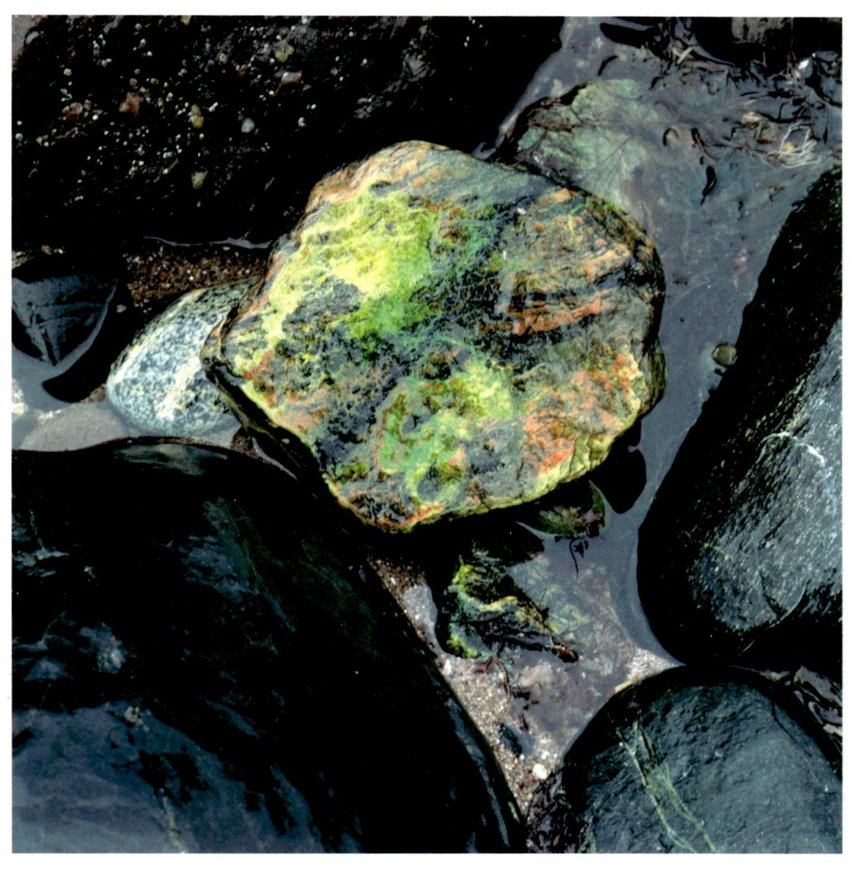

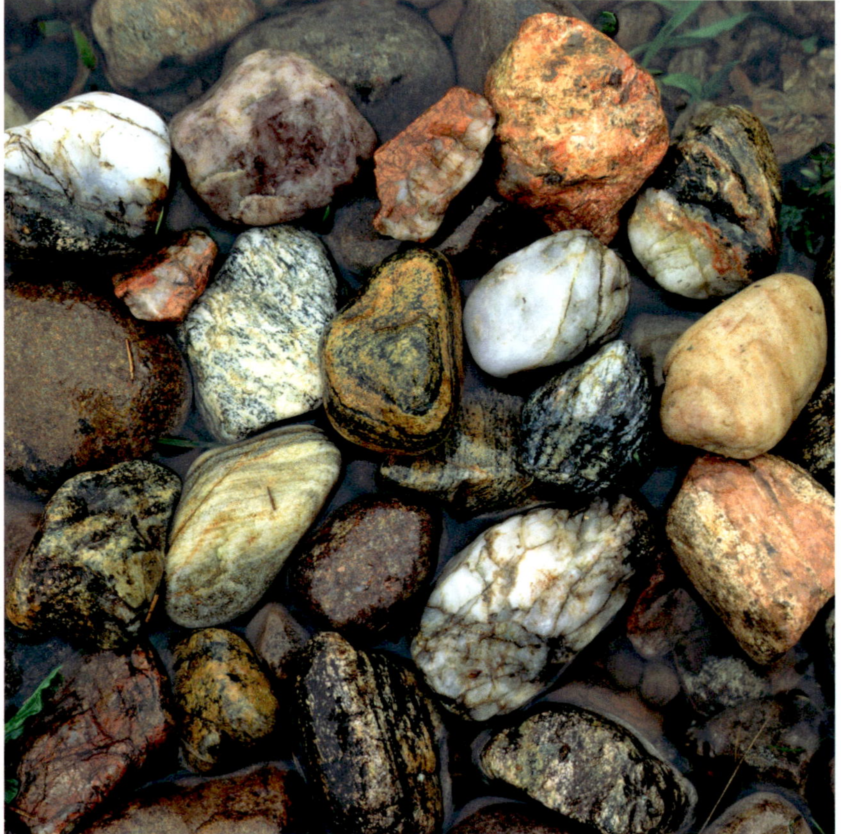

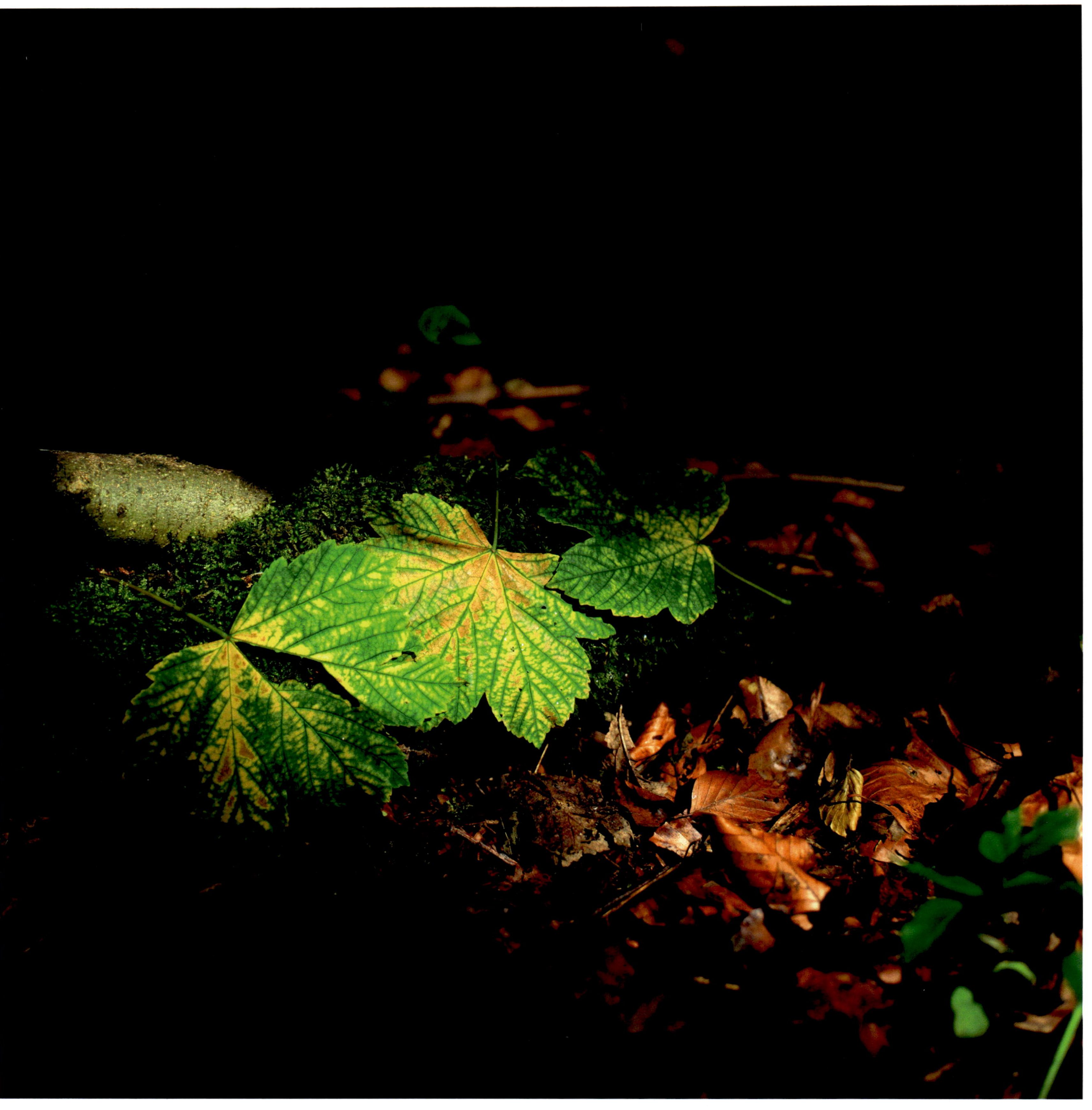

NEVER FAR FROM HOME

I'm often seen on the streets around where I live with a camera round my neck and a rucksack on my back.

In past years, my home town was your typical coal-mining and steelworks village, although much of that has long gone. However, scenically it still retains that kind of identity and, to most eyes, it would have no photographic potential whatsoever.

My mother's old uncle who lived in Nidderdale, Yorkshire never left the dale, (except for the occasional funeral) and many would say he needed to broaden his horizons. However, he could see far greater horizons than some of those who travel thousands of miles to see theirs. His knowledge and the things he could see while others walked by them was incredible and his skills at noting such things, remains imprinted in my mind.

I believe the quote from Marcel Proust sums this up succinctly.

The real voyage of discovery consists not in seeking new landscapes but in having new eyes.
MARCEL PROUST

The shot opposite and the next sequence of shots (ten) are all taken within minutes of where I live.

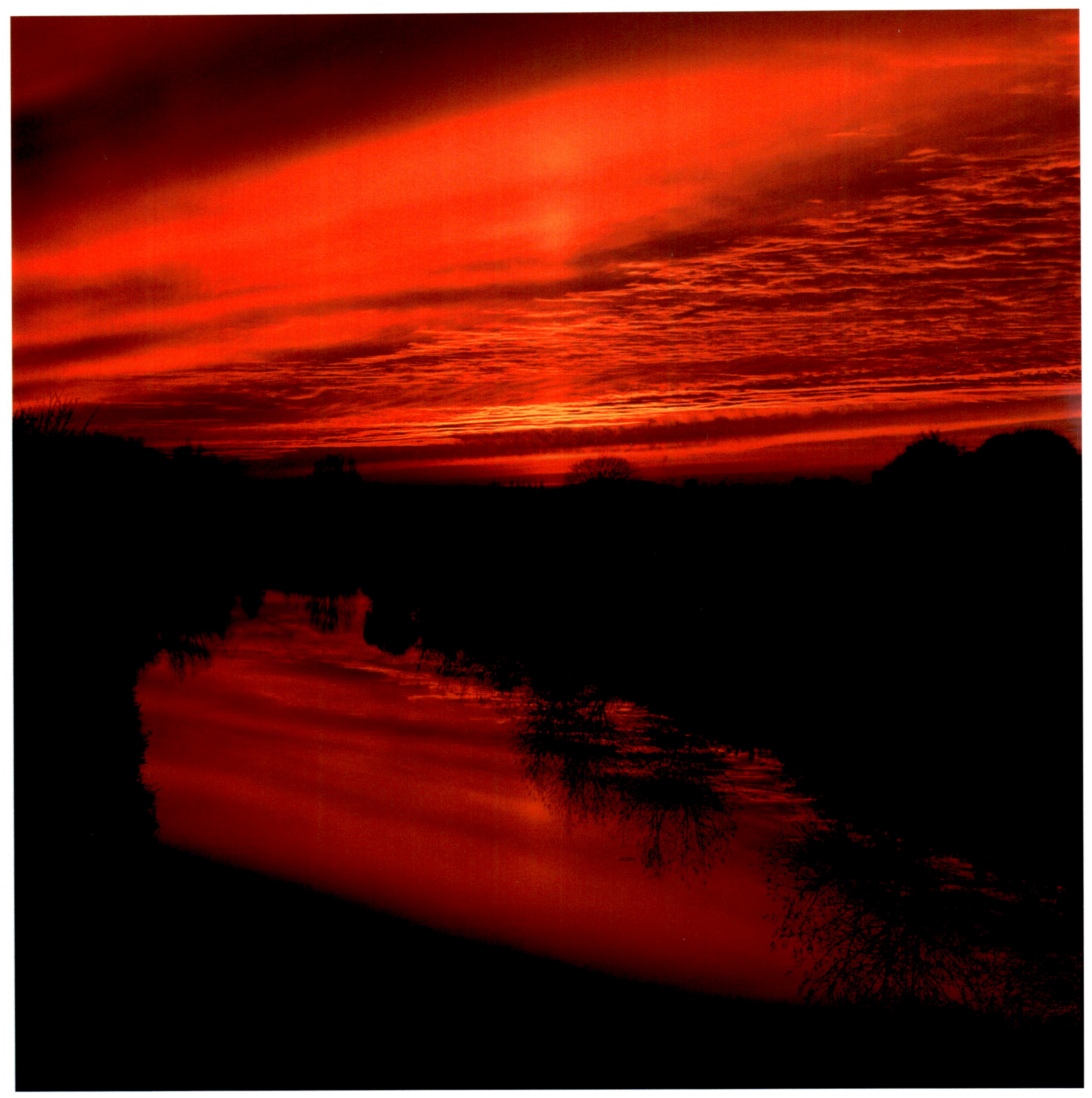

Mexborough – South Yorkshire – England

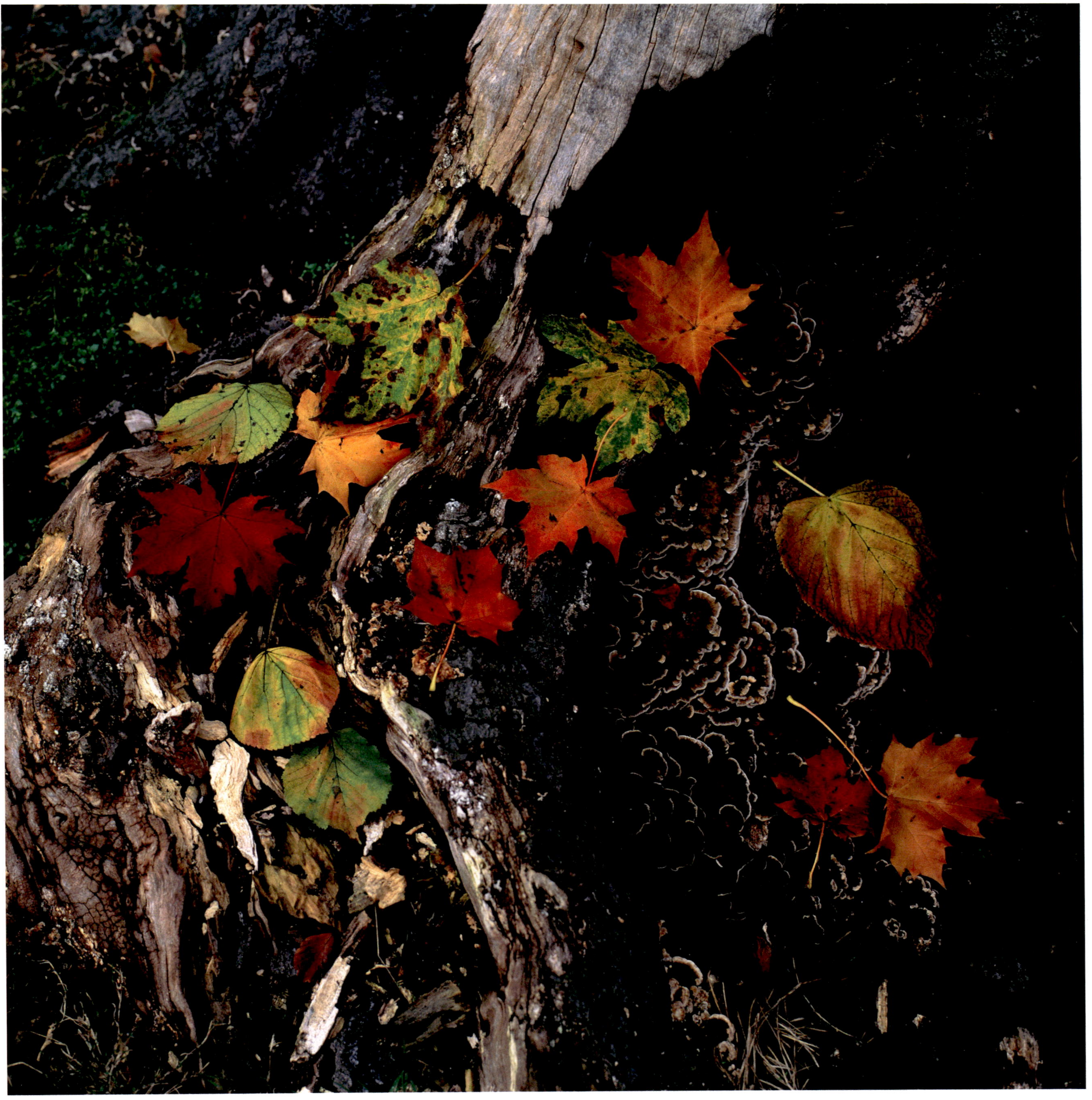

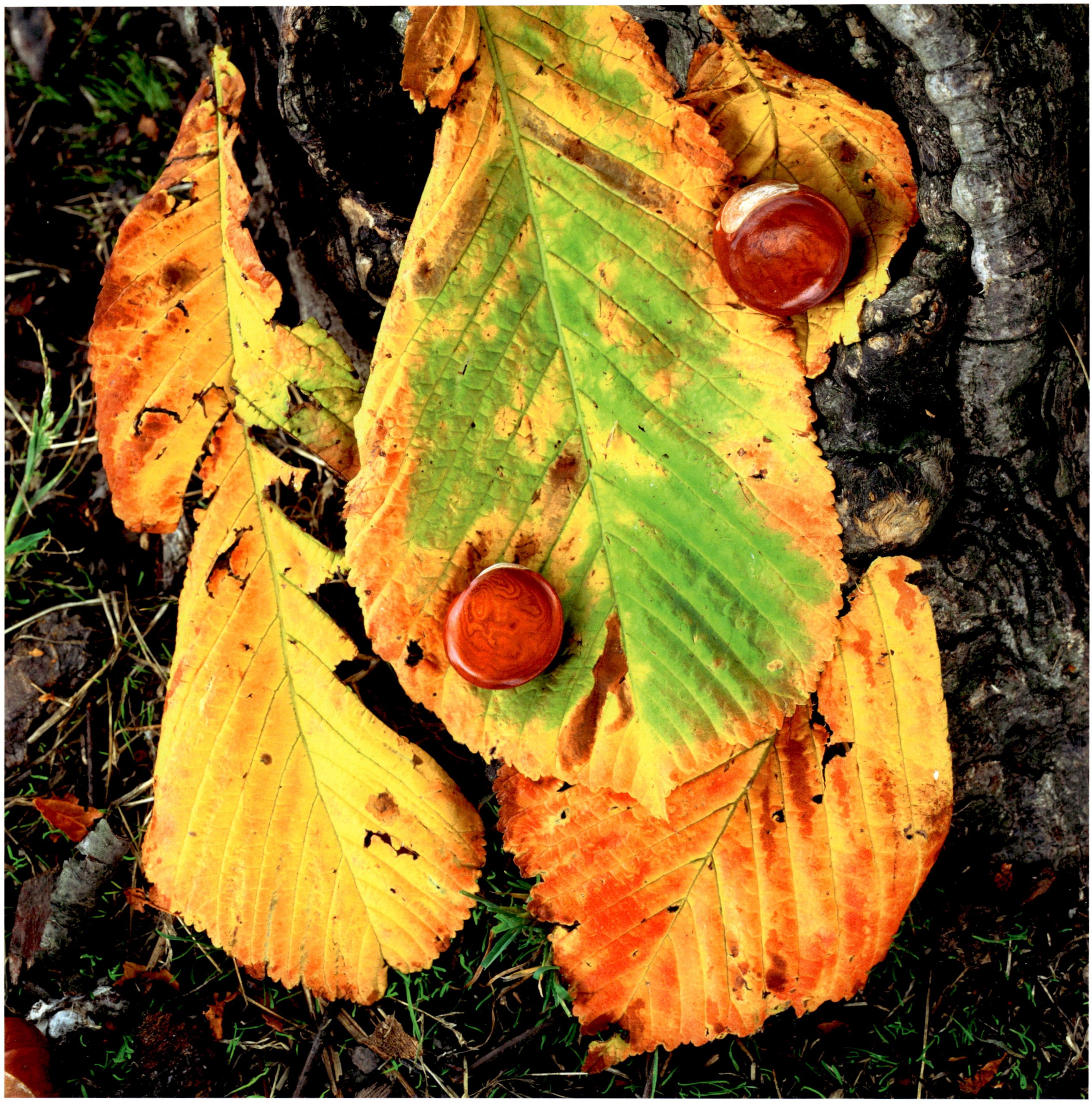

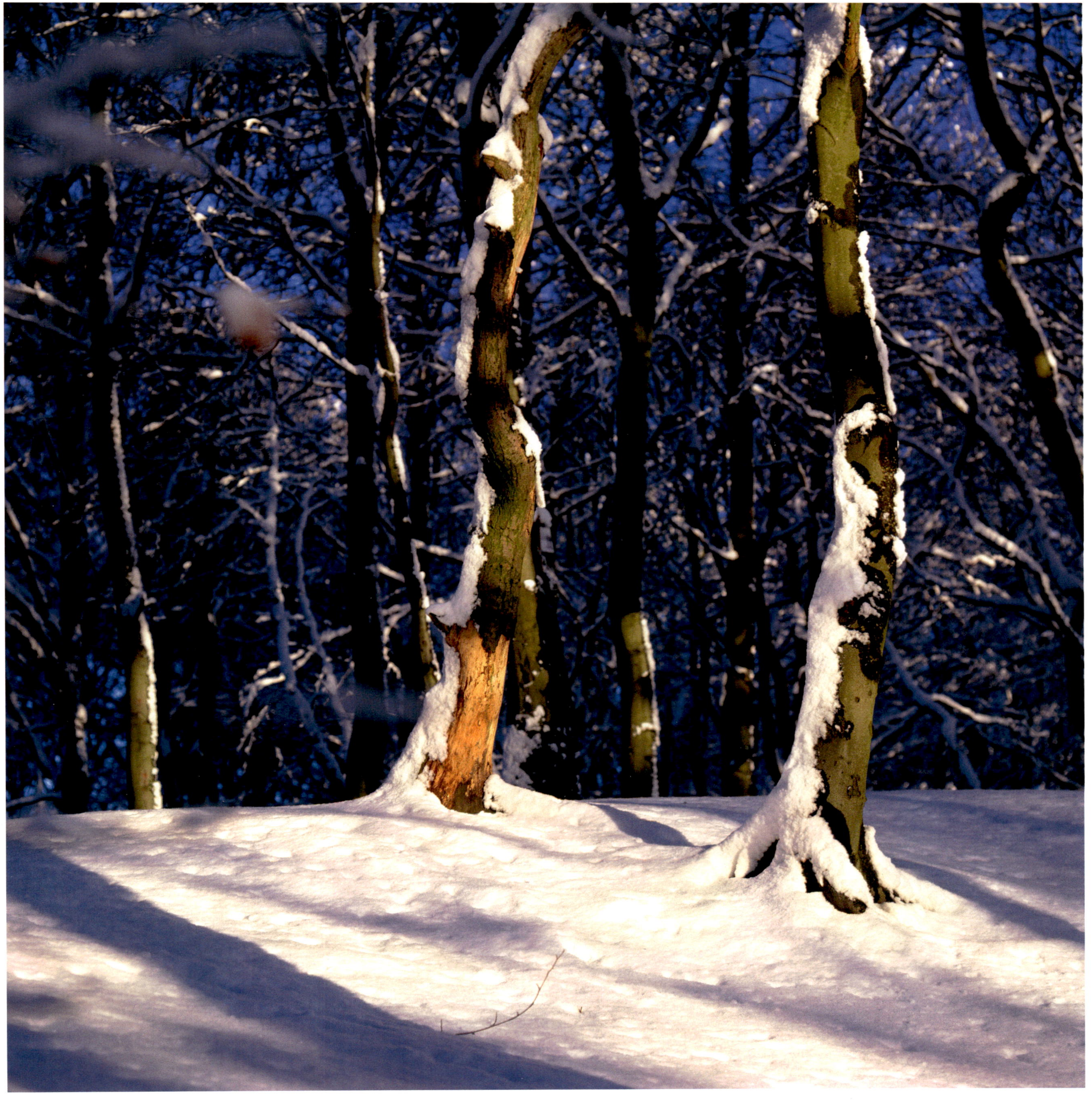

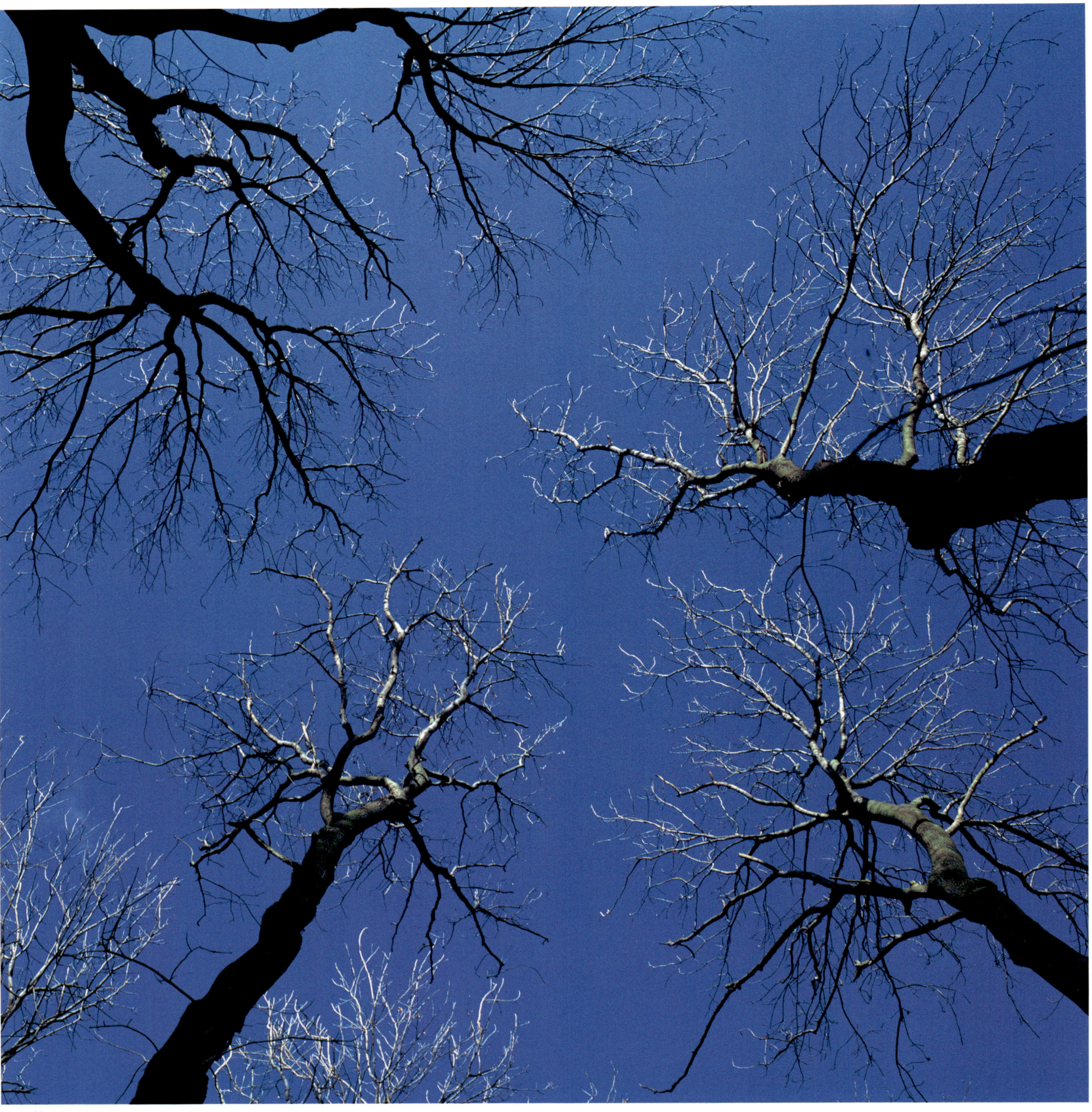

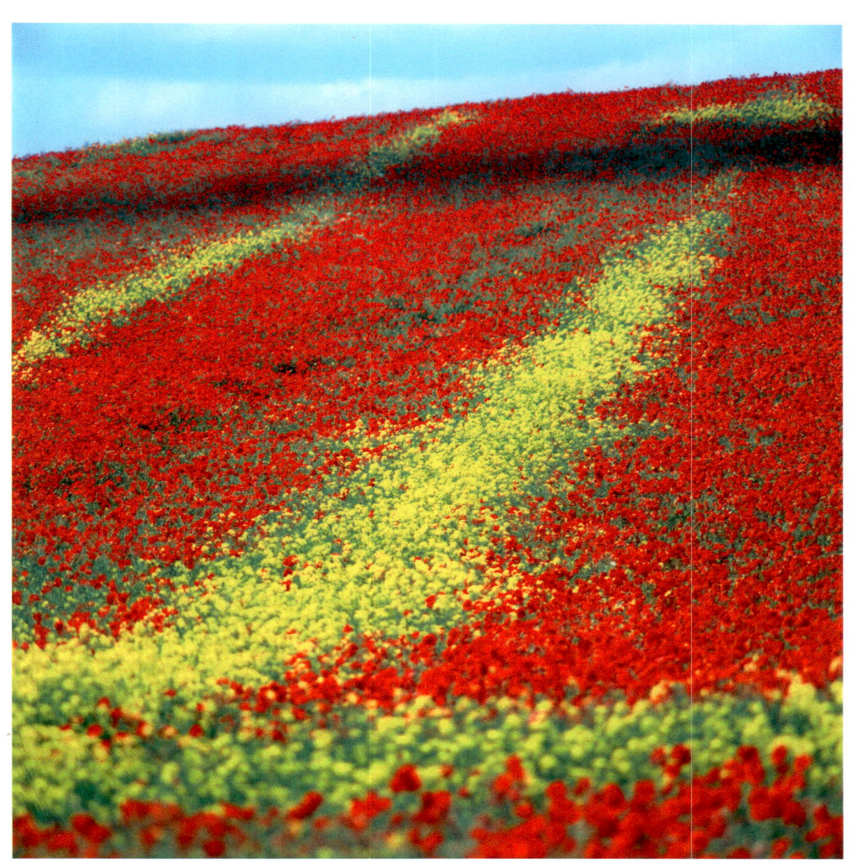

Rawmarsh – South Yorkshire – England

Rawmarsh – South Yorkshire – England

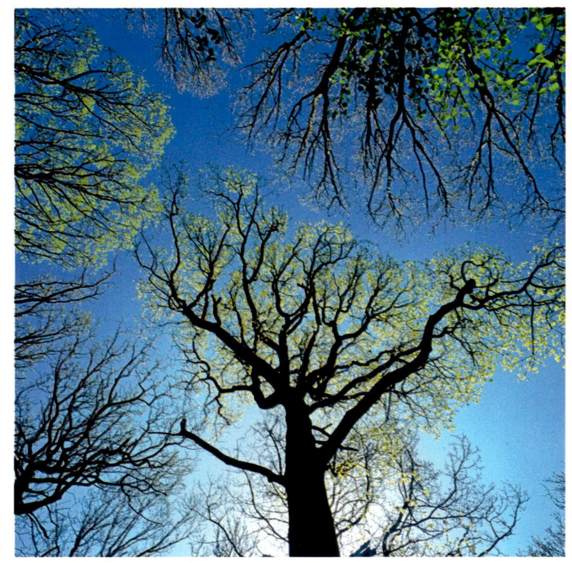

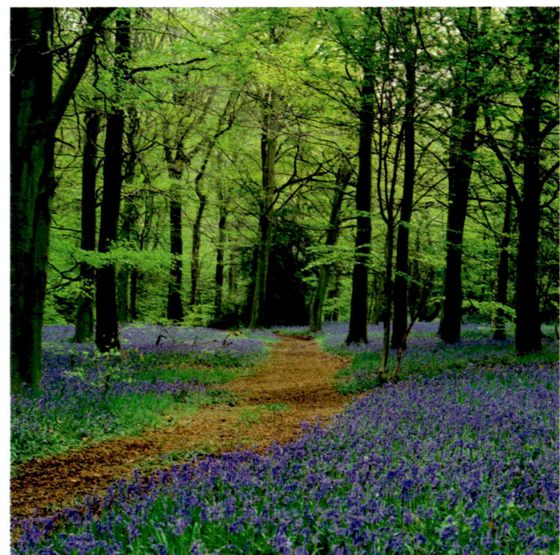

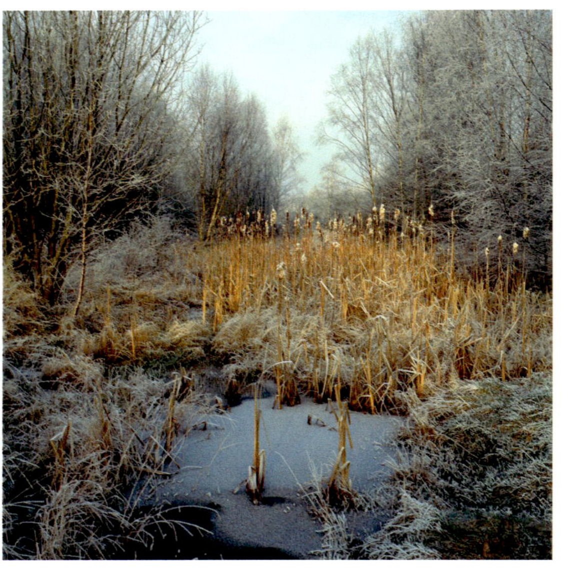

APOLOGIES

In this book, I must admit, there do seem to be many Scottish images, especially from Wester Ross, and I hope this does not spoil things for you. It's simply that I love the Scottish landscape and it never fails to inspire me. I hope this shows in the next section.

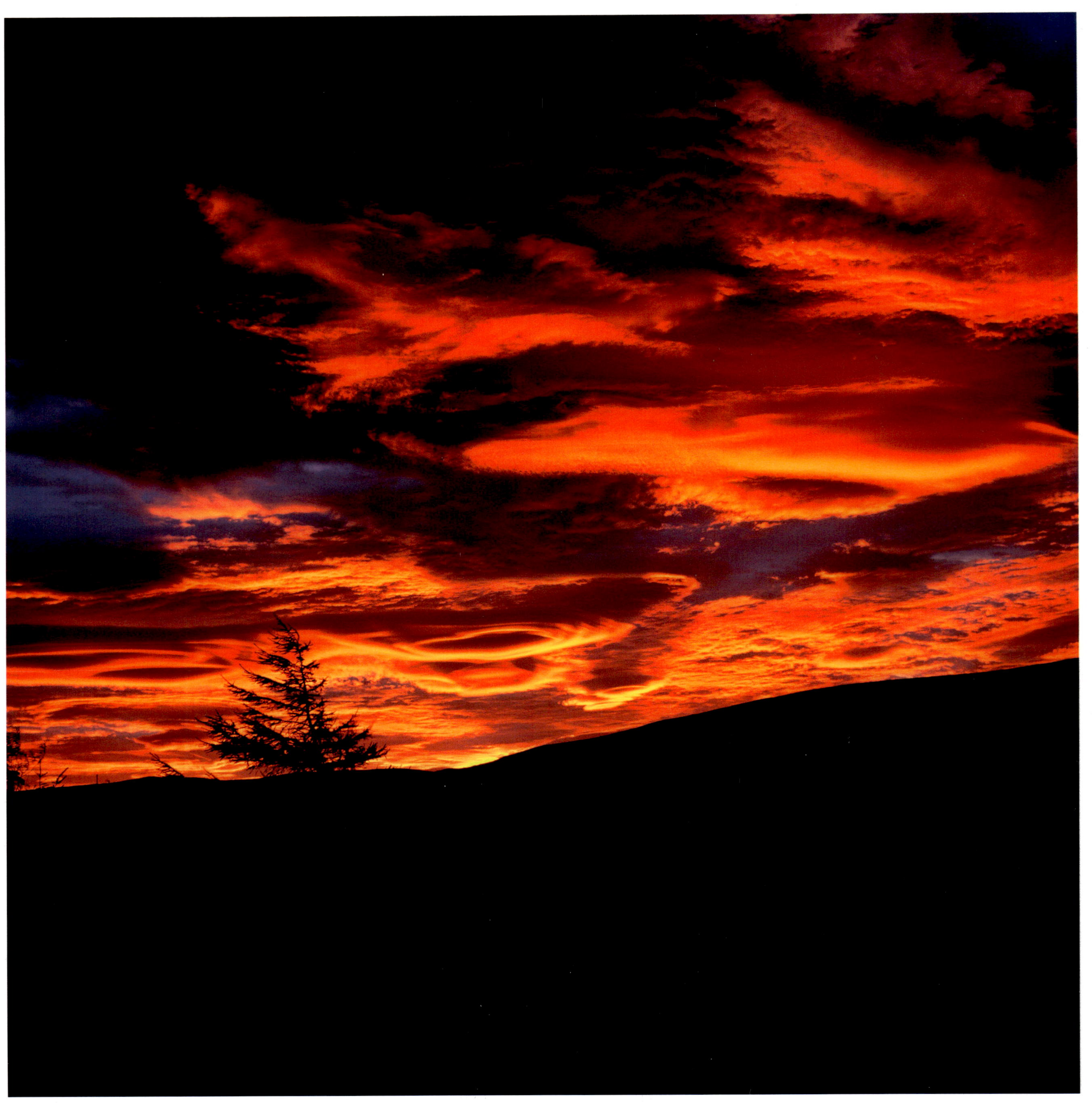

Badfearn – Wester Ross – Scotland

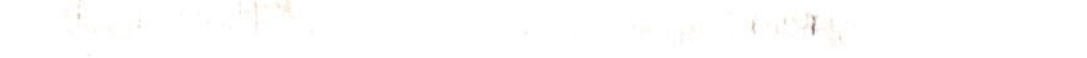

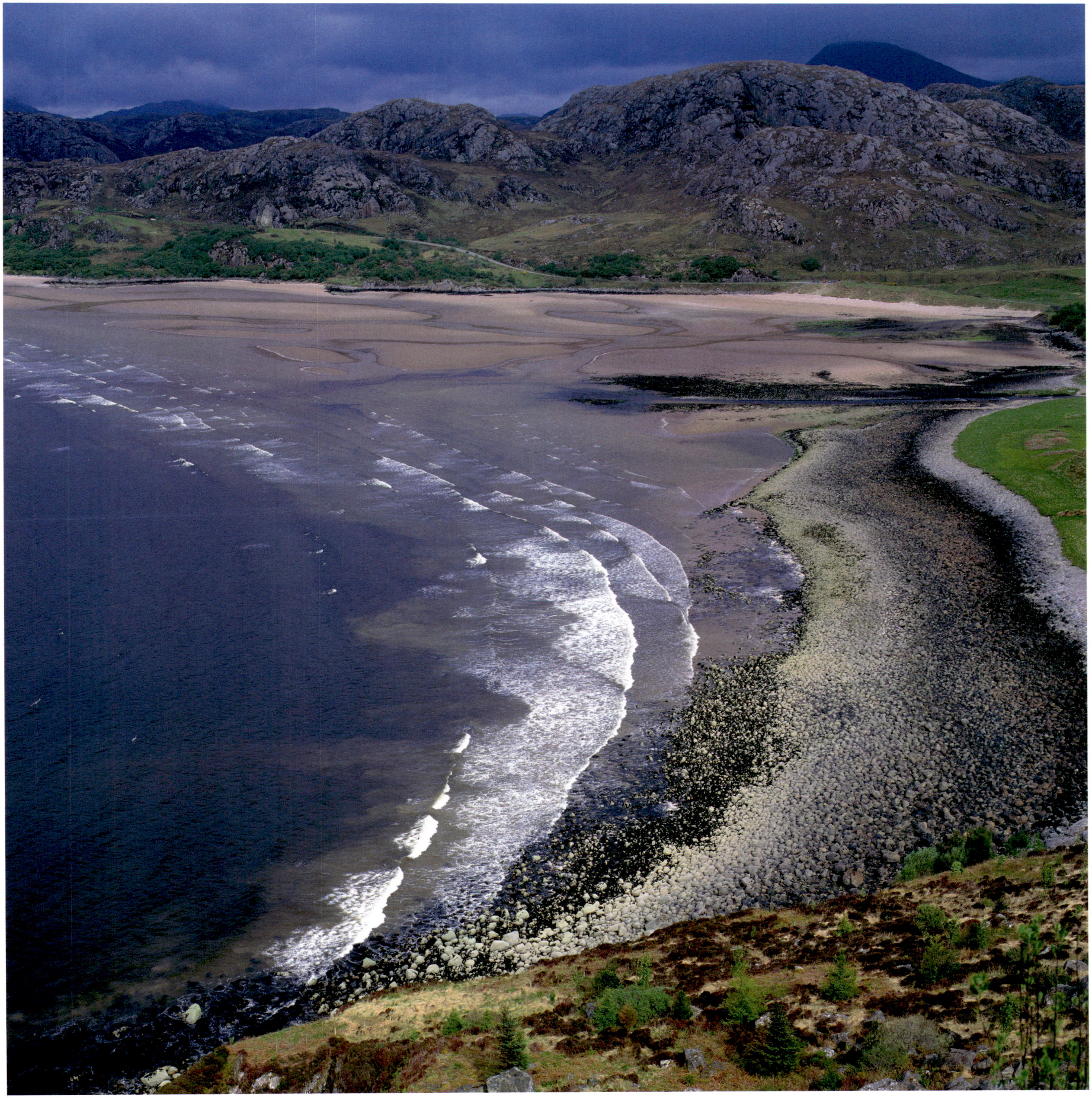

Gruinard Bay – Wester Ross – Scotland

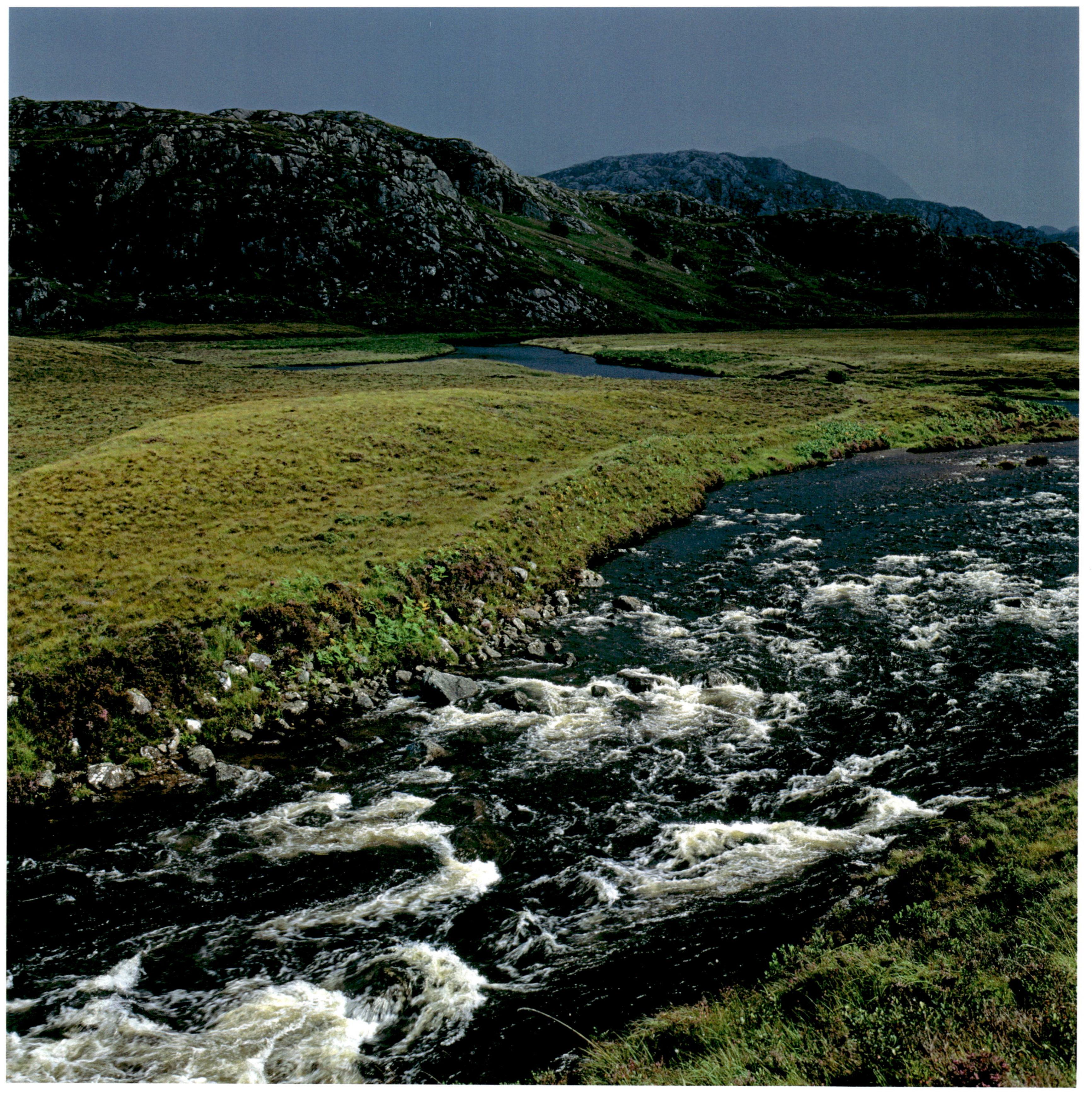

River Gruinard – Wester Ross – Scotland

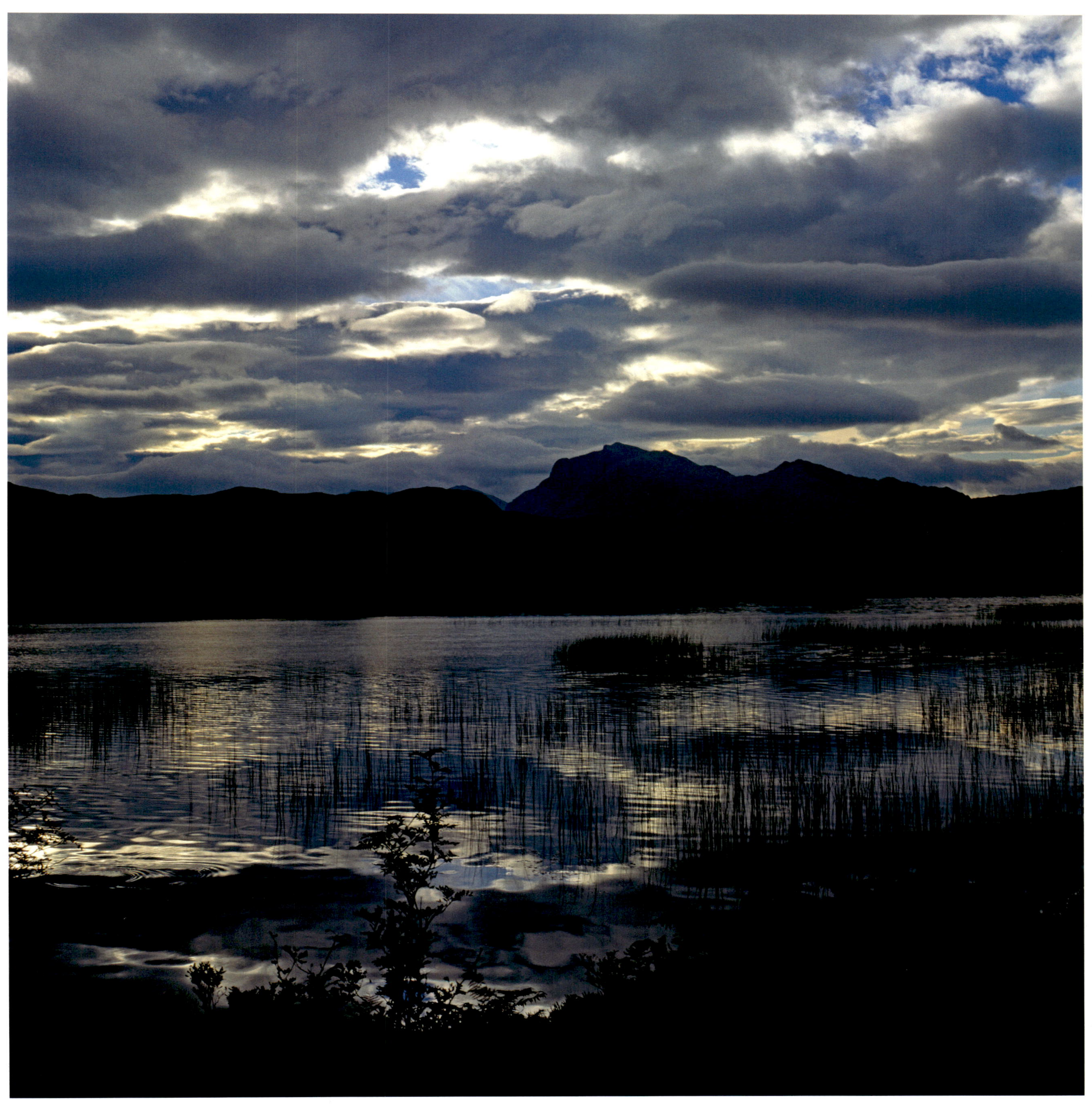

Loch nan Dailthean – Wester Ross – Scotland

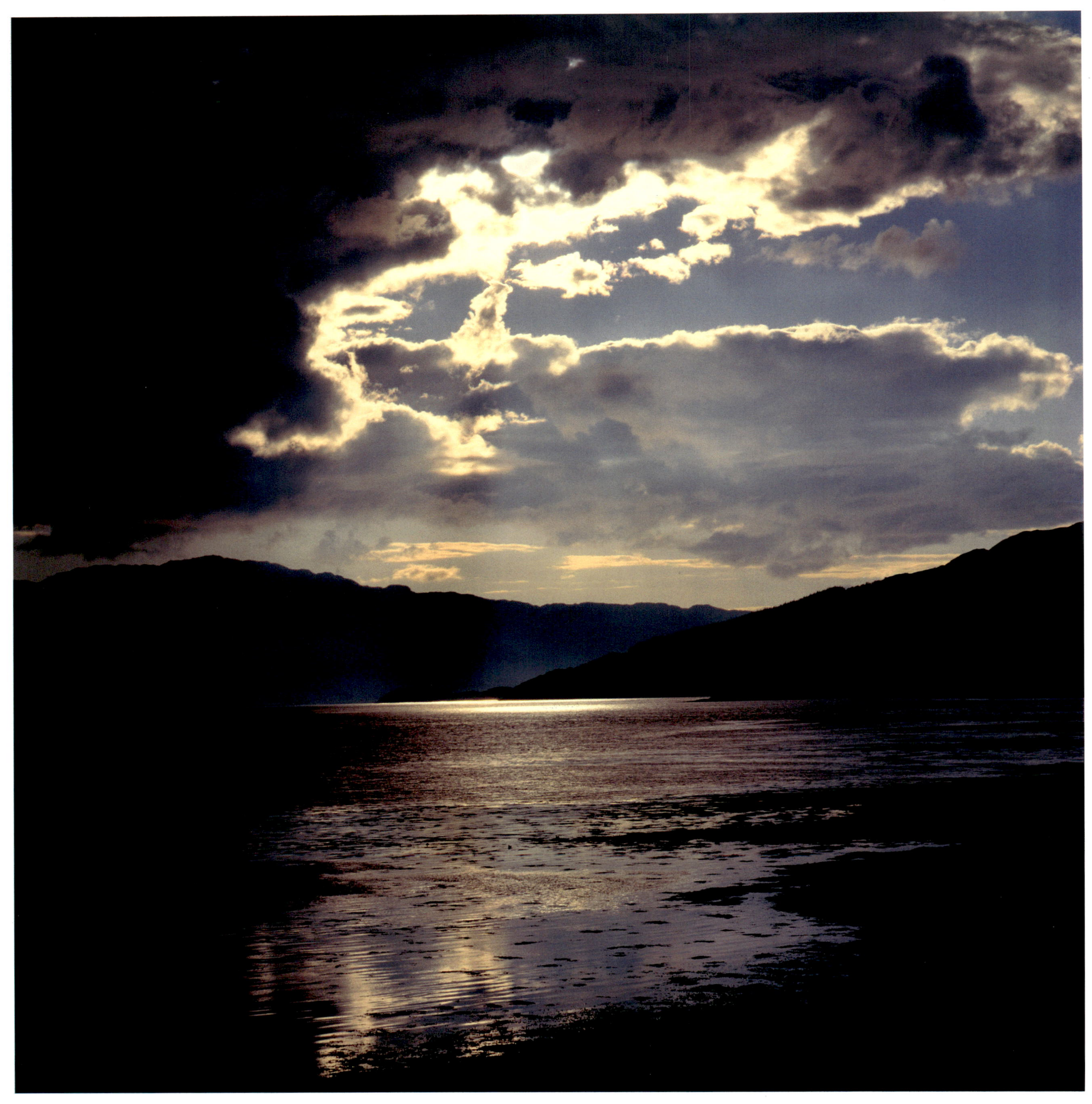

Loch Sunart – Lochaber – Scotland

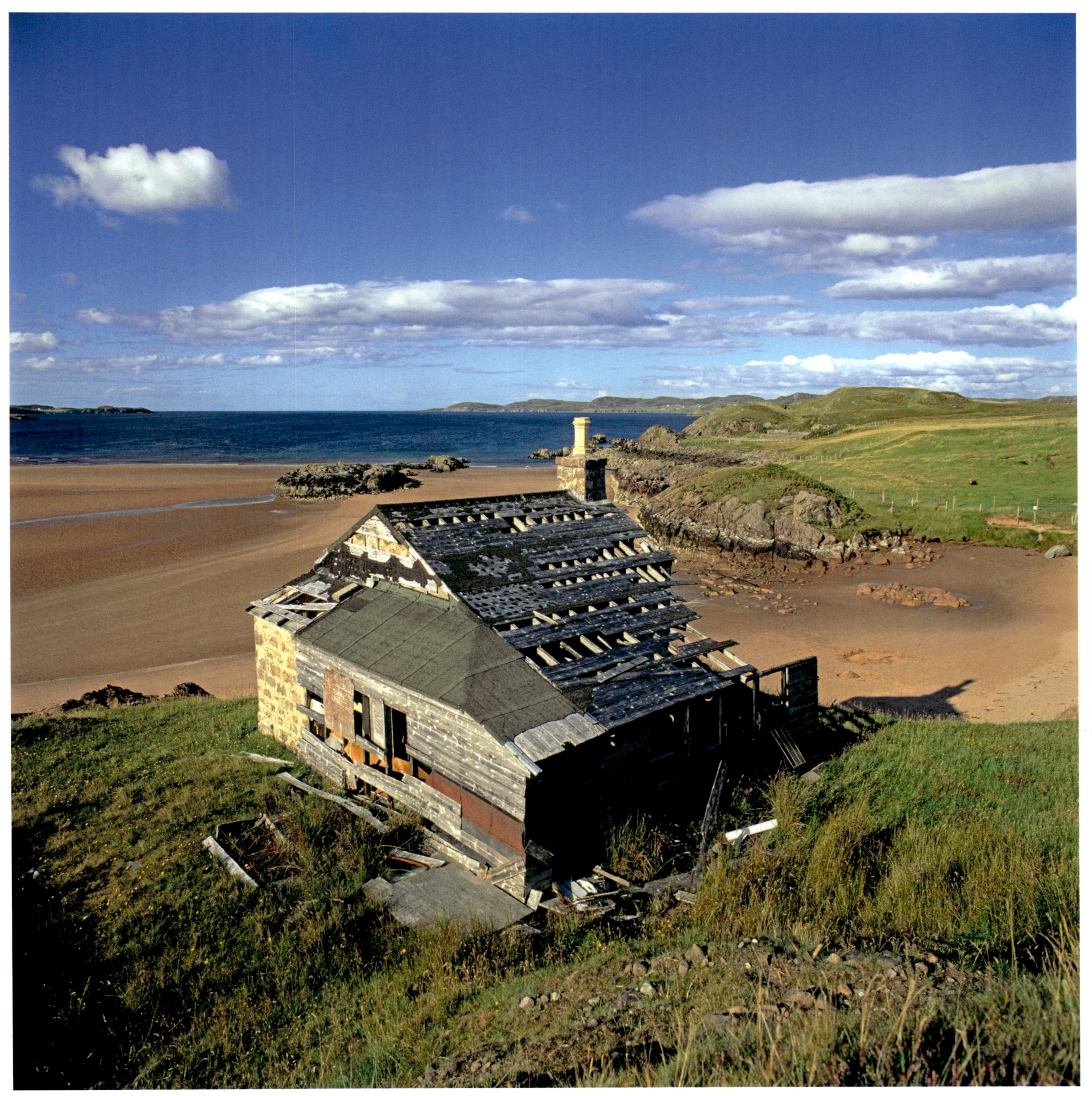

Firemore Bay – Wester Ross – Scotland

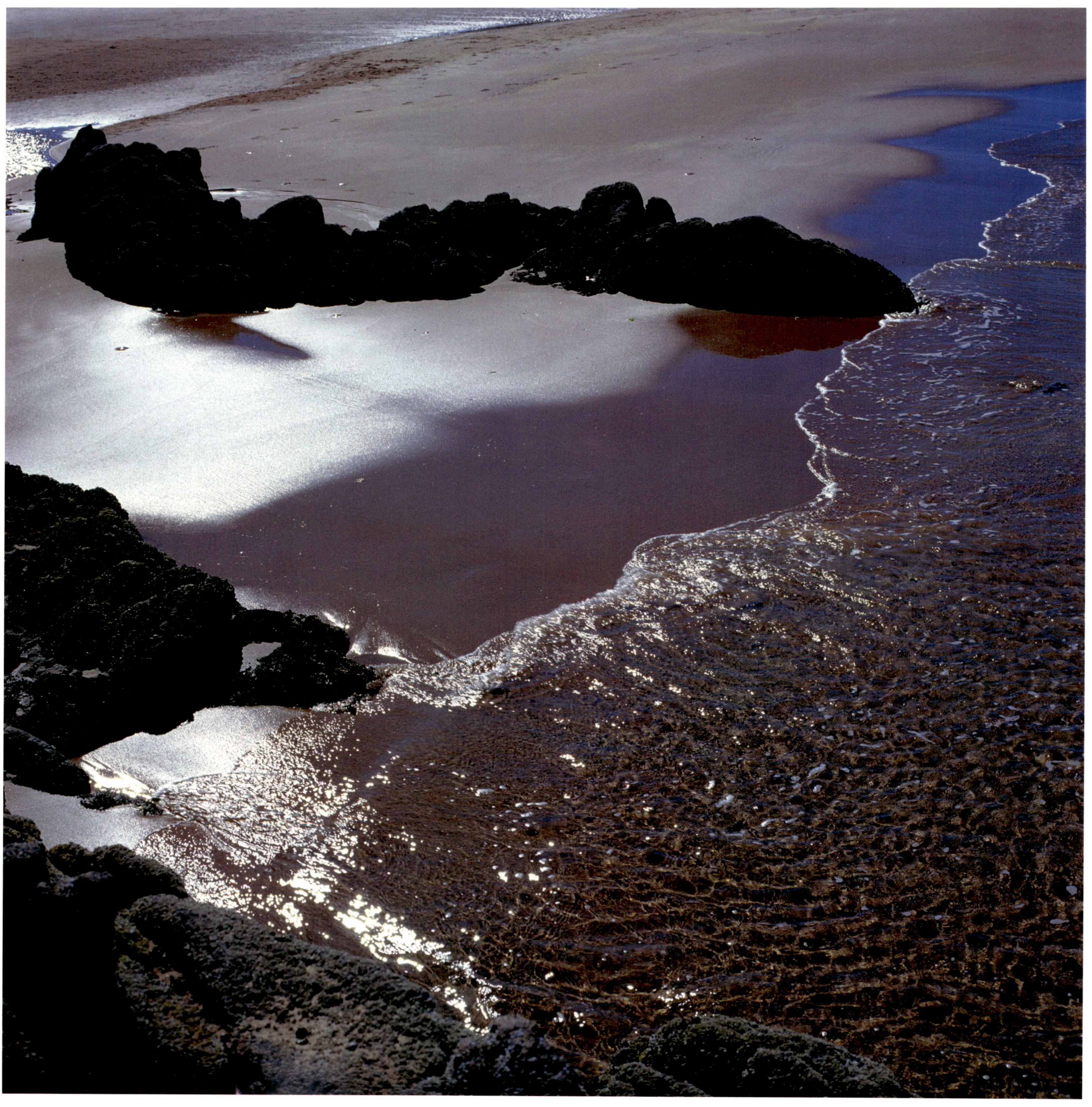

Mellon Udrigle – Wester Ross – Scotland

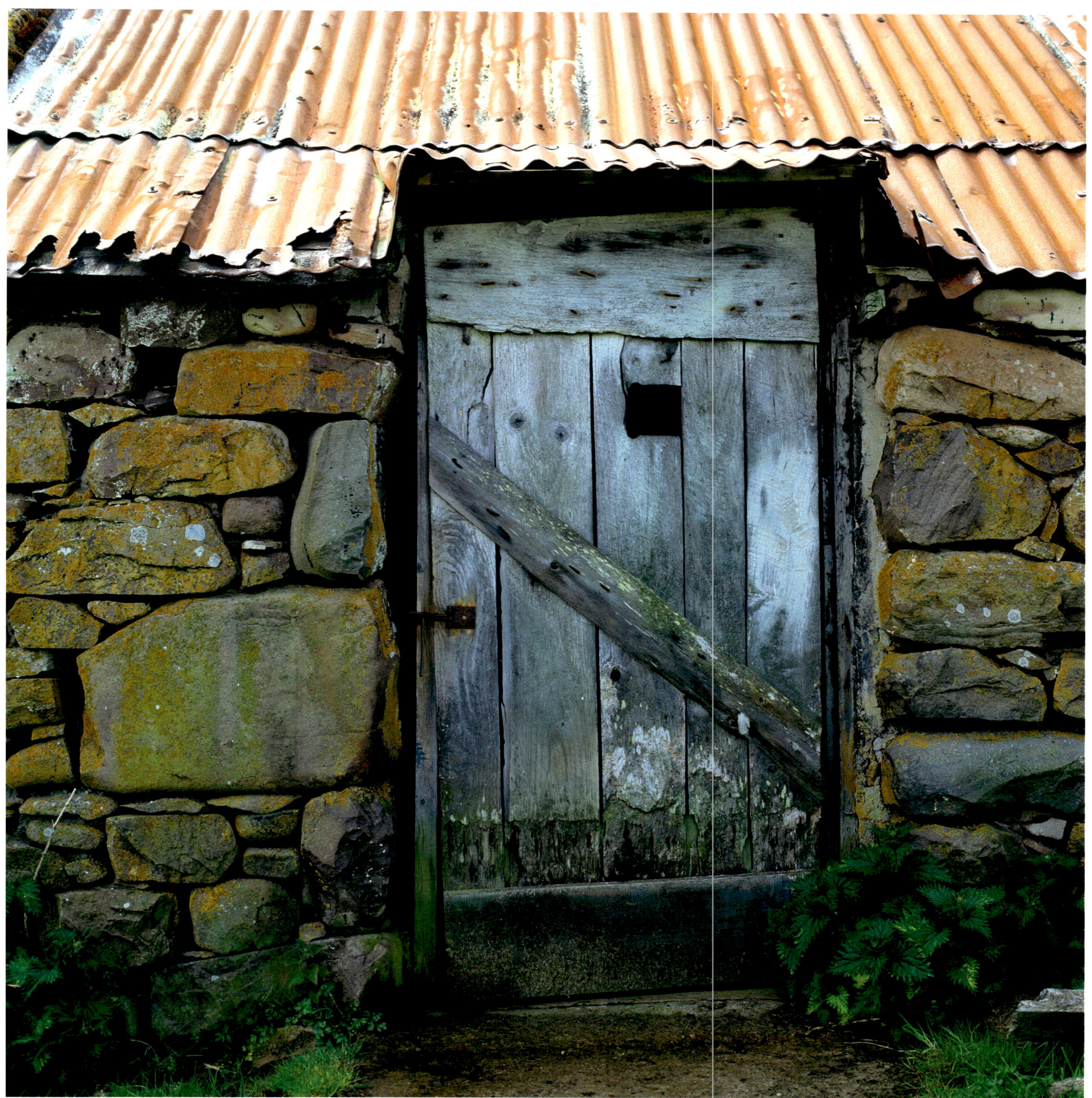

Mellon Udrigle – Wester Ross – Scotland

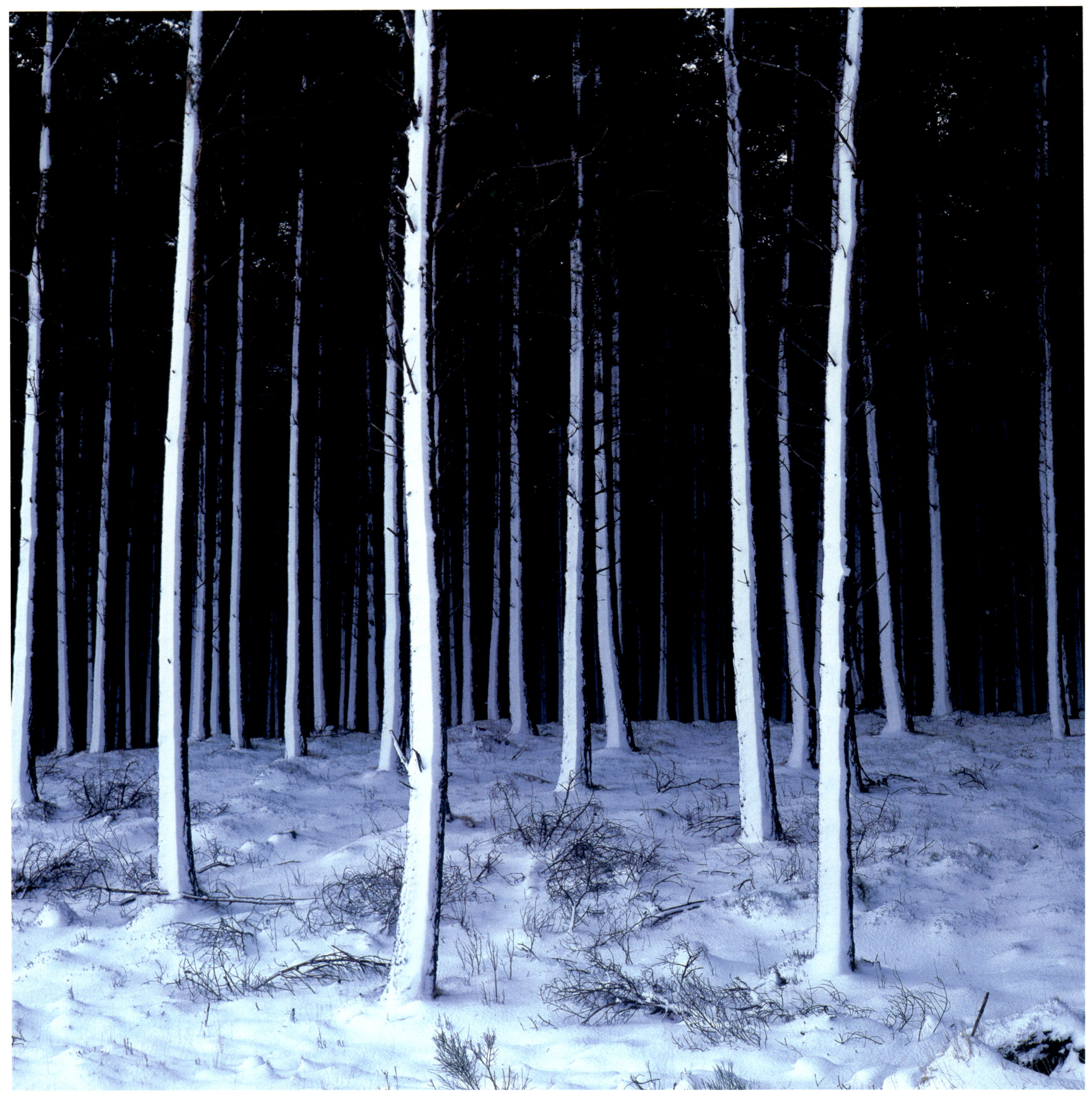

Tomfarclas Wood – Speyside – Scotland

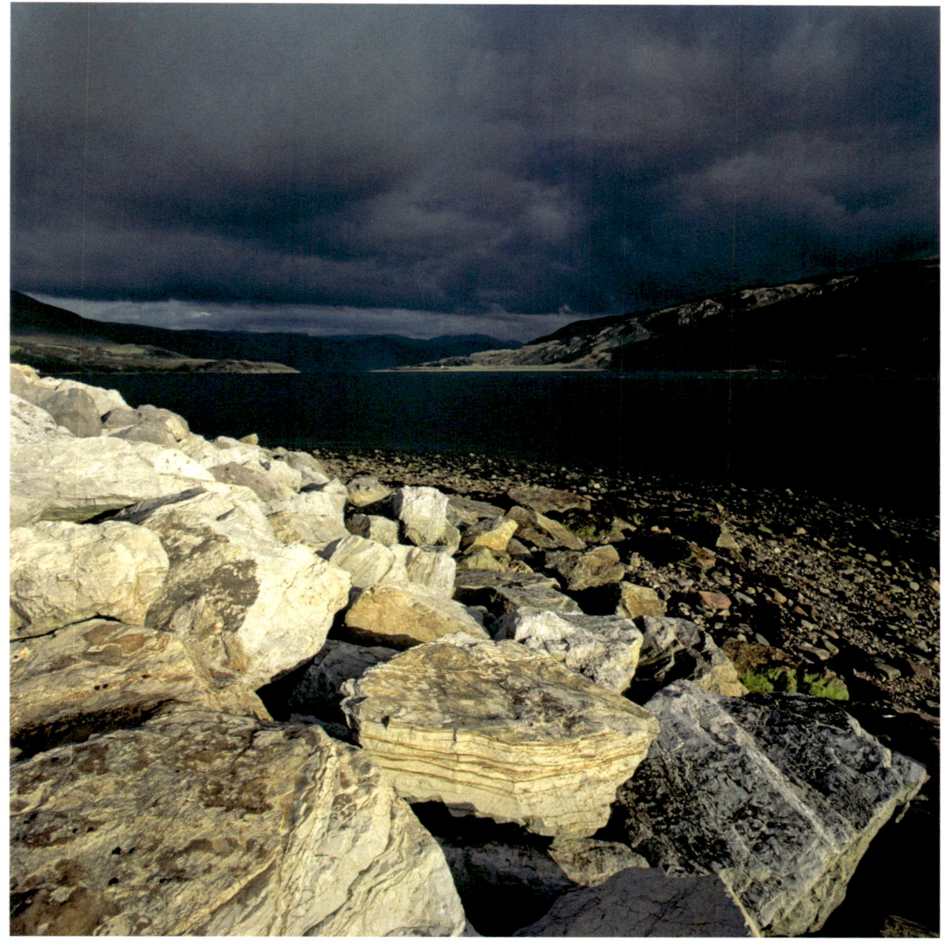

Loch Broom – Wester Ross – Scotland

I remember many evenings spent on Loch Broom. There is often a late evening burst of light on the harbour at Ullapool, while at the top of the loch, at Braemore, a brooding, dark, stormy sky provides the backcloth.

One year I witnessed British Leyland bringing their 'Road Train', a huge articulated lorry, onto Ullapool harbour in order to photograph it in the late evening light. The lorry was snow-white and pristine, and the scene was all set. The photographic crew obviously knew the effect they were after and waited with anticipation for the perfect burst of light in the foreground, with dark sky providing a dramatic contrast. Unfortunately, nothing happened.

Neither did the light appear the following night, nor the next and, after several further unsuccessful attempts, the crew returned home. Unfortunately for them, on the day of their return the evening light looked exactly as in this shot above.

I suppose in this day and age, to save on costs, the lorry would be photographed in a yard and a computer-manipulated sky added sometime afterwards. Although the result would be guaranteed, it doesn't quite hold the same attraction for me.

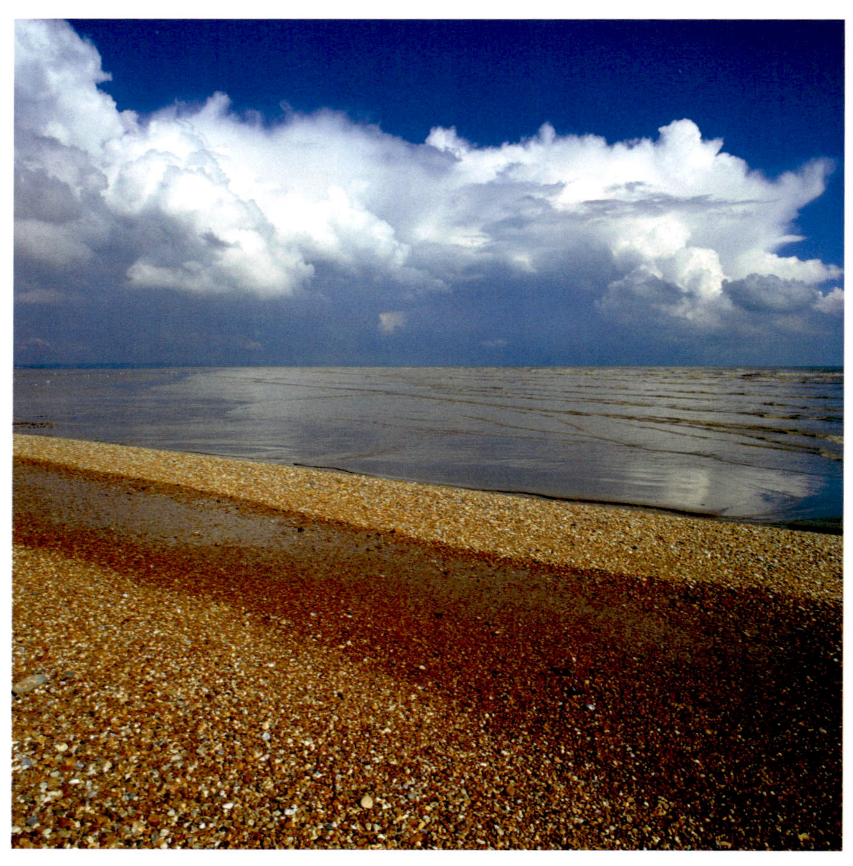

Dungeness – Kent – England

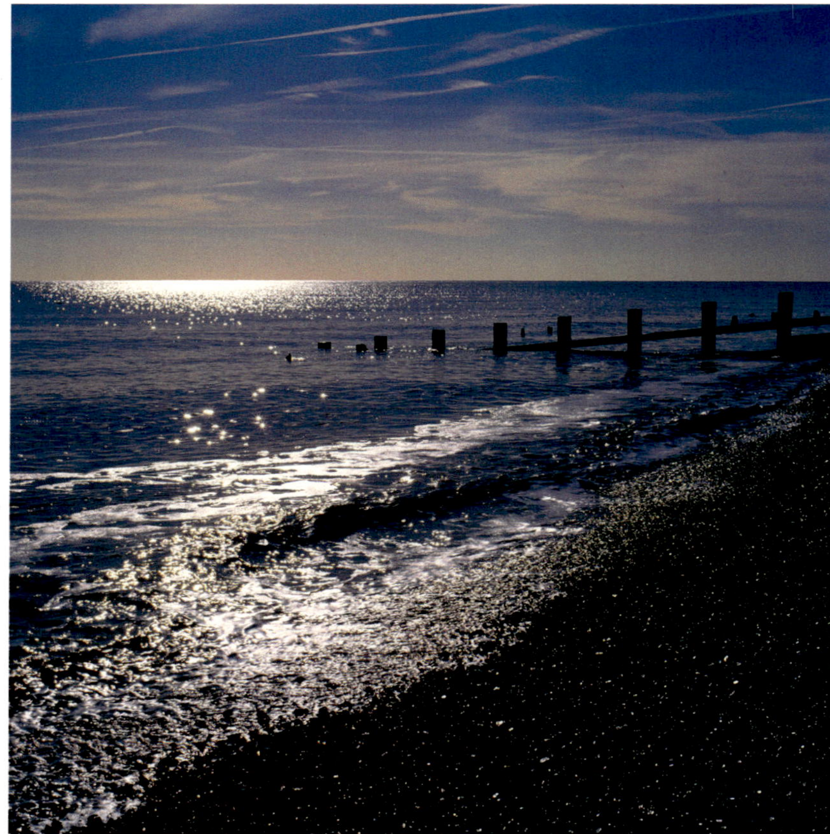

Pett Level – East Sussex – England

GUILTY AS CHARGED

At the risk of offending people south of Yorkshire, I do seem always to be heading one way on a trip, north, and I'm very guilty of not taking holidays 'down' the country. To try and rectify this imbalance in my photographic repertoire, I've included three shots here from a visit to a friend who lives in Kent, although one is actually in Sussex.

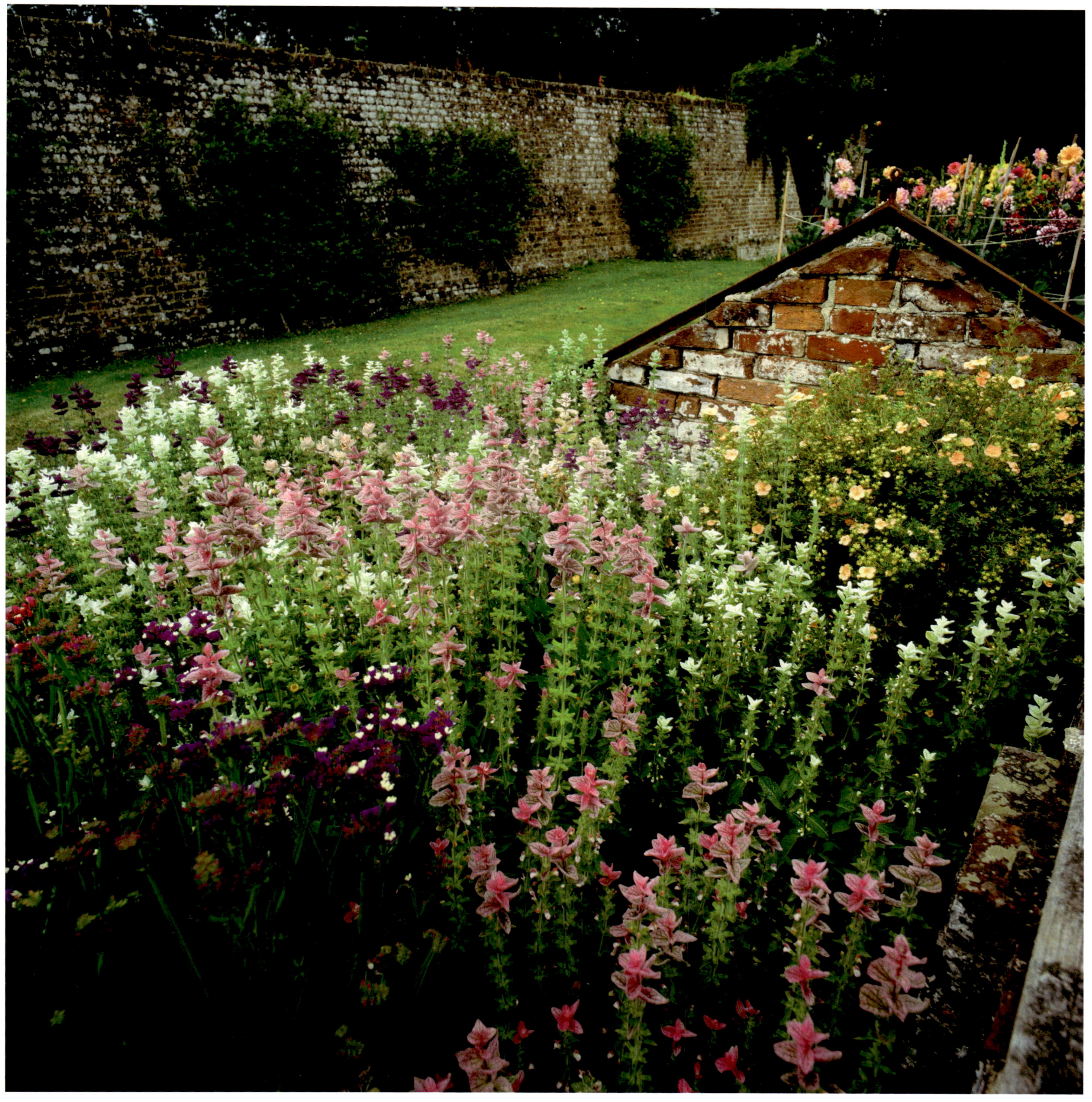

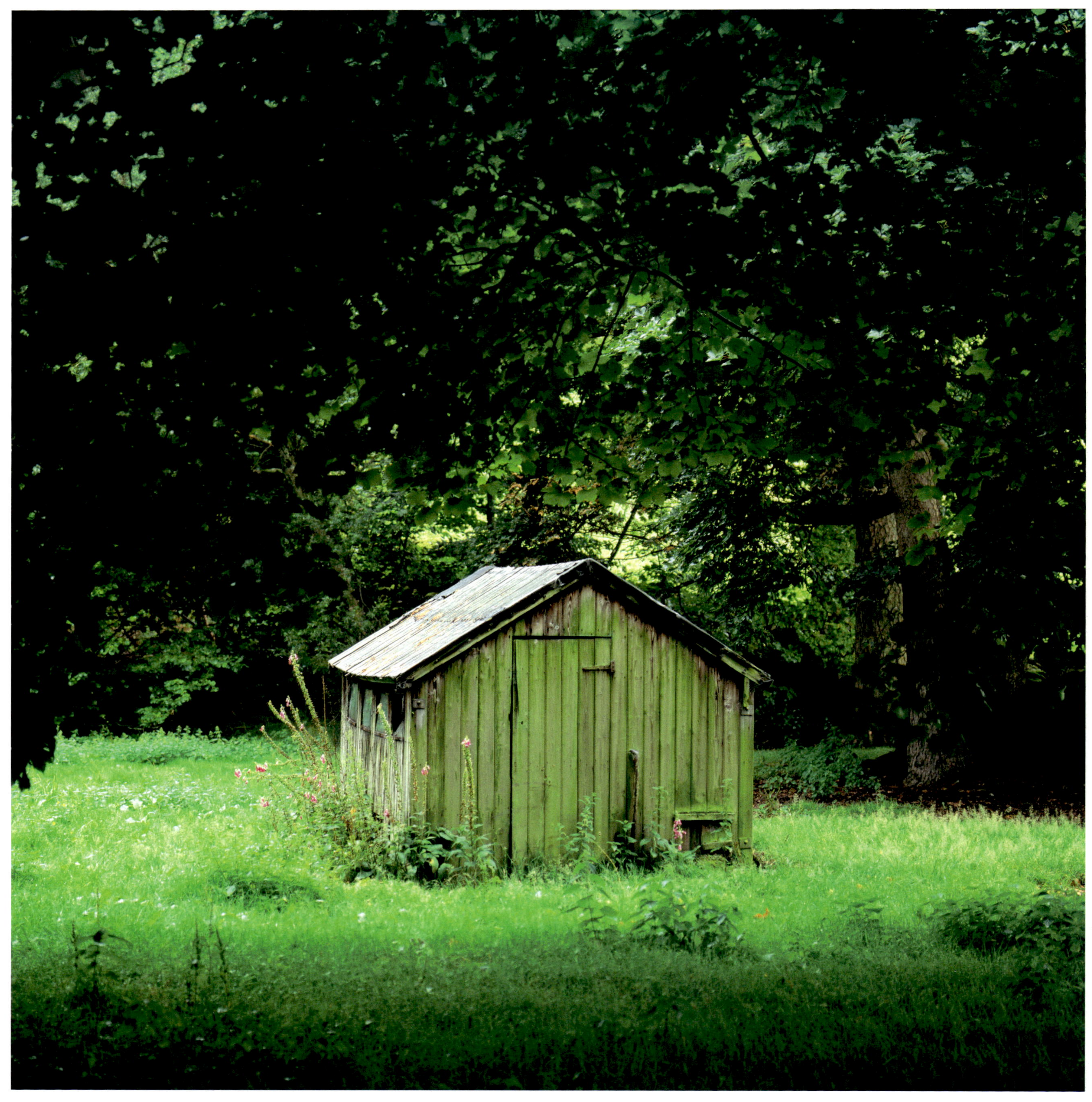

Broadgate – Cumbria – England

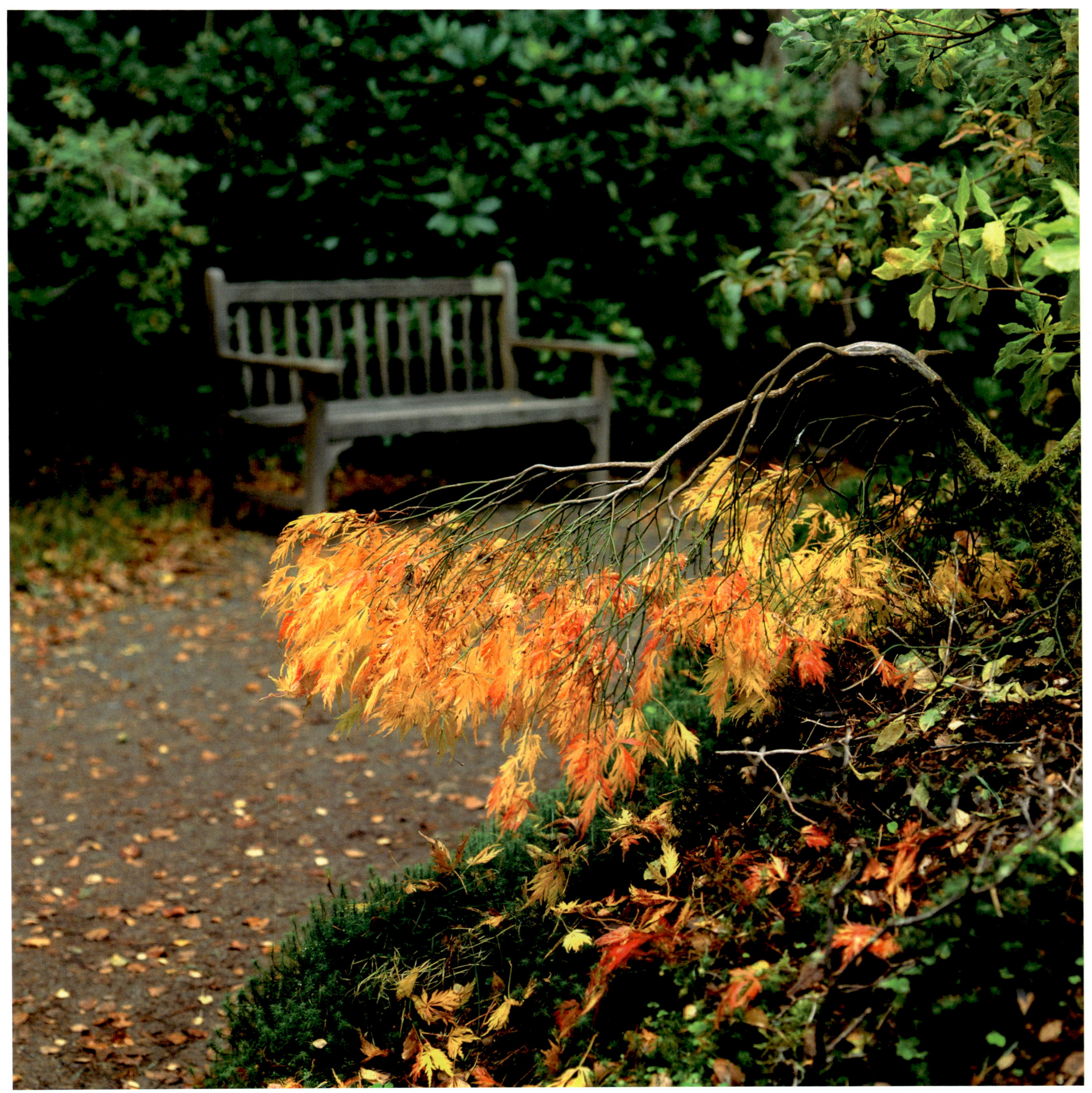

Inverewe Gardens – Wester Ross – Scotland

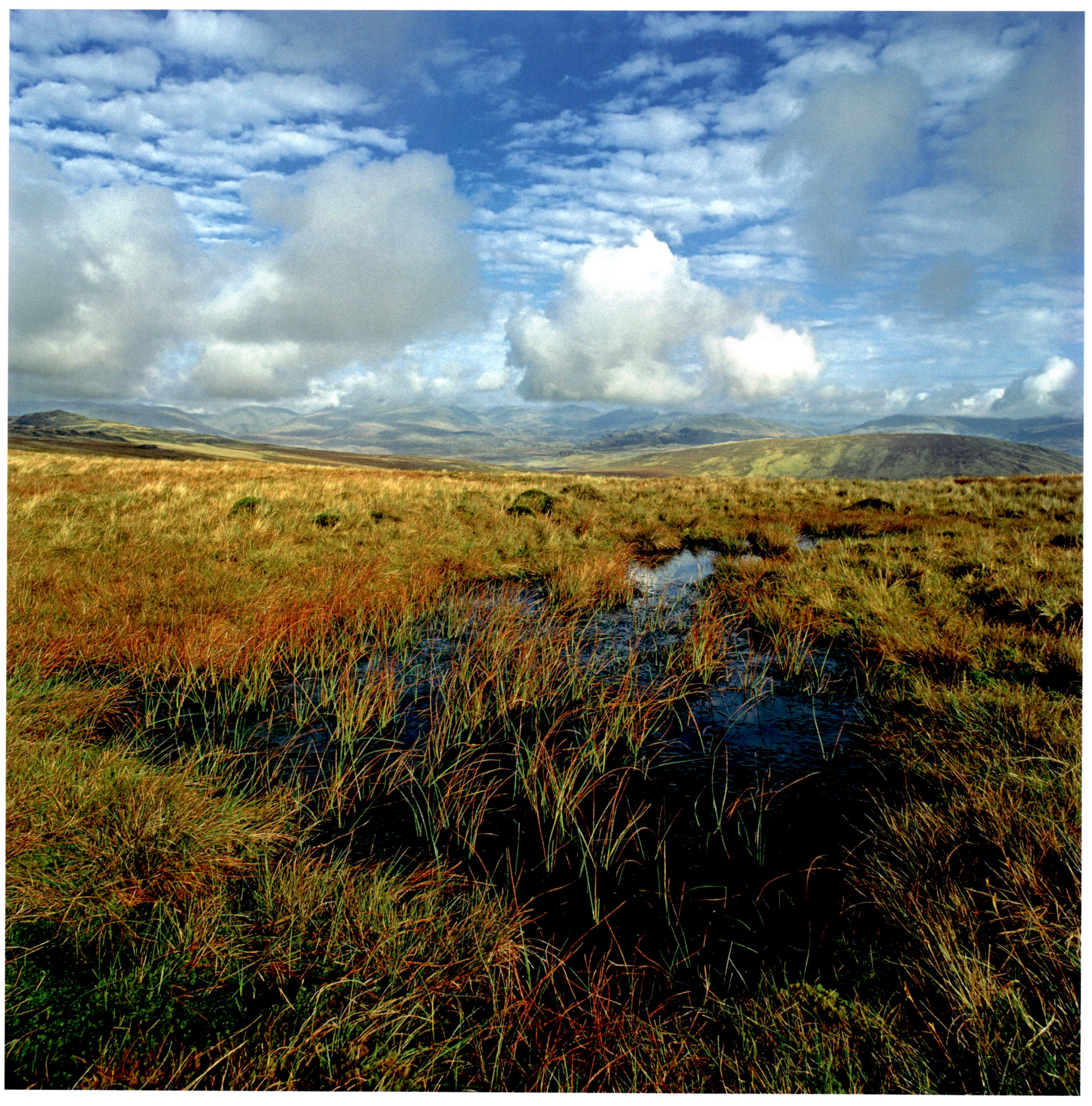

Stainton Fell – Cumbria – England

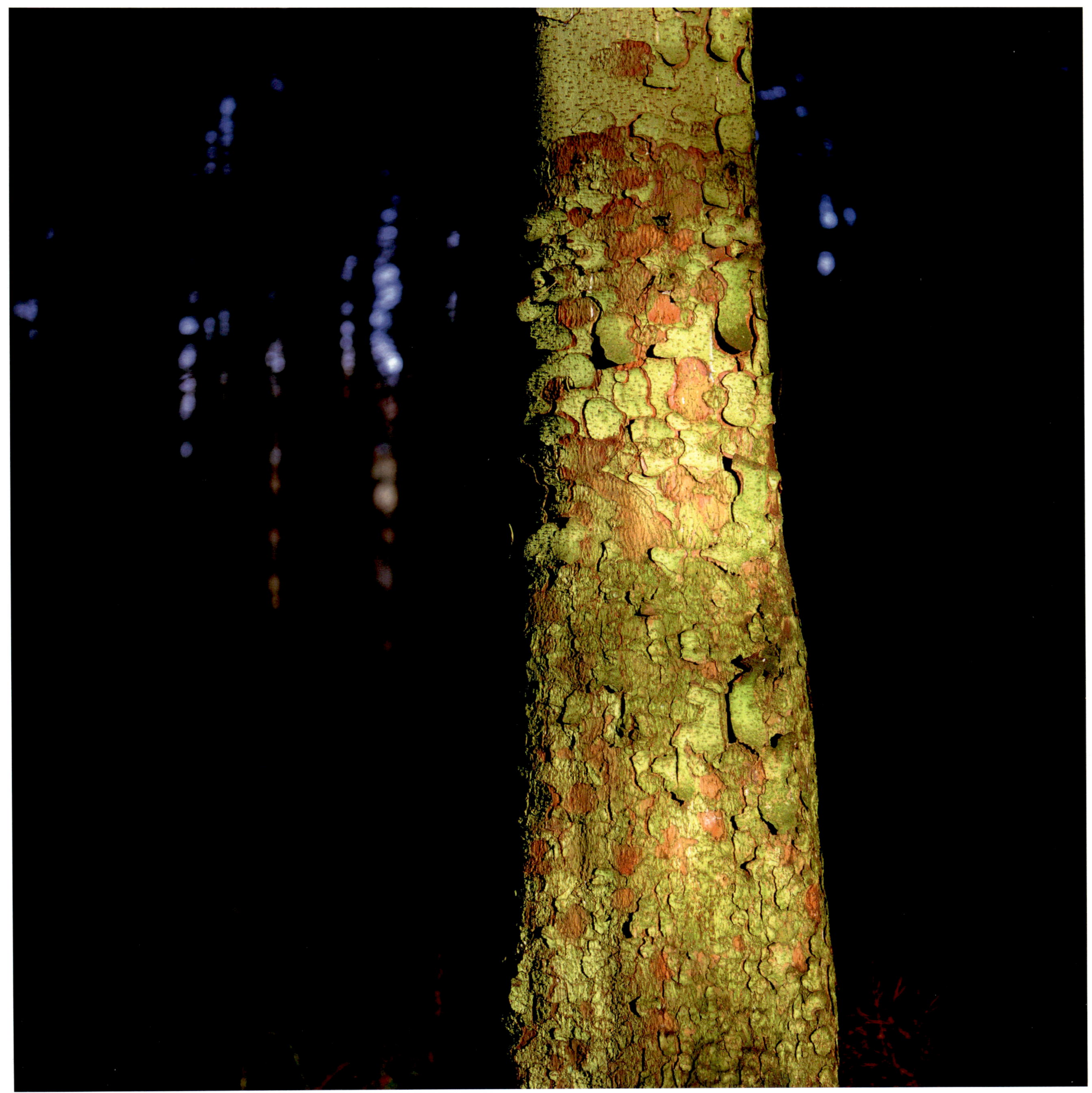

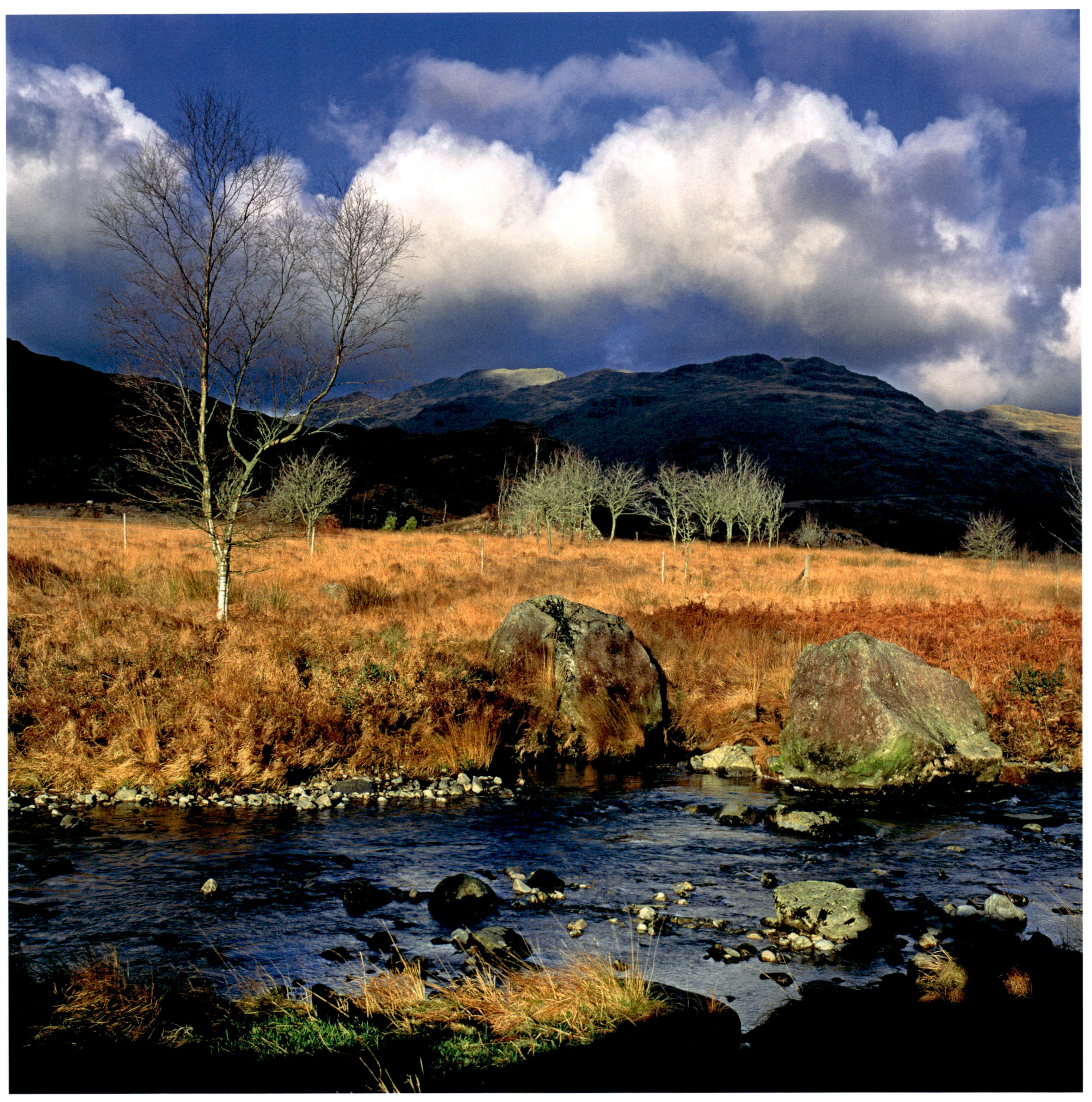

Duddon Valley – Cumbria – England

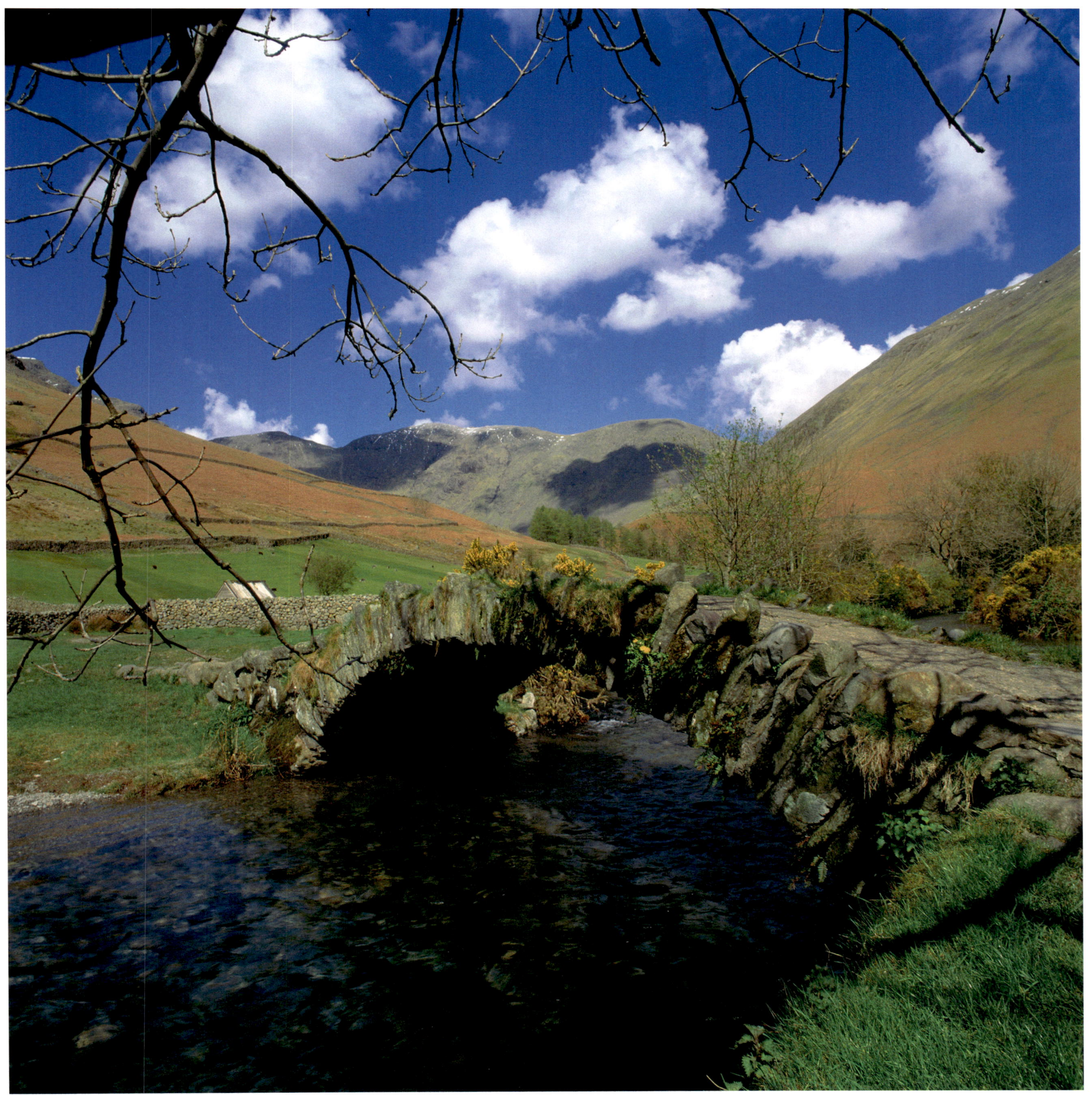

Wasdale – Cumbria – England

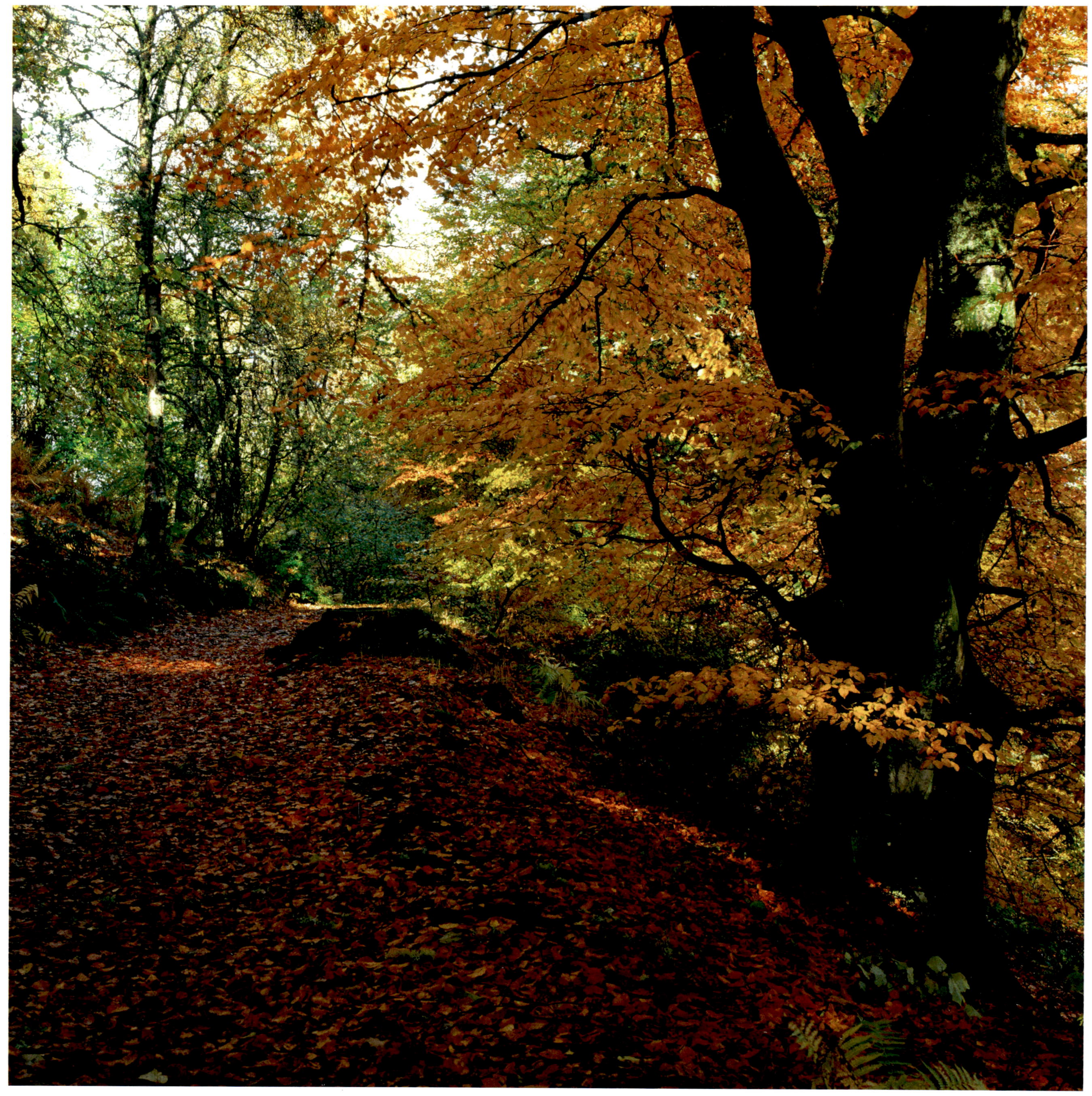

Tayside – Perthshire – Scotland

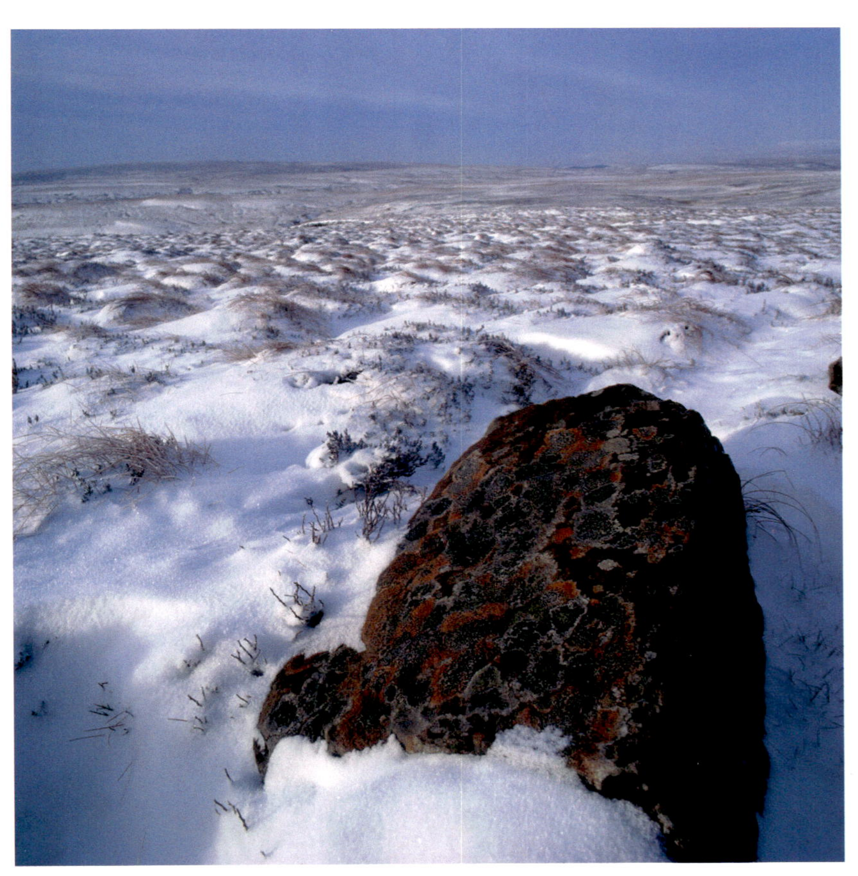

Gunnerside – North Yorkshire – England

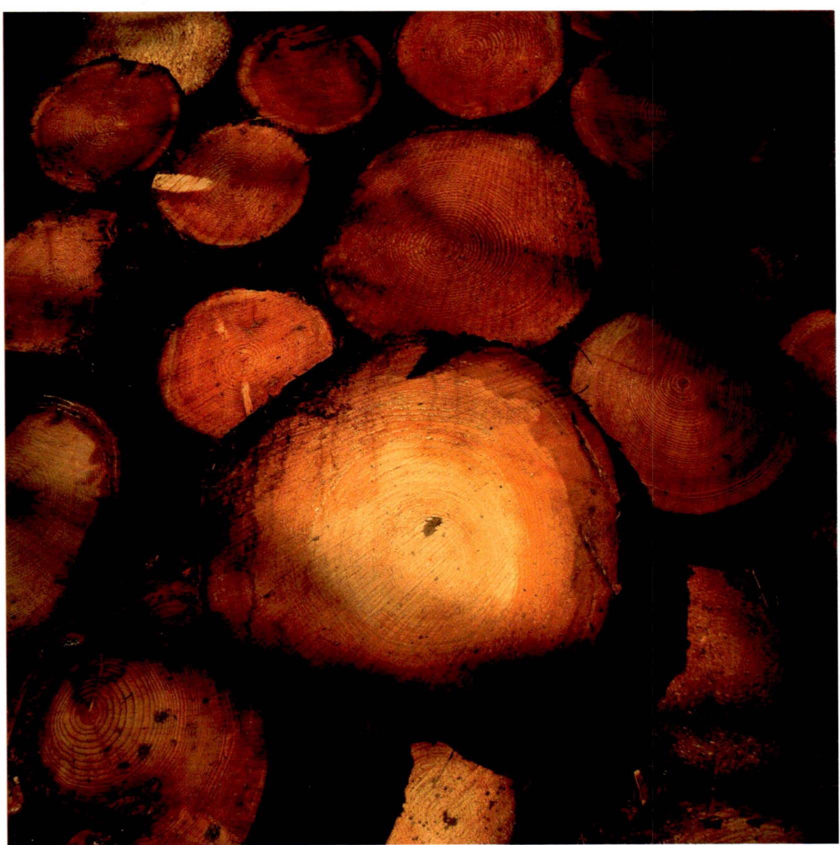

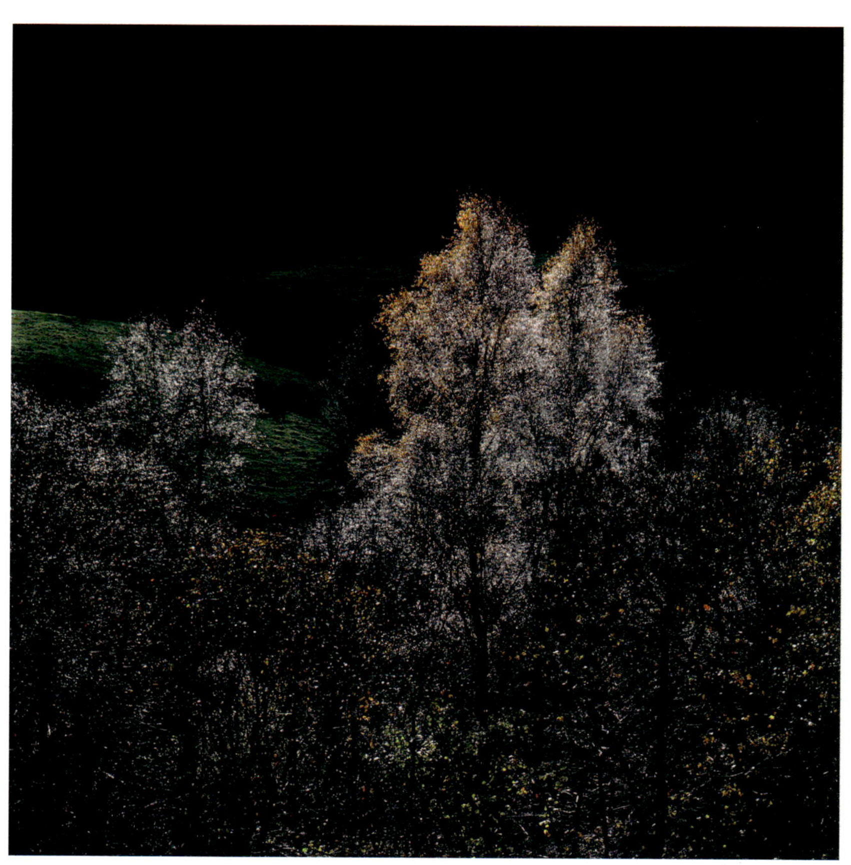

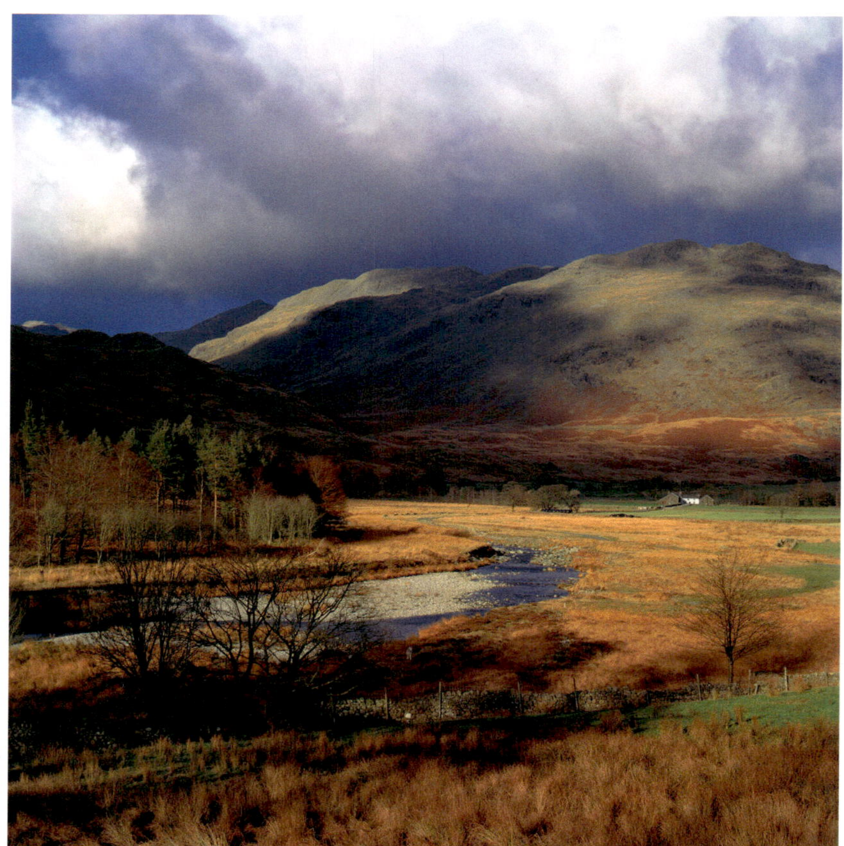

Duddon Valley – Cumbria – England

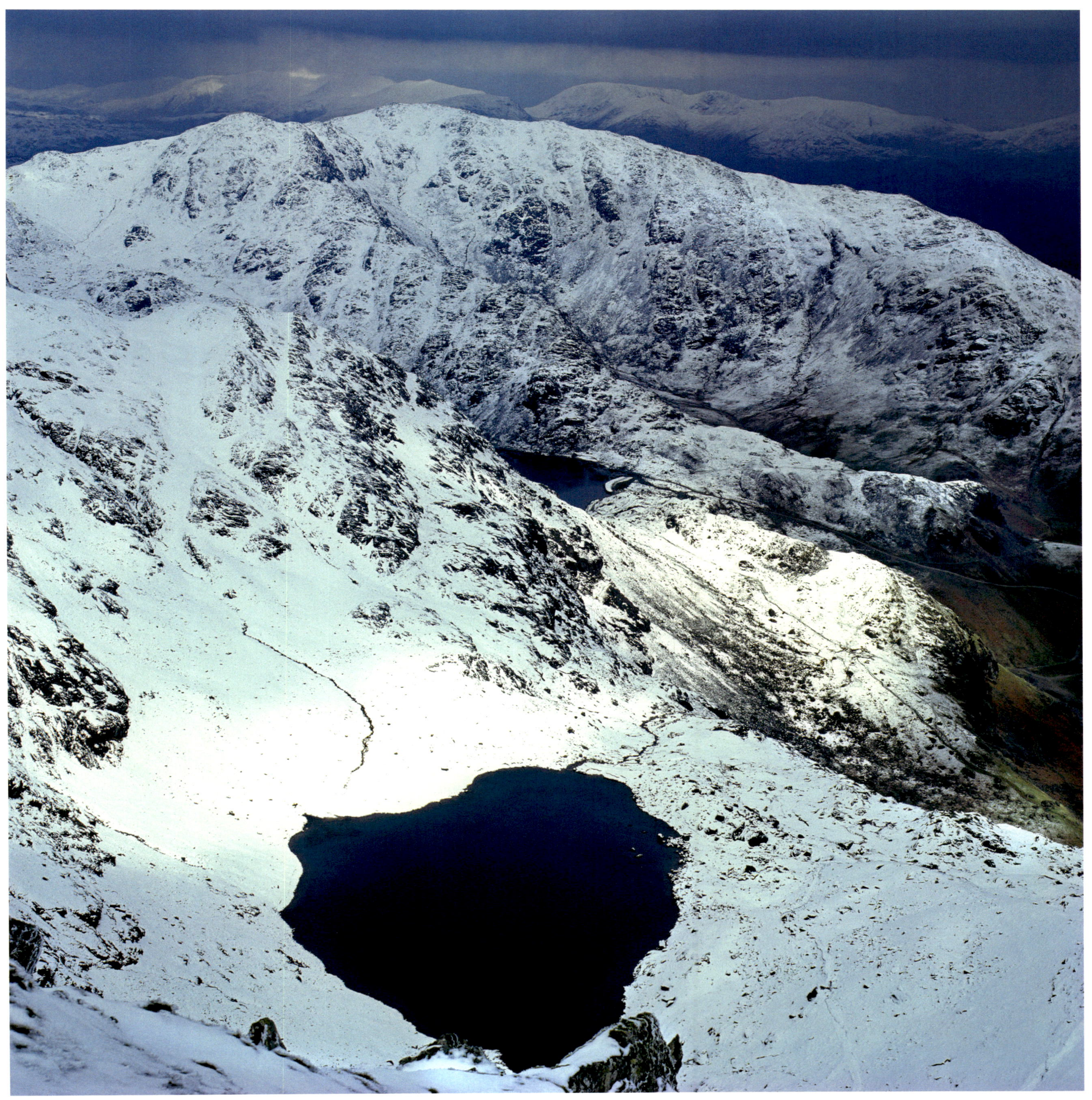

Low Water – Cumbria – England

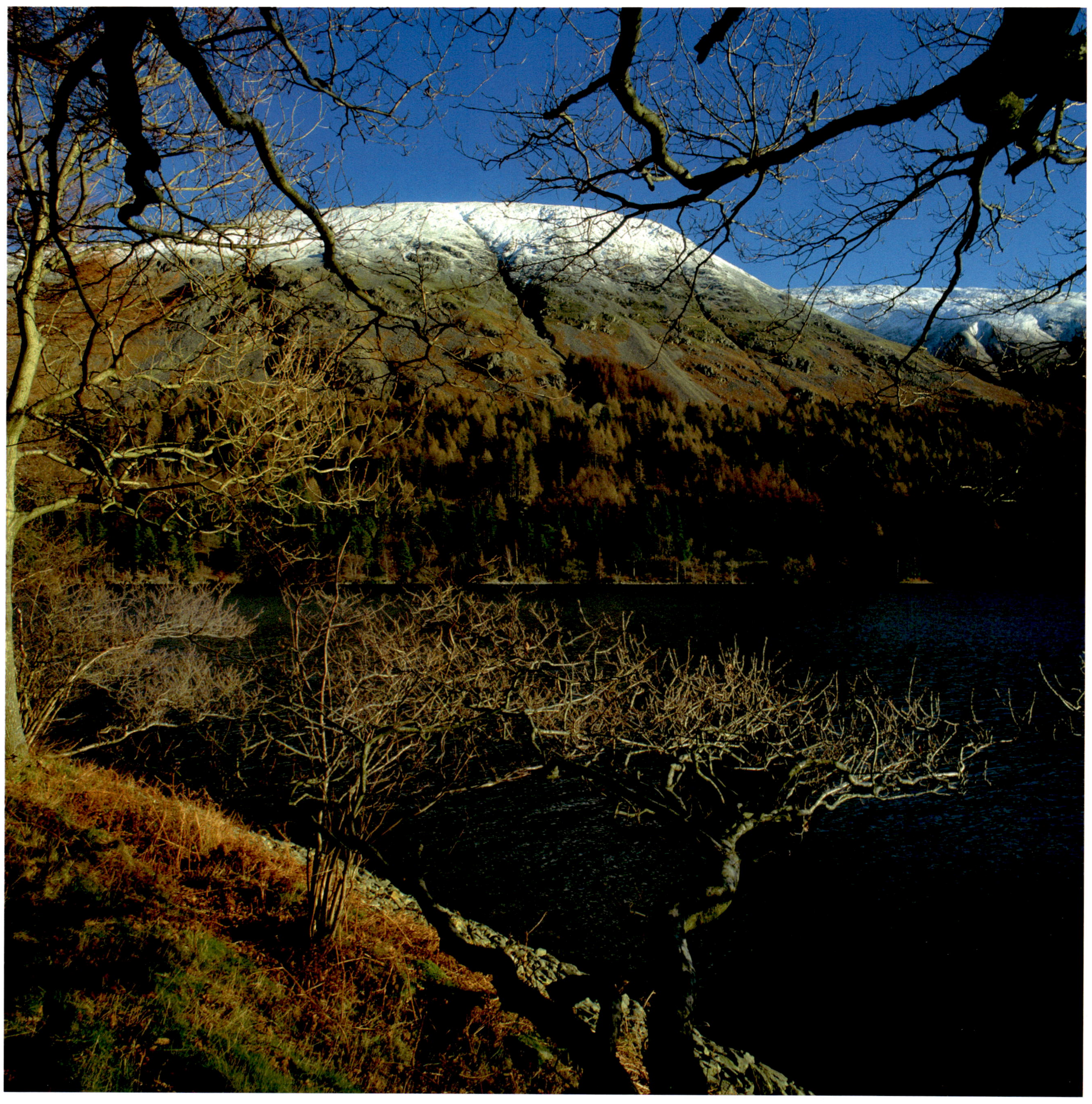

Thirlmere – Cumbria – England

MANIPULATION

Many describe working with transparencies as one of the hardest disciplines in photography, for the captured image has to be correct at the taking stage.

Here's a brief explanation of how I overcame difficulties in the shot opposite and the following two shots overleaf. This will be my only technical bit in the book I promise.

THIRLMERE

It was 25 December and a man within a few yards of me was trying out his Christmas present, a new Nikon. He said if I moved to where he was standing I would avoid the trees and I'd be able to see more of the lake. The trouble was, though, I didn't want to see more of the lake, because it was just a dark-blue mass in the foreground. It was the striking light on the main trees that was my goal, with the other trees at the top, framing and enhancing what was a plain blue sky.

KIRKBY MALZEARD

There was a setting sun creating a washed-out highlight almost on the horizon, thus spoiling the image. To eliminate this, I ran down the road to get the solitary tree in front of the sun.

FROST ON THE WINDOW

Some people don't appreciate what this shot is at first. It's ice on a window, but across the road, probably fifteen metres away, are terraced houses, the walls of which provide the different colours in the shot. To ensure I didn't see the details of the houses, I selected a large aperture to ensure shallow depth of field, which meant only the frost was sharp.

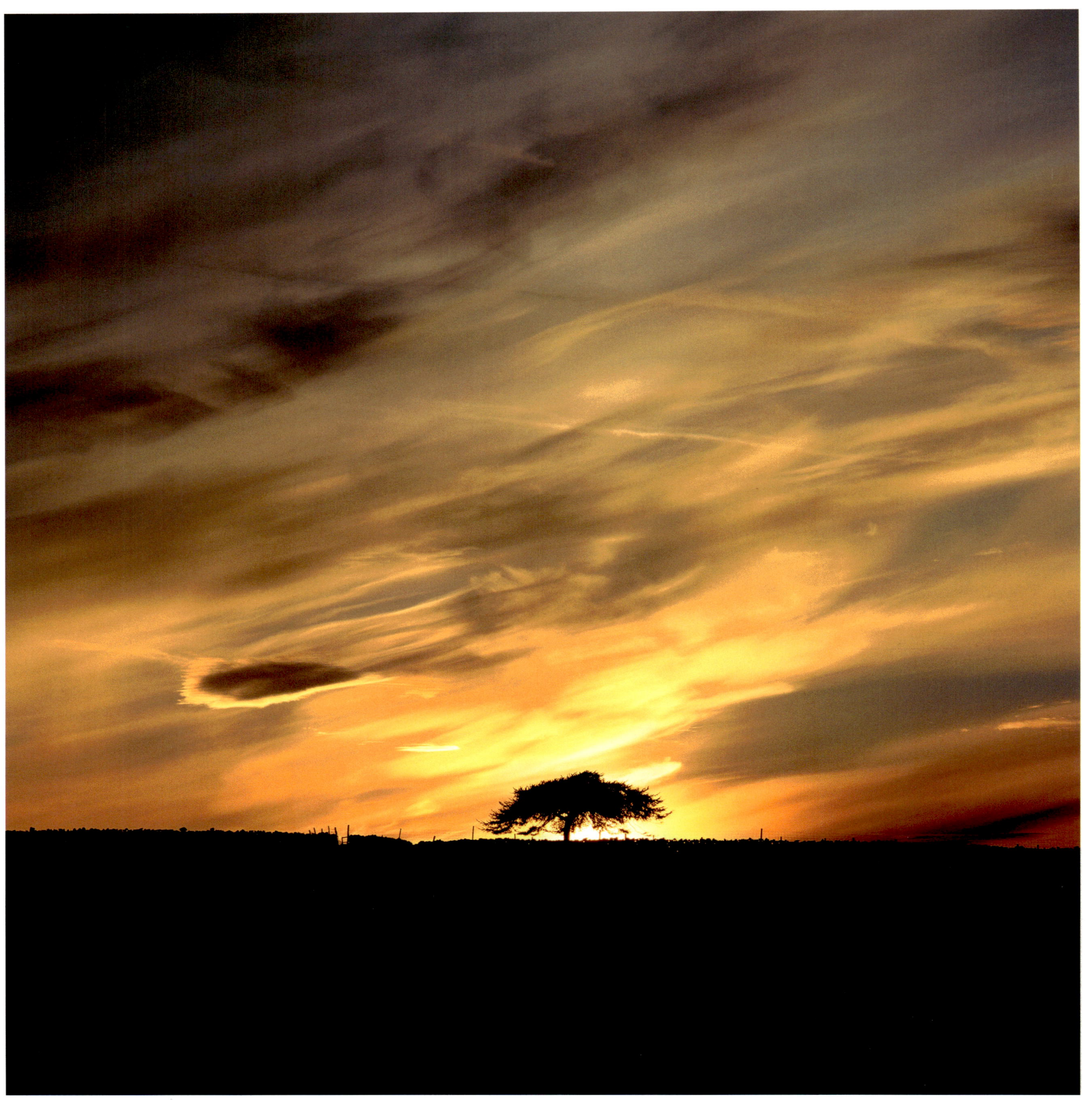

Kirkby Malzeard – North Yorkshire – England

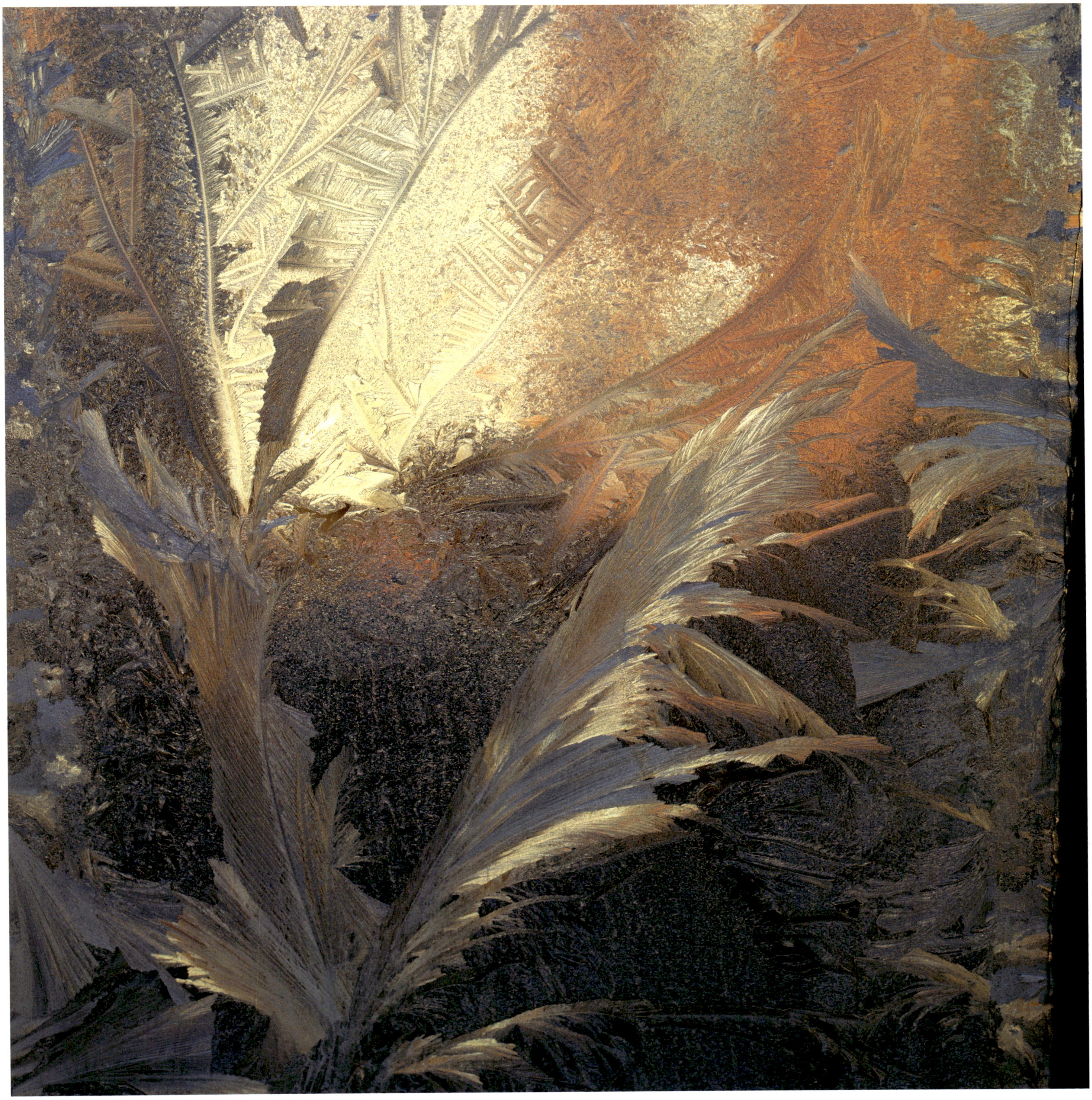

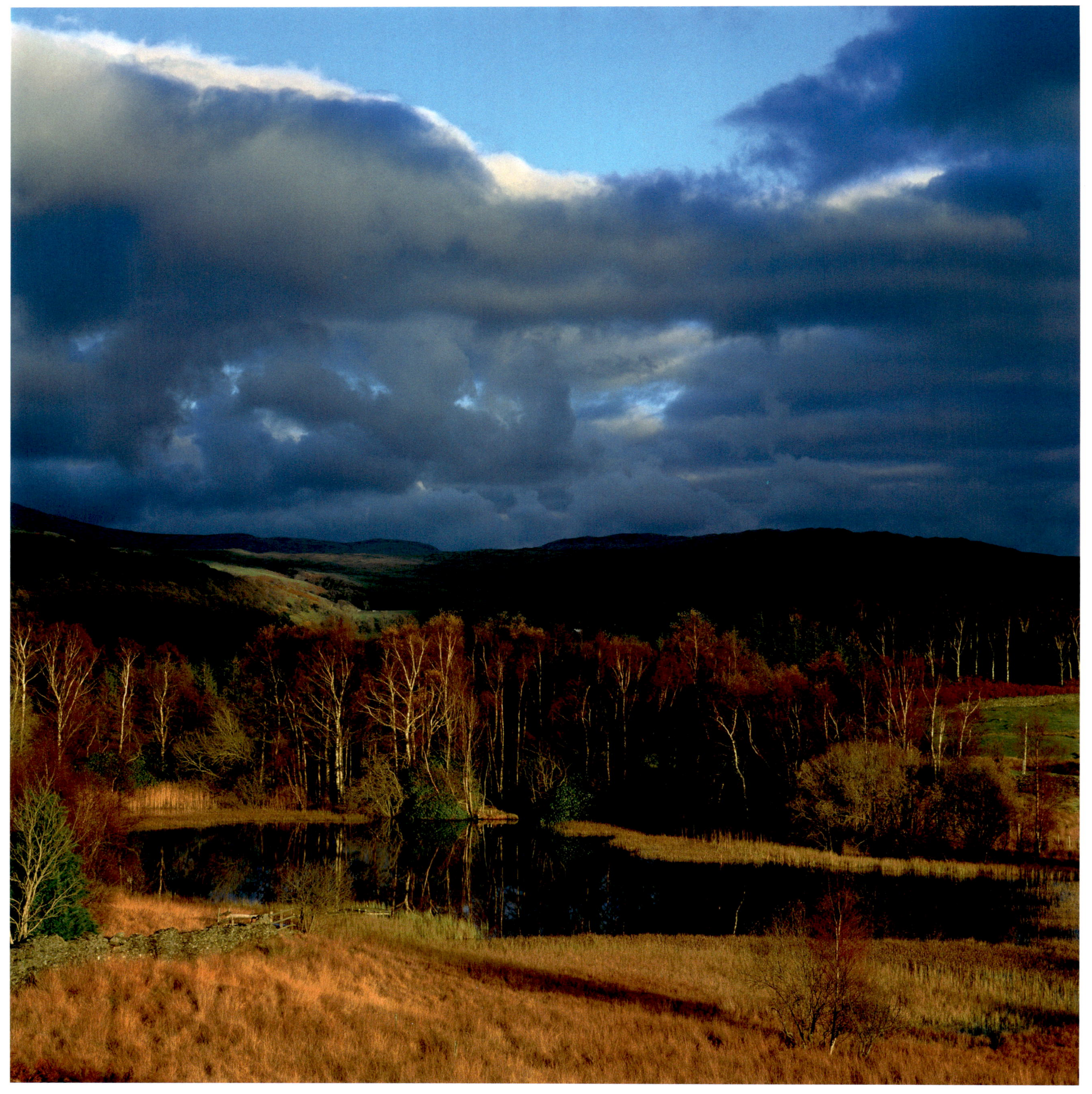

Barngates – Cumbria – England

PURE PHOTOGRAPHY

When I'm presenting a show or an exhibition I take with me a display panel explaining my photographic technique and it's simply entitled 'Pure Photography'.

One 'blogger' wrote that he loved my work, but explained how he believed there was no such thing as 'Pure Photography'. So maybe my title is incorrect, but I hope that from the following you'll be able to understand the basics of what I mean.

All the photographs in this book are shot on film, using analogue cameras. My cameras have two main 'working' features on them: a dial for the aperture and one for the shutter speed, and that's all. There are no confusing menus, no autofocus lenses, no zoom lenses and no batteries. So hopefully, not a lot to go wrong!

I rarely use a light meter, only in extreme circumstances such as very low light. I'm so used to working with 50 ISO film that invariably the exposure is programmed into my brain. Experience is a great tool!

I don't use filters on the camera as I've not yet perfected photography without them, so I don't intend trying to confuse the issue. Plus, I'm a big believer in the fact that, whenever a filter is used, something has to 'give' in terms of reproduction. I do read of how certain filters are probably 'the best on the market' and don't suffer too badly from colour casts etc., but one comment on the internet summed up my own feelings: 'There's something not quite right about using a Zeiss lens and sticking a bit of resin (which many filters are) at the front of it.'

On my workshops, one of the main topics photographers concern themselves with is post production, i.e. work done on a computer *after* the photograph is taken. My post production is simple – I take the film out of the camera. As explained previously, with transparency (slide) film there is very little latitude, which means that you have to get the exposure perfect (or very near to it) in the camera. You can't lighten or darken a slide in processing because once the film is placed in the chemicals, that's it. I believe the art of capturing correct exposure and perfect composition in the camera is dying with too many people relying on being able to manipulate a photograph after it has been taken.

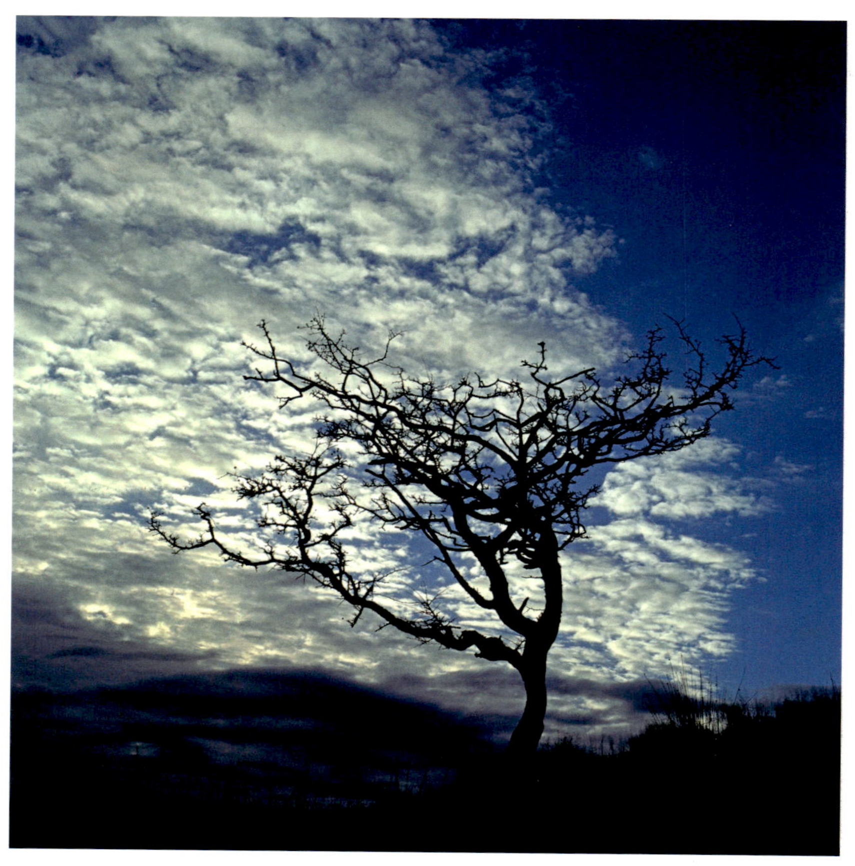

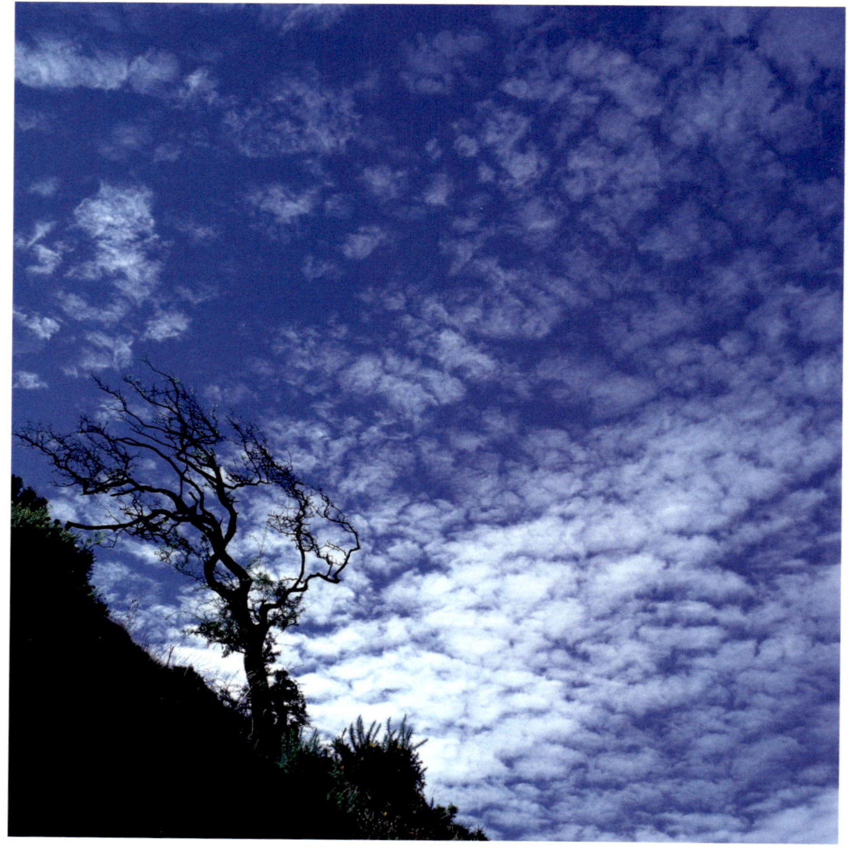

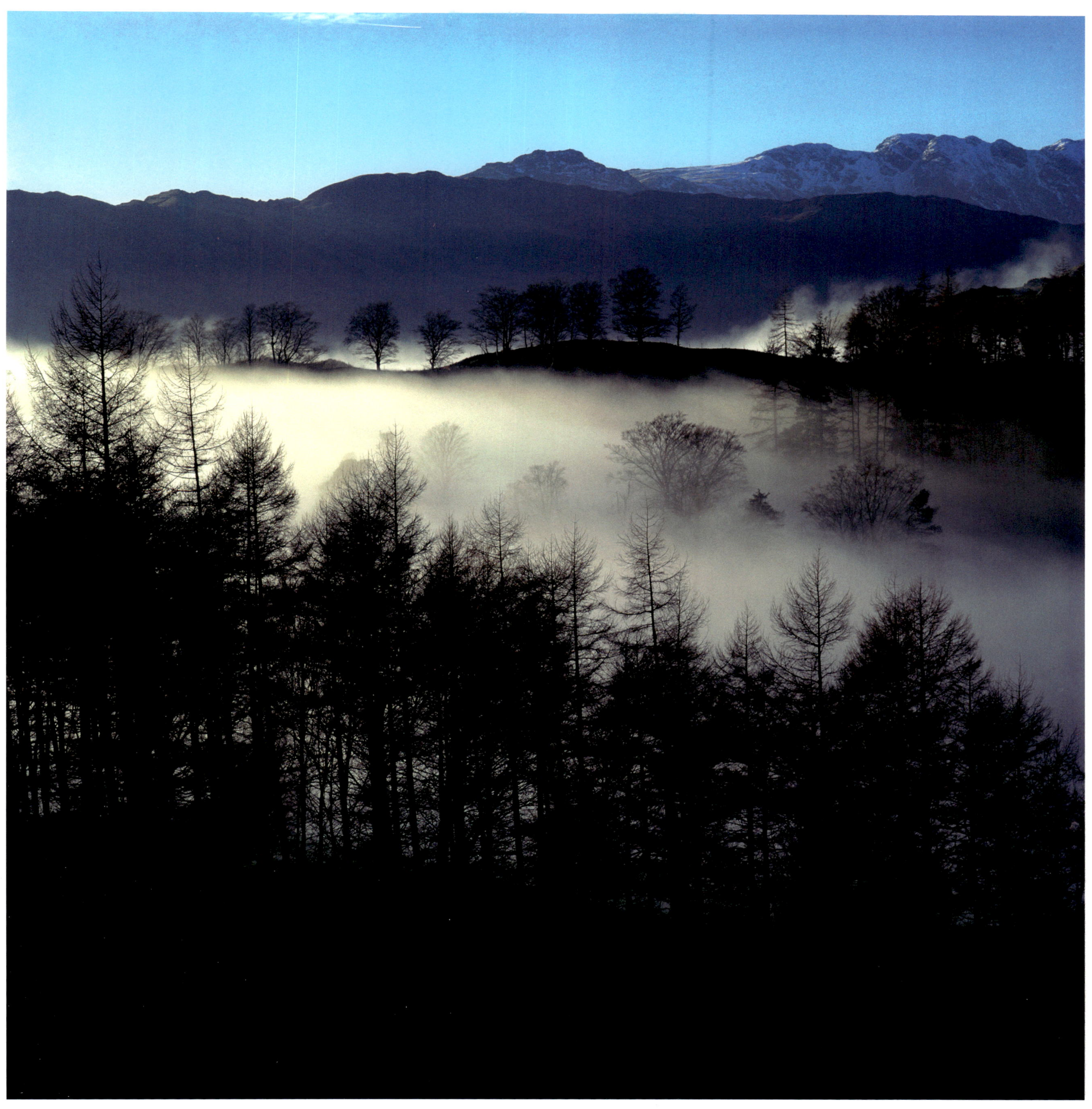

Loughrigg Fell – Cumbria – England

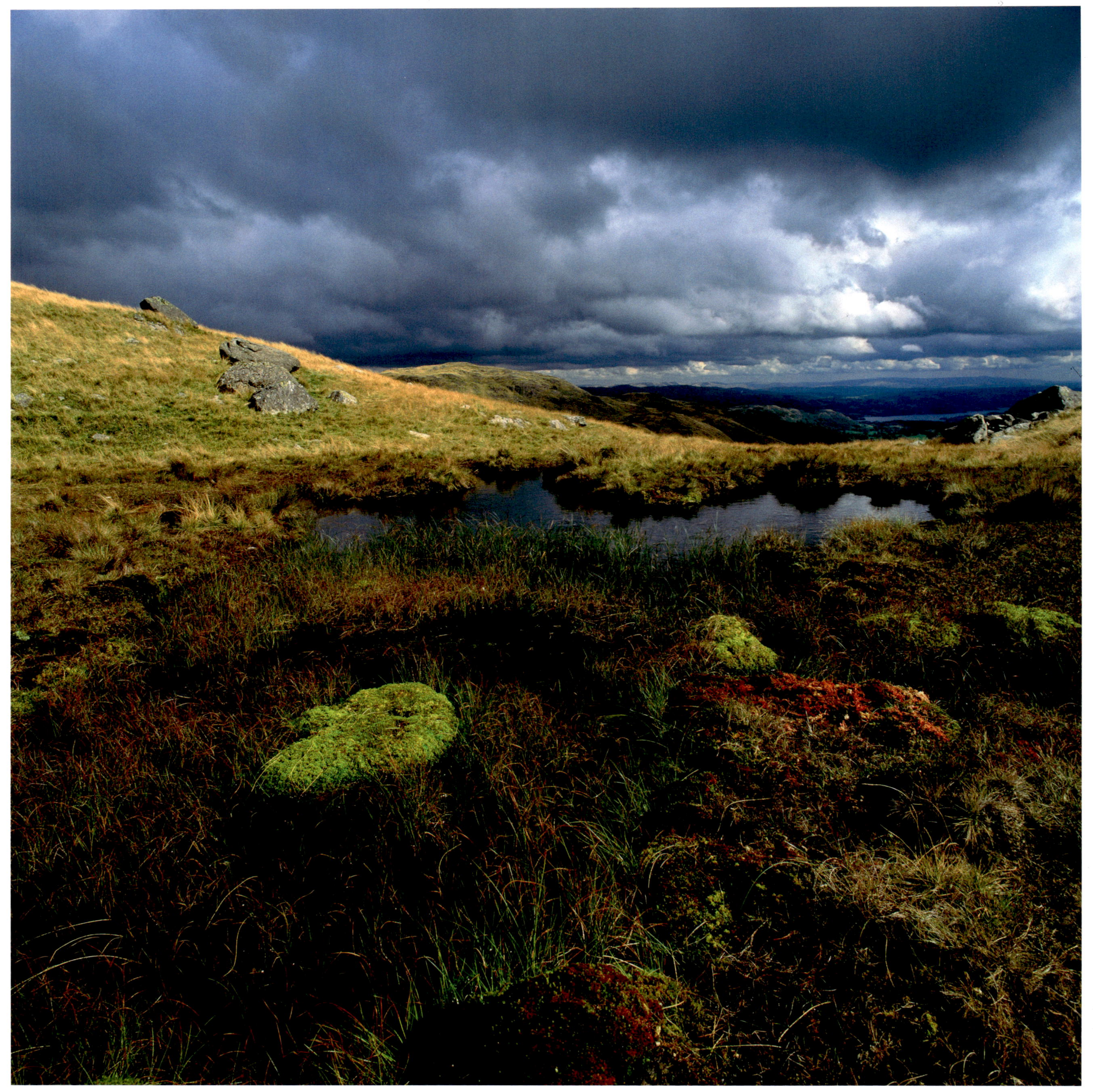

Langdale – Cumbria – England

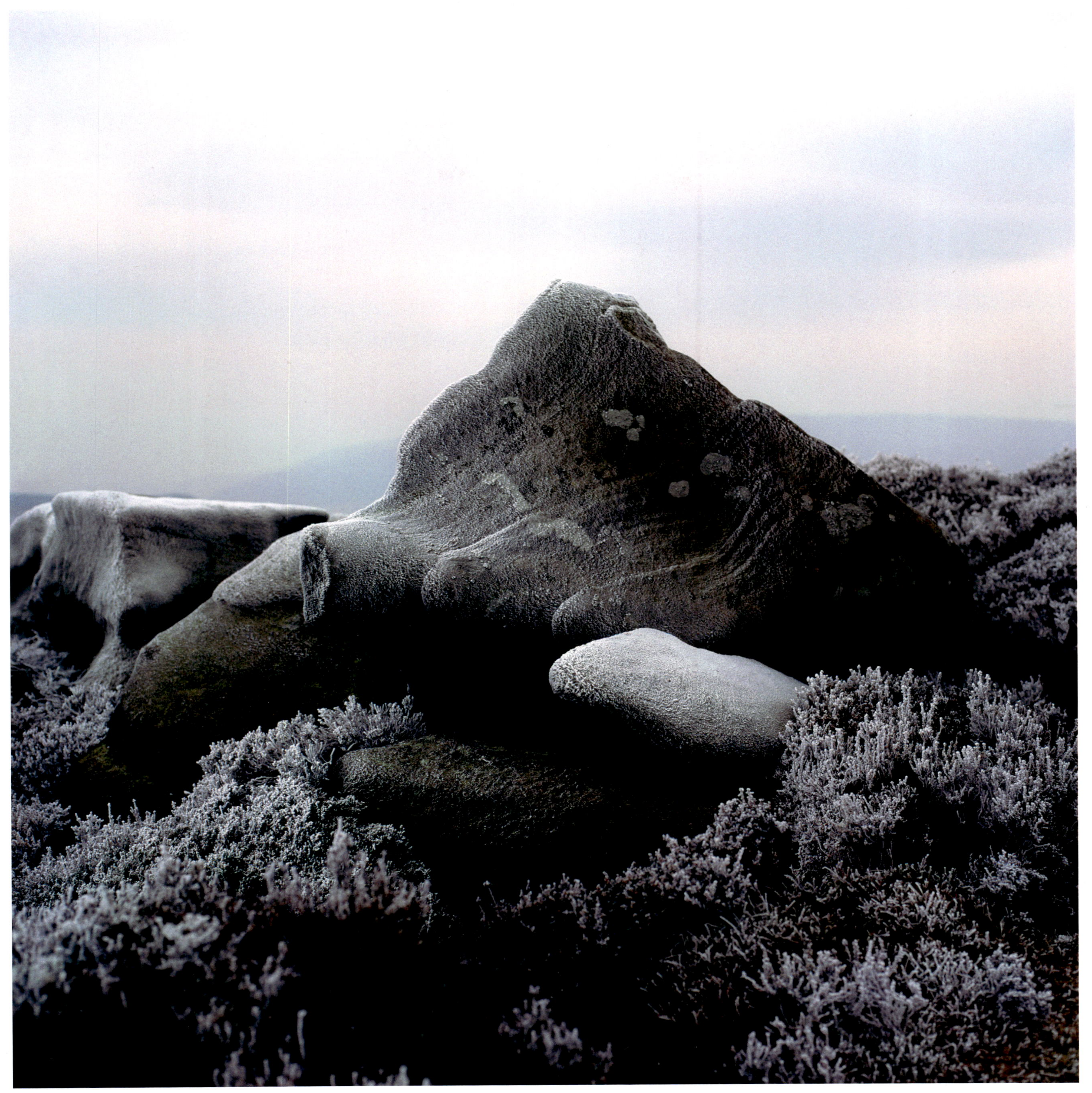

Millstone Edge – Derbyshire – England

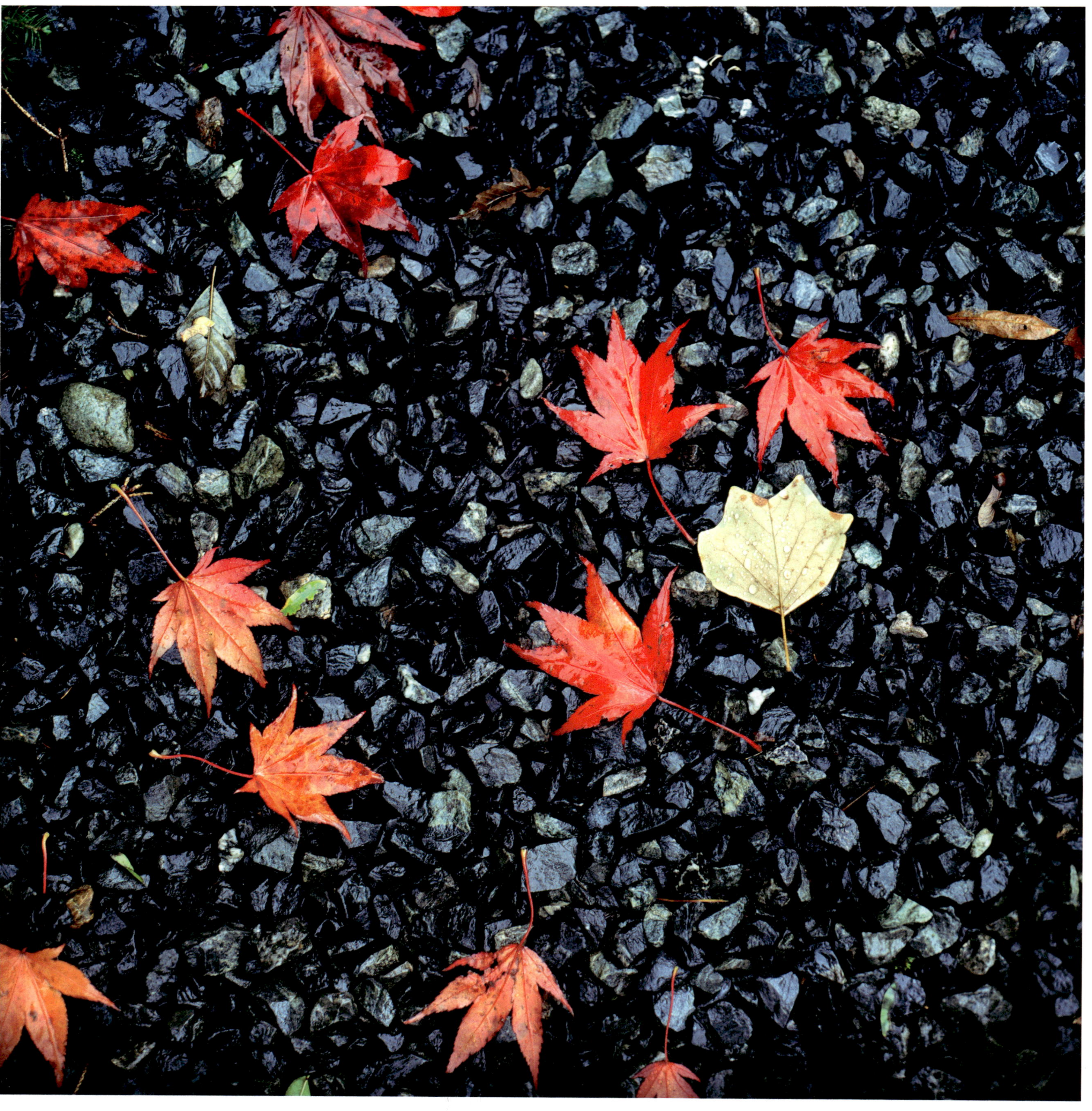

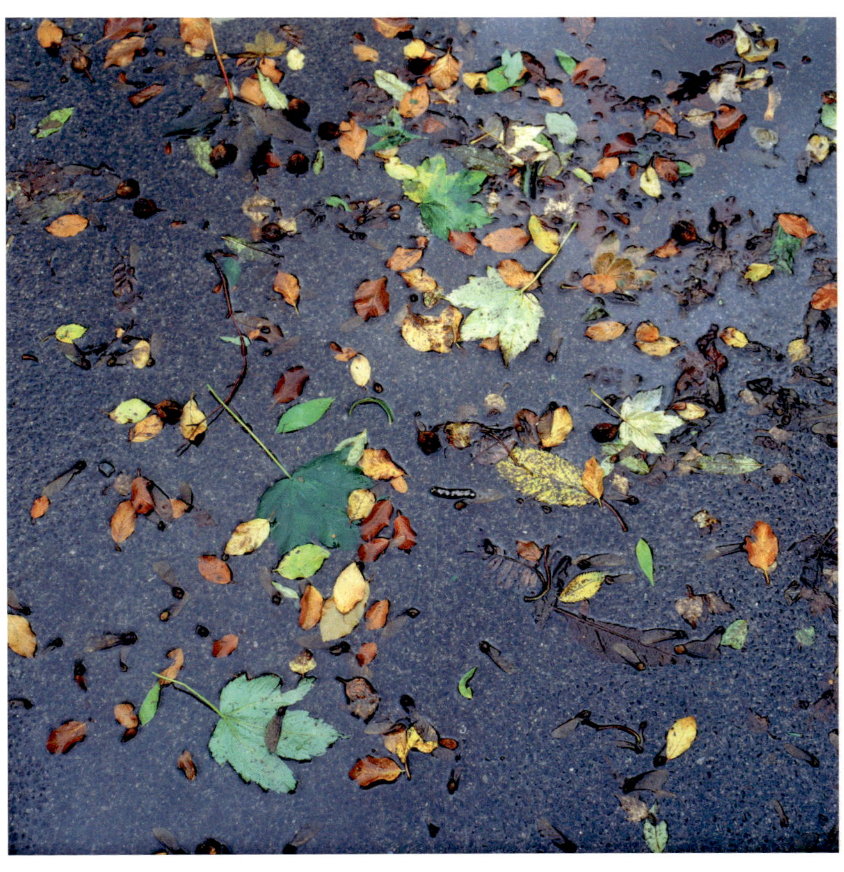

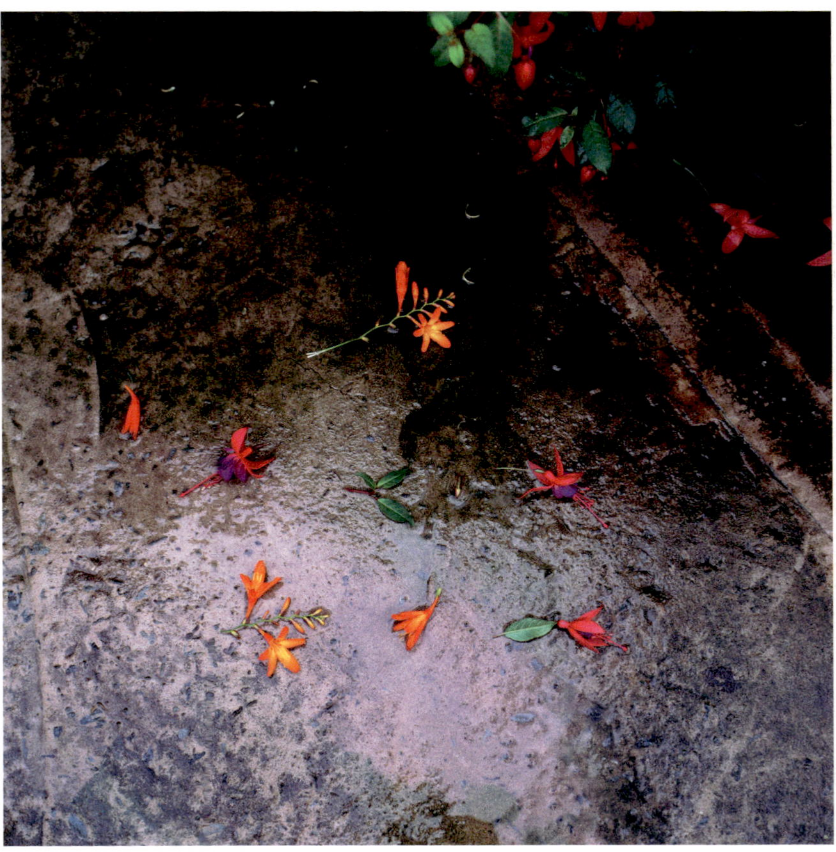

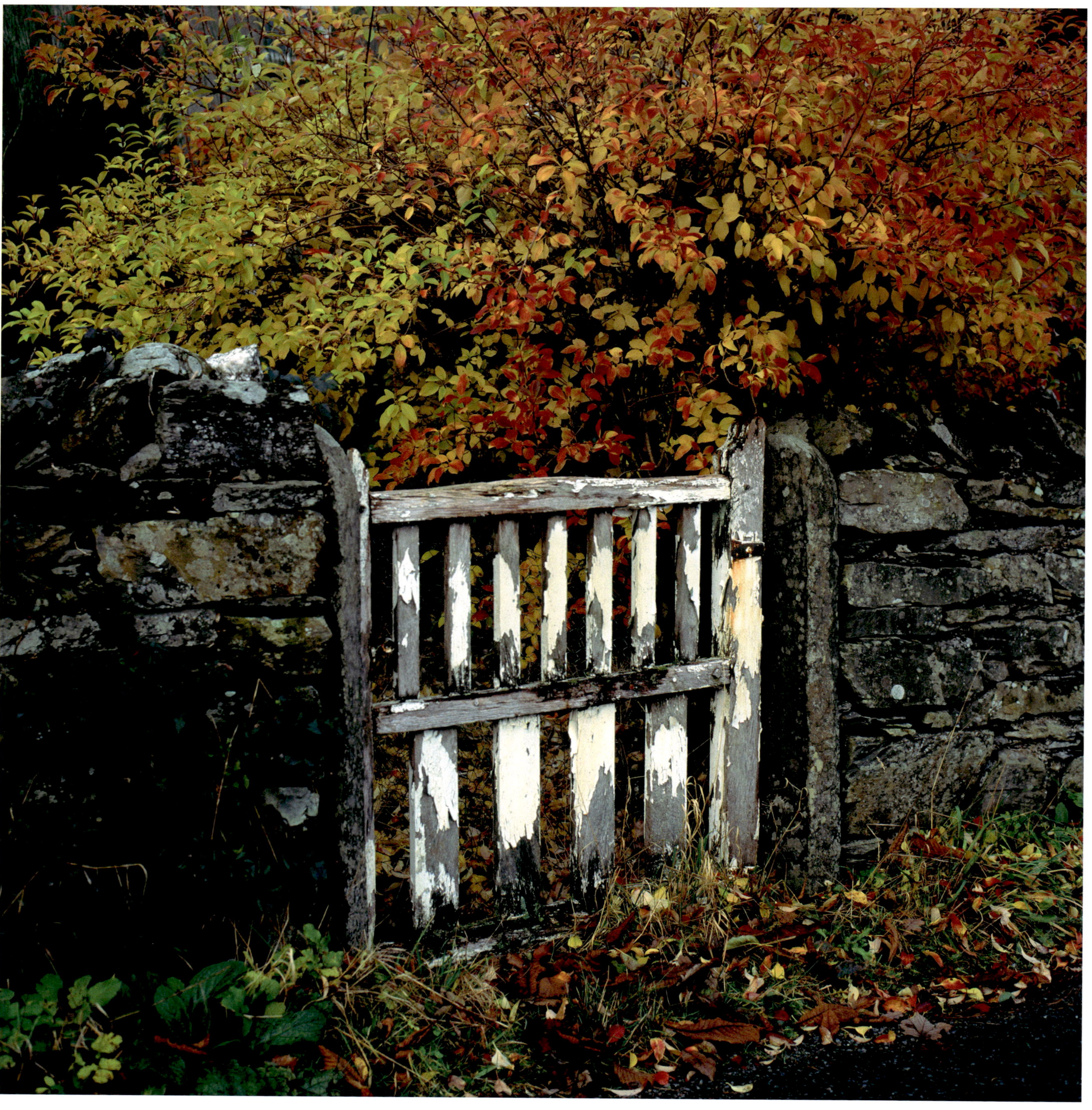

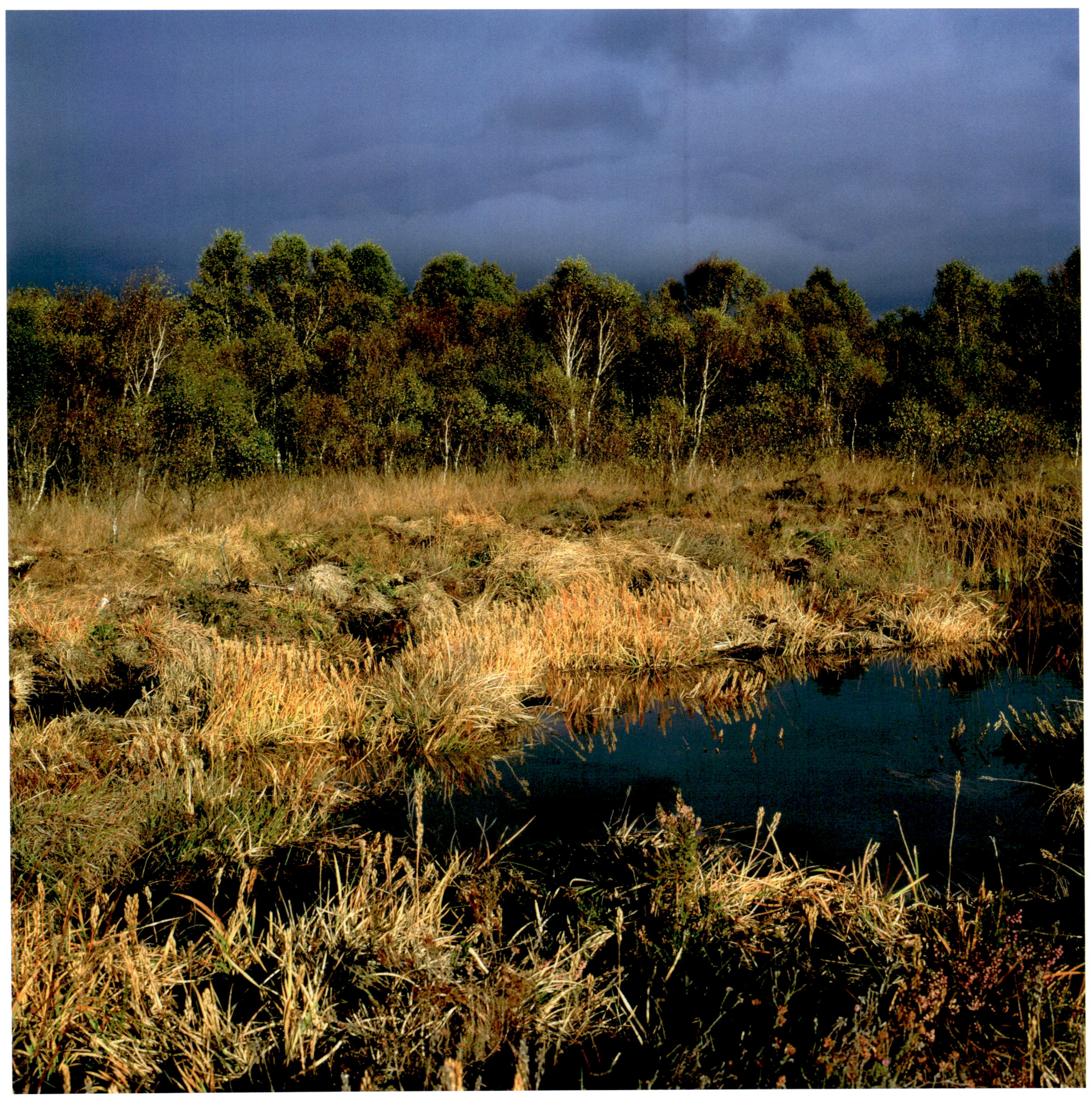

Duddon Moss – Cumbria – England

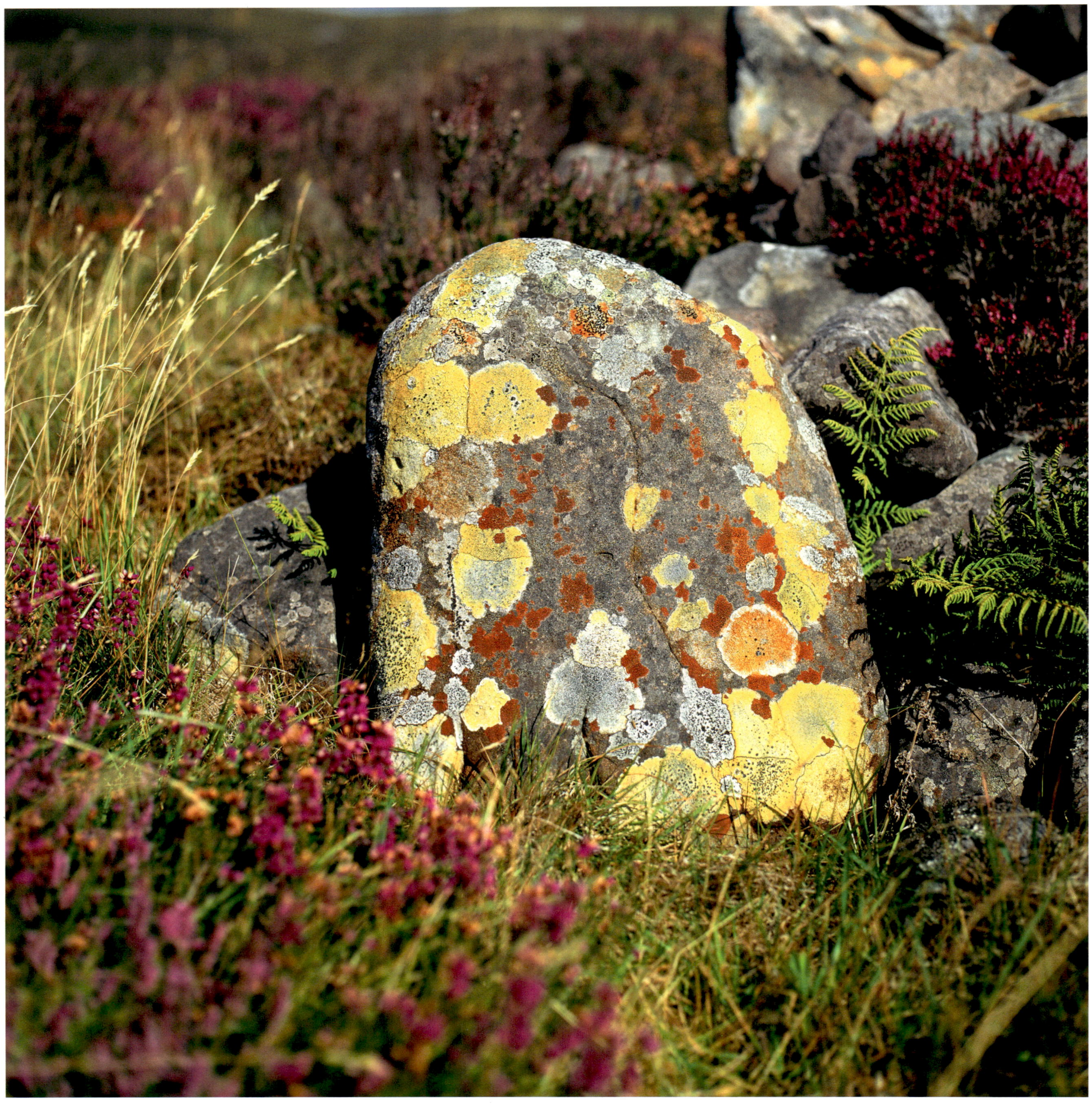

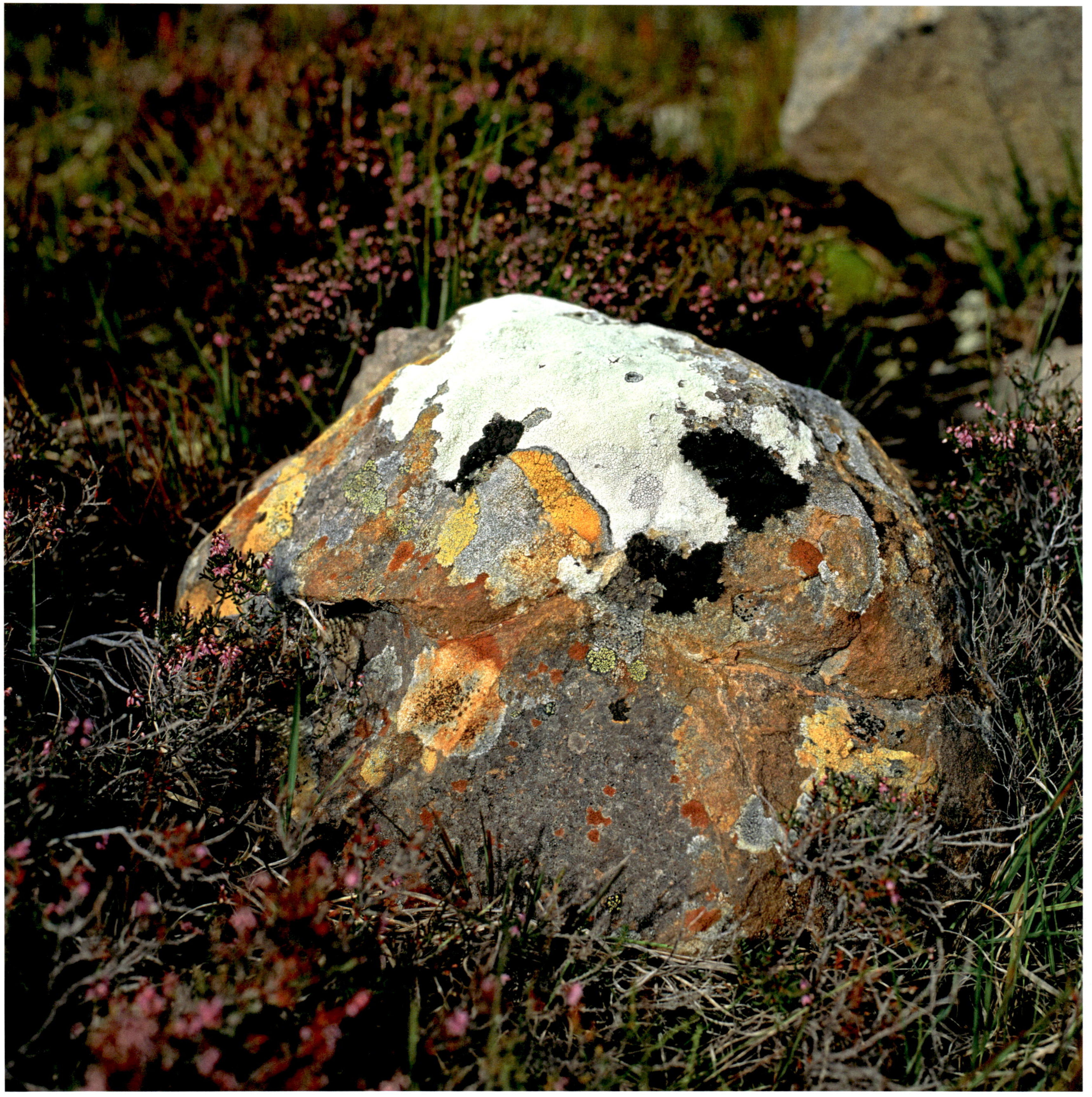

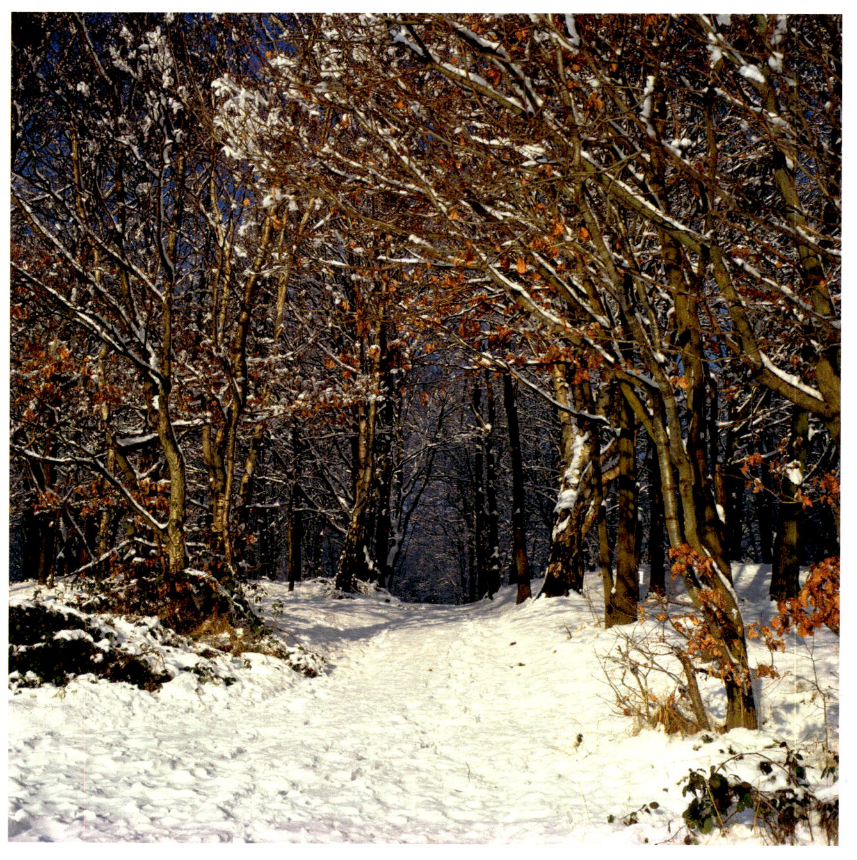

Hesley Wood – South Yorkshire – England

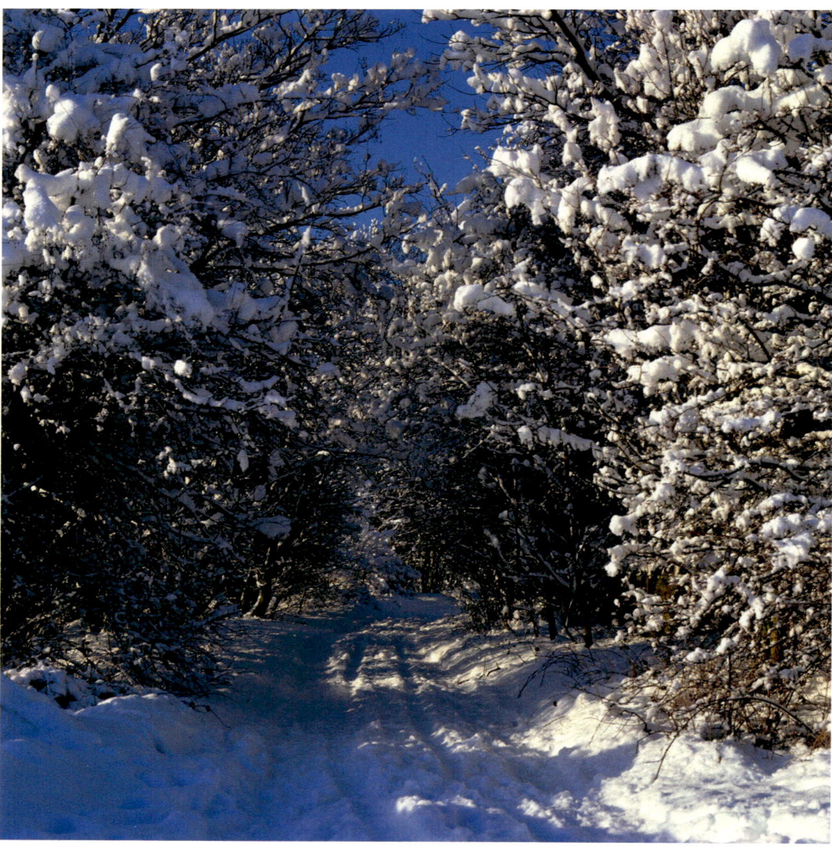

Hoober – South Yorkshire – England

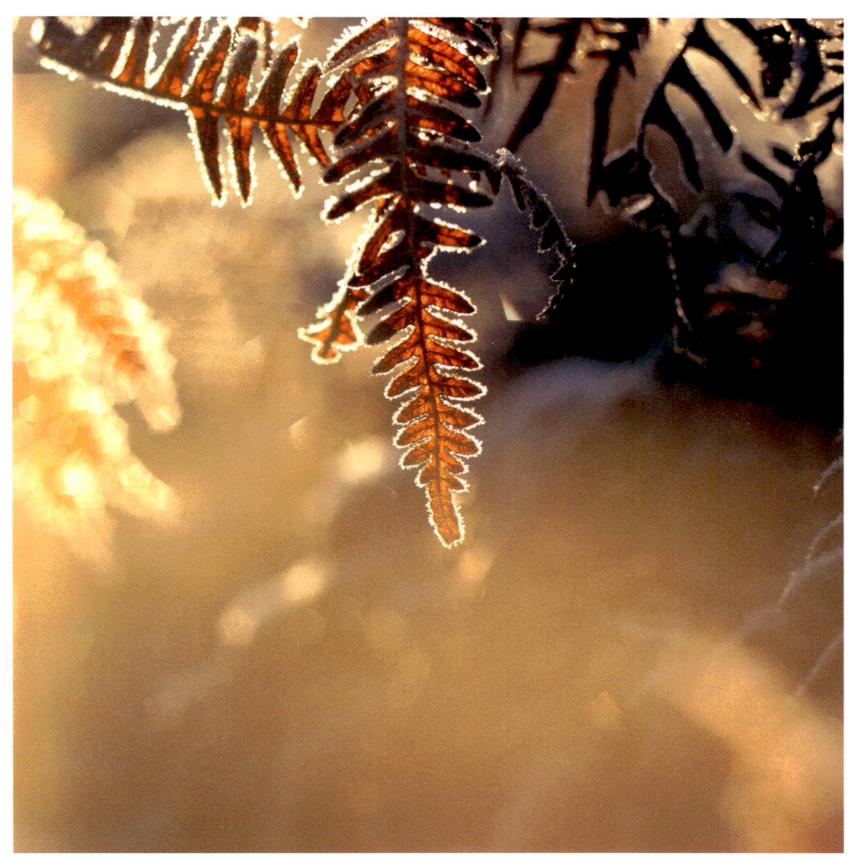

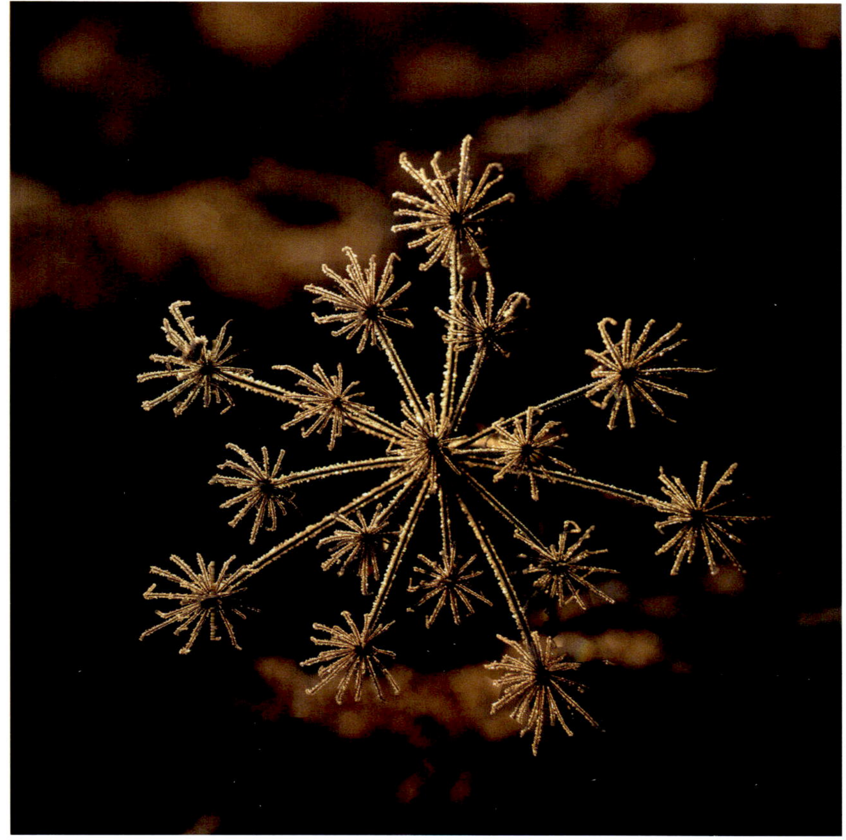

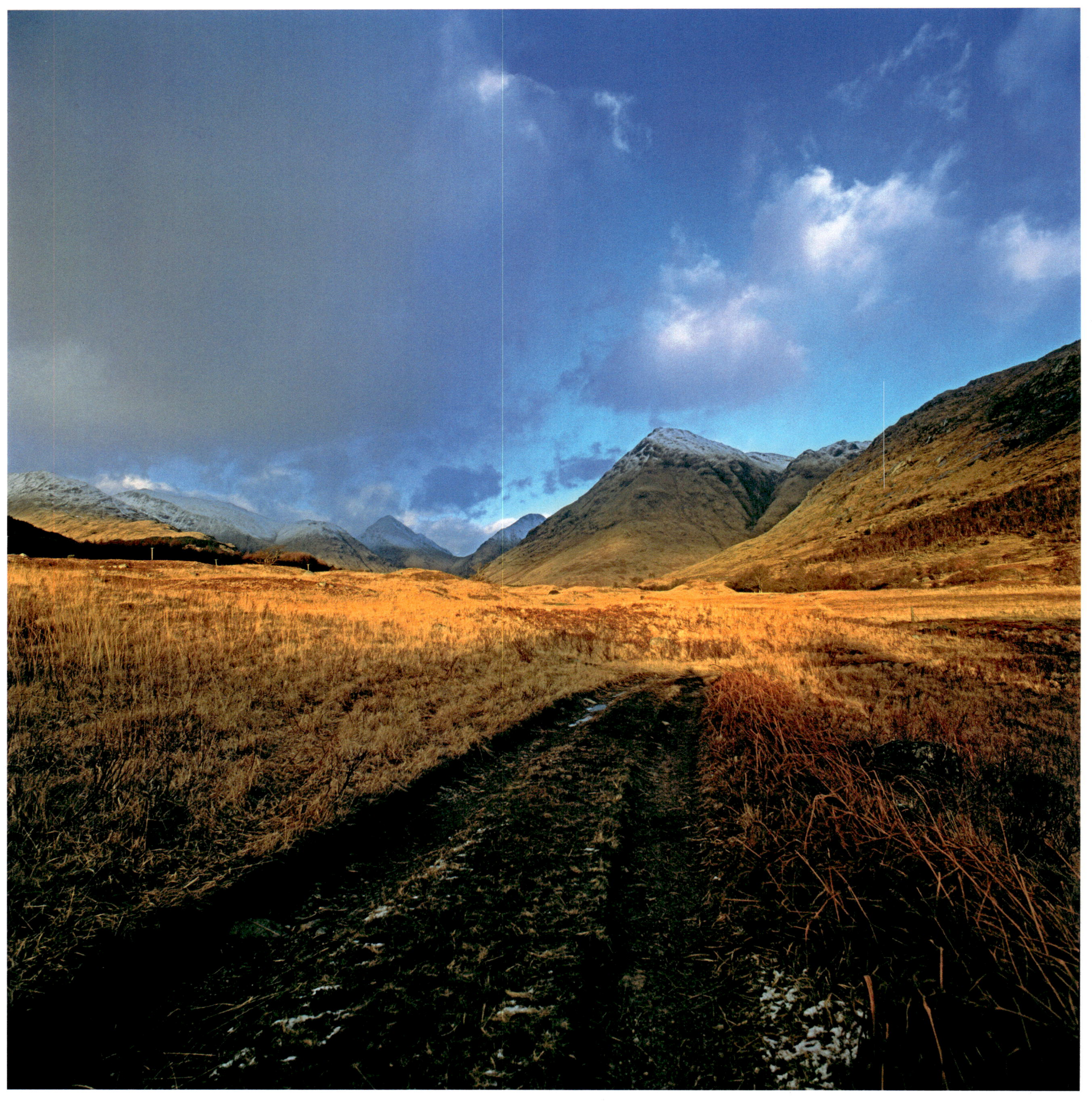

Glencoe – Highlands – Scotland

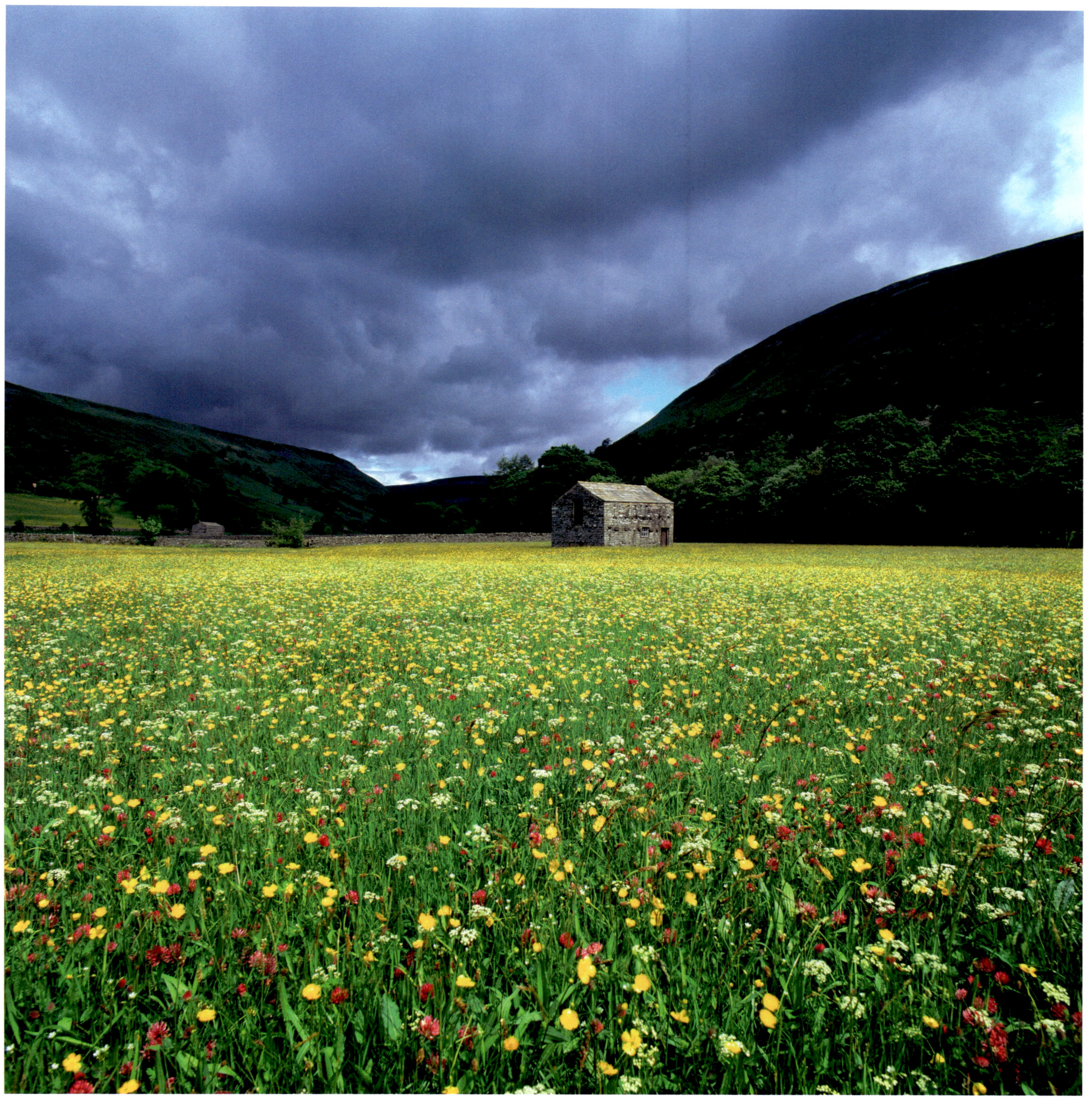

Muker – North Yorkshire – England

Only when the last tree has died and the last river has been poisoned and the last fish has been caught will we realise that we cannot eat money
OLD CREE PROPHECY

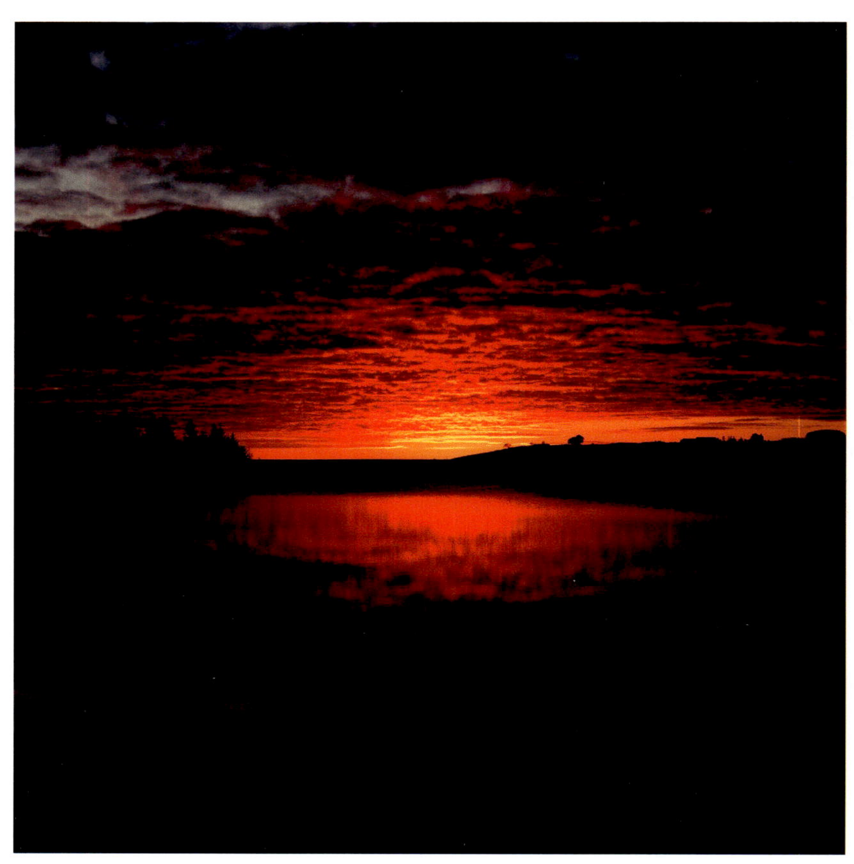

Redmires Reservoir (7:05 a.m.) – South Yorkshire – England

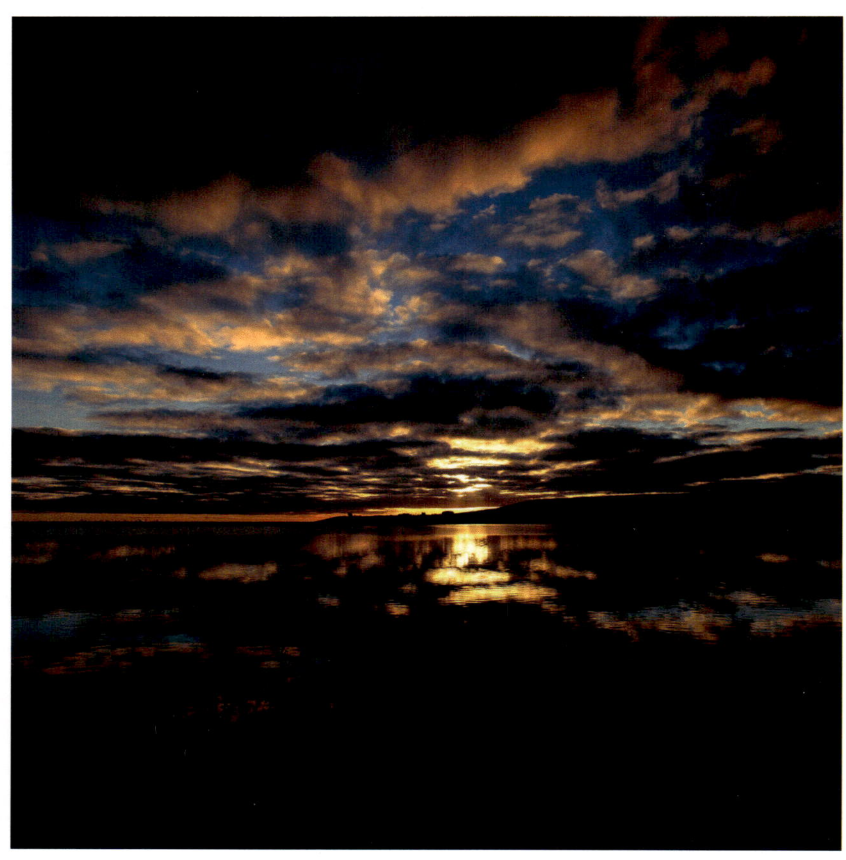

Redmires Reservoir (7:15 a.m.) – South Yorkshire – England

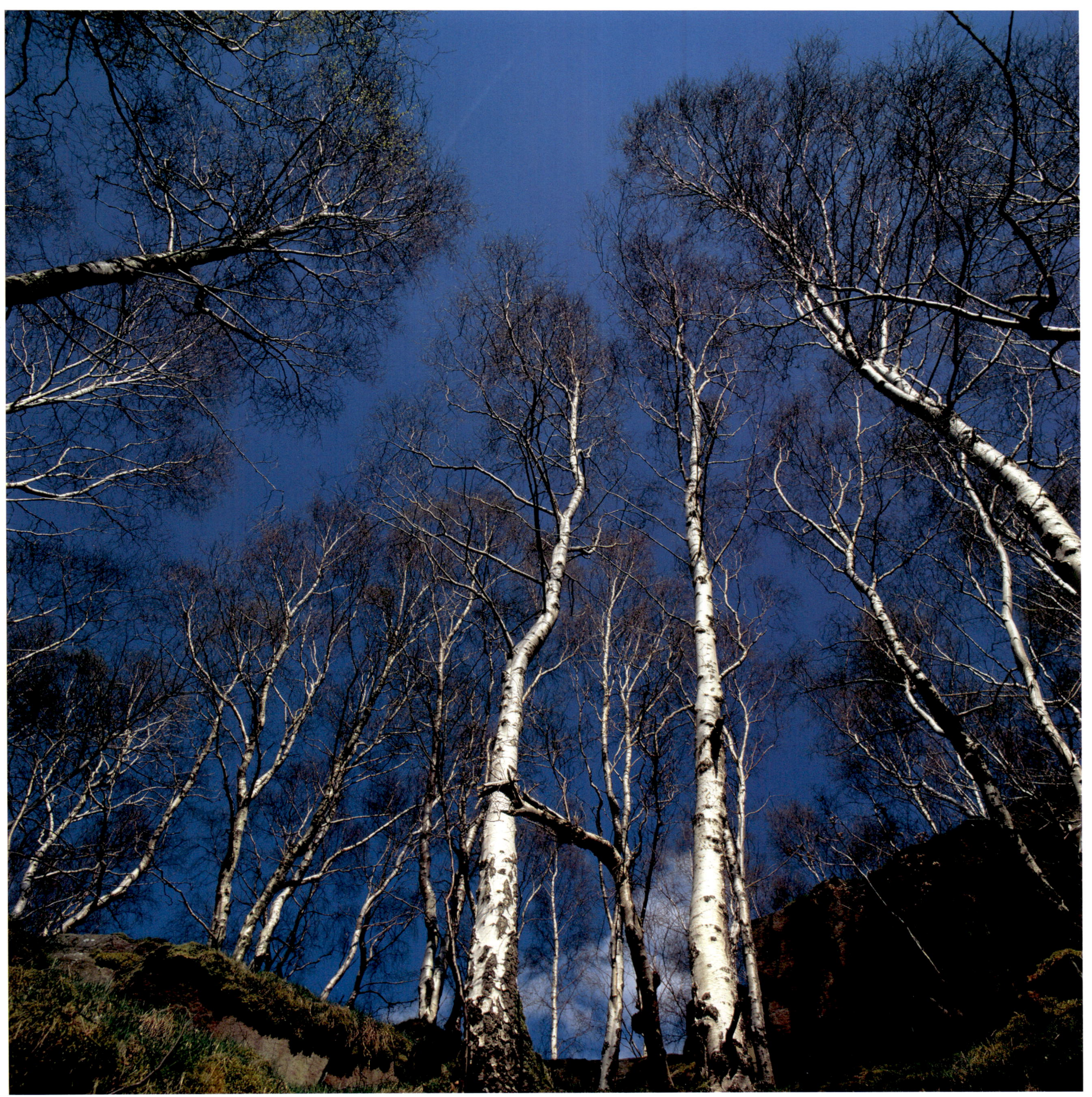

Bole Hill Quarry – Derbyshire – England